AIDS Issues in the
Workplace

AIDS Issues
in the
Workplace

**A RESPONSE
MODEL
FOR
HUMAN RESOURCE
MANAGEMENT**

Dale A. Masi

Q

QUORUM BOOKS
NEW YORK • WESTPORT, CONNECTICUT • LONDON

Library of Congress Cataloging-in-Publication Data

Masi, Dale A.
   AIDS issues in the workplace : a response model for human resource
management / Dale A. Masi.
      p.   cm.
   Includes bibliographical references and index.
   ISBN 0-89930-516-4 (lib. bdg. : alk. paper)
   1. AIDS (Disease)—Social aspects.   2. Industrial hygiene.
3. Employee rights.   4. AIDS (Disease)—Law and legislation.
5. Personnel management.   I. Title.
RC607.A26M364   1990
362.1'9697'92—dc20   90–8912

British Library Cataloguing in Publication Data is available.

Library of Congress Catalog Card Number: 90–8912
ISBN: 0-89930-516-4

First published in 1990

Quorum Books, 88 Post Road West, Westport, CT 06881
An imprint of Greenwood Publishing Group, Inc.

Printed in the United States of America

The paper used in this book complies with the
Permanent Paper Standard issued by the National
Information Standards Organization (Z39.48–1984).

10 9 8 7 6 5 4 3 2 1

Copyright Acknowledgments

The author and publisher gratefully acknowledge permission to use the following
copyrighted material.

Sam B. Puckett and Alan E. Emery, *Managing AIDS in the Workplace*, © 1988 by Sam B.
Puckett and Alan E. Emery. Reprinted with permission of Addison-Wesley Publishing Co.,
Inc., Reading, Massachusetts.

EAP Digest, May/June 1988, with permission of Performance Resource Press, Inc., 2145
Crooks Road, Suite 103, Troy, Michigan 48084.

Constance B. Wofsy, "Human Immunodeficiency Virus Infection in Women." *Journal of the
American Medical Association* 257, no. 15 (April 17, 1987): 2074, 2075, and 2076.
Copyright 1987, American Medical Association.

TP

This book is dedicated to my daughter, Renée, who symbolizes the modern, professional woman par excellence. Her love of family, her courage to try the new, and her concern for people are testimony to her ability to work in the world of business and finance and yet maintain the values that her mother, this author, hopes are reflected in this book.

CONTENTS

PREFACE

Why write another book on AIDS? Why read another book on the subject? Some people are saying: This is last year's problem (1989) in the workplace. We have other, more critical issues to give our attention to—health care, drugs, illiteracy, to name a few. The year 2000 will see a shrinking labor force as well as a changing labor force. Corporate America needs to put its energies into these concerns. AIDS affects only a small population, and few are even in the workplace.

The purpose of this book is to show how wrong such thinking is, and how such rationalizing is built upon ignorance of facts as well as a denial of one's feelings about the subject of AIDS. More importantly, the book addresses areas that have not been covered before in the literature that relate directly to the workplace. Information about AIDS is constantly changing and needs updating. Last year's information is just that. Already new facts, new legal decisions, and new medical information are pouring out into the media. All of this has implications for the work environment and that is what this book is about.

I am a professor at the University of Maryland and president of an Employee Assistance Program (EAP) consulting company for corporations. Clearly those roles affect my interpretation of the material. I consider that an advantage; I know of no other book written by an author with such a perspective. As an EAP professional I have worked for 15 years with large and small companies in the United States as well as many foreign countries. I have devoted my energy to assisting the client companies in investing in people—their most precious commodity—and thus investing in themselves. Corporate America is getting the message. It knows that its only hope to maintain a stable workforce is to provide flexible benefits, child care, drug education, and so on. As yet, Corporate America has not related the importance of an AIDS program to productivity. But soon it will have no choice. This book will provide the facts as well as offer solutions.

What is different about this book? Besides addressing the needs of persons with AIDS (PWAs), this book takes a broader perspective to include the needs of other employees affected by AIDS, such as family members and loved ones; and of special work populations in need of a unique approach such as minorities, women, and drug abusers. The book provides a program for the workplace that covers all aspects of the problem. This stems from my social work training in human service program design and implementation.

Chapters 1 and 2 cover the latest medical and legal information. For two years I lectured to executives on AIDS in a number of cities, under the auspices of the American Management Association. This enabled me to learn about these subjects first hand as I witnessed audiences' reactions to the material. Chapter 3 discusses policy development—not only why a policy is important, but what a policy should cover and a number of examples from the public and private sector are given.

Chapter 4 moves into a major area of concern: the lack of involvement by EAPs in the AIDS issue and roles EAPs could serve. EAPs can help not only people with AIDS, but also several other work populations affected by AIDS, such as employees living with someone with AIDS. As one who has been on the cutting edge of the EAP movement, I have witnessed the initial burst of interest in AIDS, followed by diminished attention to the subject, especially by contract EAPs. Chapter 4 addresses the reasons for this decline, as well as possible solutions. Case management—the other side of the EAP coin—requires planning coordination with human resources departments and benefit managers.

Chapter 5 covers the educational component of the company AIDS package. It points out the critical importance of continuous education that includes updated material.

Chapter 6 deals with special work populations, such as health-care workers, overseas employees, and emergency service personnel, from the aspect of the nature of their work in relation to contraction of the AIDS virus.

Chapter 7 discusses persons who use drugs and their vulnerability to AIDS. Intravenous (IV) drug users are particularly at risk; however, when non-IV drug users are using alcohol and other drugs that alter one's reactions, resistance can be lowered and precautions normally taken would be dismissed. Chapter 8 discusses the subject of women, minorities, children, and teenagers. Existing literature on AIDS in the workplace has not adequately addressed the issue of AIDS among these populations. Reaching these workplace groups without appearing discriminatory is a delicate matter. Understanding the perspectives of the AIDS issue particular to them and how they relate to the workplace makes the subject more complex.

Chapter 9 is composed of interviews with individuals who were selected because of the diverse perspectives from which they approach the subject. They include a manager who had an employee with AIDS; a social worker educating workers about AIDS; a medical director educating an overseas employee population; a dentist; the president of a national business leadership task force on AIDS; and a medical writer/producer specializing in AIDS issues from an ethical perspective in the United States and Australia.

The appendixes contain resource lists and original documents from such sources as the Centers for Disease Control's (CDC) Universal Precautions; CDC's Recommendations for Health-Care Settings; and handicapped legislation. A full bibliography completes the book.

The workplace represents a vital system in our society. Not only must companies confront the issue of AIDS within their organizations, but they also must take responsibility to join the fight against AIDS in society at large. In many ways, AIDS is our society's biggest challenge. How we cope with AIDS may truly determine our generation's stature in the history of humankind. This book is written to help employers stand tall in that role.

ACKNOWLEDGMENTS

The research associate throughout this book was my daughter, Robin Masi. She made this book a reality by using her research and writing skills, as well as her organizational ability, to synthesize the material with me. Equally important was her commitment to the subject. In fact, during her work on the manuscript she was able to organize a benefit to raise awareness of the issues surrounding women, AIDS, and the arts. The event, entitled "Female Artists Against AIDS," was held in Boston in November 1989.

It is with sadness that I must acknowledge three men in my life, who were both close friends and professional associates, whom I lost to AIDS. Jim is one that I will always grieve. Benny was a friend for over 20 years who died while I was writing this book. The third will go unnamed because the cause of his death remains unnamed. I pray to God there are no more. If this book helps anyone in any way to deal with AIDS, then it was well worth the effort.

Certain chapters had special assistance from others. Chapters 1 and 2, on medical and legal issues, respectively, rely heavily on material from my fellow lecturers, Dr. Virginia Anderson and Adin Goldberg, from the American Management Association's Executive Briefings on AIDS. We lectured in a number of cities together and the professional acumen and humanitarian value orientation they brought to the subject was an inspiration to me. I also wish to acknowledge Harold Green, LLB for his careful review of the legal chapter, and Michele Jones, MSW for her additional research work for the chapter.

Glenn Haughie, MD, Medical Director from International Business Machines (IBM) and Joseph Meade, EAP Administrator, Internal Revenue Service (IRS), are from two of my client organizations who graciously shared their material for Chapter 3 on policy development. Another client, Kathleen McGloin, assistant vice-president, National Fire Protection Association, gave permission to participate in an actual AIDS education session that helped us immeasurably for Chapter 5.

The special populations in the workplace and issues surrounding AIDS and drugs covered in Chapter 6 through 8 were a major challenge as it was the first time such material is presented in one comprehensive publication. Robin Masi did an exceptional job in tracking down the various source material and synthesizing it.

Michael Irwin, MD, the medical services director for the World Bank and former medical director for the United Nations, kindly shared material developed for United Nations employees serving overseas. This material could easily be adapted for the private sector.

Chapter 9 is composed of interviews held with experts. I thought they could express their views much better than I could paraphrase them. I am grateful for the time each of them gave.

Many thanks to Sharon Brody and Jay Avella for the final review and editing before the manuscript was sent to the publisher.

CHAPTER 1

MEDICAL INFORMATION

INTRODUCTION

This chapter will cover the medical aspects of the AIDS virus. Most important for the workplace, this chapter will discuss the transmission/ nontransmission of the disease and its implications for the work setting. The definition of the virus will include a description, its origin, and the history of the virus since its discovery. Following a discussion of the epidemiology of the disease and its geographical patterns of transmission, the chapter will present predictions of the disease's future path, including a discussion of the limitations of accurate documentation and worldwide underreporting. The virus then will be discussed from a biological perspective, and traced as the disease progresses within the body. Symptoms of AIDS will be presented.

The recommended preventive measures will be drawn directly from Surgeon General C. Everett Koop's pamphlet sent to every American household in 1986. Employers are recommended to urge their employees to reread this pamphlet as it is timely, informative, and essential in beginning to understand the virus and the implications of the disease to every American. A discussion of the importance of condoms and sterilized needles and their proper uses will be presented. The chapter will conclude with medical treatment of the AIDS virus, drugs presently used, and the search for a vaccine and cure.

The presentation of the medical material has relied heavily on third-party sources because it is important that the medical facts be presented as accurately as possible in order to set the stage for an appropriate workplace response.

NONTRANSMISSION/TRANSMISSION

Everyday living does not present any risk of infection. One *cannot* get AIDS from casual social contact. Casual social contact should not be confused with casual *sexual*
contact which is a major cause of the spread of the AIDS virus. Casual *social* contact
such as shaking hands, hugging, social kissing, crying, coughing, or sneezing, will not
transmit the AIDS virus. Nor has AIDS been contracted from swimming in pools or
bathing in hot tubs or from eating in restaurants (even if a restaurant worker has AIDS
or carries the AIDS virus). AIDS is not contracted from sharing bed linens, towels,
cups, straws, dishes, or any other eating utensils. You cannot get AIDS from toilets,
doorknobs, telephones, office machinery, or household furniture. You cannot get
AIDS from body massages, masturbation, or any nonsexual contact.[1]

The transmission of the AIDS virus occurs only in a few ways: through
sexual contact; through the sharing of needles and syringes when injecting
illicit drugs; through the transfusion of blood or its components; and
through perinatal exposure—exposure from mother to child or to fetus.
The risk of infection with the AIDS virus is increased by having multiple
sexual partners, either homosexual or heterosexual, and the sharing of
needles among drug users.

DEFINITION

A-I-D-S is a shortened term for Acquired Immune Deficiency Syndrome.
When individuals are diagnosed with AIDS they are in the final stages of a
series of health problems caused by a virus. This virus primarily infects
certain cells of the immune system. The latest research from the Centers for
Disease Control concludes that "AIDS is characterized by a defect in the
body's natural immunity against disease. People who have AIDS are vulnerable to serious illnesses which would not be a threat to anyone whose
immune system was functioning normally. These illnesses are referred to as
'opportunistic' infections or diseases."[2]
The virus is one of a particular class of viruses called retroviruses. Retroviruses are relatively rare in number; only a few have been discovered
to date. "This new form of retrovirus has been named by various researchers
as 'Human T-Lymphotropic Virus Type III' (HTLV–3), 'Lymphadenopathy
Associated Virus' (LAV) and 'AIDS Retro Virus' (ARV). In 1986 an international scientific committee gave it the official designation 'Human Immunodeficiency Virus,' or 'HIV'."[3]
Two major strains of the HIV virus are now recognized in this country:
HIV–1 and HIV–2.

HIV–1 infects T-lymphocytes which are white blood cells that have a central role
in the immune response. The virus causes a rare, highly malignant cancer called

adult T-cell leukemia. Two years after the discovery of HIV–1, in 1986, its close relative, HIV–2 was isolated and probably causes some cases of a disease called hairy-cell leukemia as well as T-cell leukemias and lymphomas of a more chronic type than those associated with HIV–1.[4]

Both strains of the virus share some key features: each strain is spread by blood, sexual intercourse, and from mother to child. Both cause disease after an extended latency, and both infect T-lymphocytes, a group of white blood cells. In addition, "both viruses can replicate in certain cells of the central nervous system which may be involved in the neuropathogical features of AIDS."[5] HIV–1 is the most prevalent strain in both numbers of cases and geographical distribution, having infected millions of people worldwide. It currently manifests itself as AIDS Related Complex (ARC). The HIV–2 strain has so far been found primarily in West Africa.

STAGES OF THE DISEASE

The course of the disease has been defined into six stages by Robert A. Redfield of the Walter Reed Army Institute of Research in Washington, D.C. After the initial infection with the virus, a person may appear to remain healthy for up to eight to ten years. In the first stage an unknown proportion of infected people do experience an early, brief, mononucleosis-like illness with fever, malaise, and possibly a skin rash. Such symptoms, when they are present, develop at about the time antibodies produced by the body against HIV can first be detected. This usually occurs between two weeks and three months after infection.

The second stage occurs with a condition called lymphadenopathy, a chronic lymph node disease, which may last several years without any other signs of the disease. After these two stages the virus can remain dormant for many years.

The third and fourth stages are defined by a marked decrease in the body's immune system, which is measured by T4 counts.

Stage four is also characterized by an abnormal reaction to a skin test called delayed hypersensitivity response, which measures T-cell activation following an injection of foreign proteins. As T4 levels continue to decline, patients enter stage five, when they develop symptoms of immune collapse. These symptoms most often involve chronic infections of the skin and mucous membranes. . . .

The sixth and final stage is AIDS itself, when once exotic and often life-threatening infections may strike a wide variety of organs. These illnesses often begin with persistent coughing and shortness of breath, symptoms of PCP, a virulent form of pneumonia caused by a protozoan called Pneumocystis crinii that is harmless to people whose immune system is sound. According to the CDC, PCP is the primary cause of death for three out of five AIDS patients. . . .

The prognosis is grim once patients have entered stage six, with most dying within two years. Many researchers hoped that not all HIV-infected people would progress to the immune collapse represented by stages four through six, but long-term studies of AIDS have shown that the course of illness appears inevitable. A Walter Reed study found that 90 percent of a group of HIV-infected patients progressed one or more stages over an average of three years.[6]

Infection with the HIV virus always seems to lead to AIDS. While people infected with the virus remain in good health, they are referred to as asymptomatic. When they develop illnesses varying in severity from mild to extremely serious, the illnesses are designated AIDS Related Complex. However, the term ARC is not widely used since the concepualization of the six stages of the disease.

Although a large enough dose of the right strain of HIV can cause AIDS on its own, cofactors can clearly influence the progression of the disease. People whose immune systems are weakened before HIV infection may progress toward AIDS more quickly than others; stimulation of the immune system in response to later infections may also hasten disease progression.[7]

Specifically, when other sexually transmitted diseases (STDs) have been found in an individual infected with HIV, HIV causes AIDS to accelerate more rapidly than if the STDs were not present.

ORIGIN OF THE AIDS VIRUS

It is not definite if the virus originated in Africa or somewhere else. The virus has been traced by scientists to Africa where the virus is thought to be present before 1970. In several countries in south central Africa, the AIDS virus has been found in stored blood supplies that date as far back as the 1960s. Robert C. Gallo of the National Cancer Institute in Bethesda, Maryland, codiscovered the virus. In theorizing about the long-term existence, he proposed that, "HIV originated in Africa, where both people and African primates were infected, and was spread to the Americas by the slave trade and to the southwestern islands of Japan (the virus's other endemic area) by oceangoing Portuguese traders."[8]

This theory is supported by the French scientist who codiscovered the virus. Luc Montagnier of the Pasteur Institute in Paris agrees that the AIDS virus is indeed very old. "We're boarding a train already in motion. The AIDS virus's complexity shows that it has undergone an arduous process of selection. With nine genes, it is the most complex retrovirus known to man."[9]

Like other viruses, retroviruses cannot replicate without taking over the biosynthetic apparatus of a cell and exploiting it for their own ends. What is unique about retroviruses is their capacity to reverse the ordinary flow of genetic information—from DNA to RNA to proteins (which are the cell's structural and functional molecules). The genetic material of a retrovirus is RNA. In addition, the retrovirus carries an enzyme called reverse transcriptase, which can use the viral RNA as a template for making DNA. The viral DNA can integrate itself into the genome (the complement of genetic information) of the host. Having made itself at home among the host's genes, the viral DNA remains latent until it is activated to make new virus particles. The latent DNA can also initiate the process that leads to tumor formation.[10]

AIDS is an epidemic today because it is a disease of civilization and is dependent on behavior. The virus is so old that it may have well appeared earlier in history to wipe out previous civilizations. Since then, the virus has been biding its time in isolated populations, masking its existence behind other fatal diseases, until the cofactors of modern life united to spur it into its current epidemic proportions. These cofactors, weakening the immune system, include sexual promiscuity, industrial pollution, drug use, and the mingling of people into a world culture. According to Montagnier, since "the whole world is married to one another, the globalization of culture has globalized our germs."[11]

CHRONOLOGY OF AIDS

1960–70s	AIDS virus surfaces in Africa.
1977	AIDS virus arrives in New York.
1978	AIDS virus arrives in Los Angeles and San Francisco
1981	First medical cases reported to CDC.
1982	First organization on AIDS created in New York.
1983	The name "AIDS" established.
1984	The AIDS virus discovered: Montagnier, Pasteur Institute (France) announces LAV; Gallo, U.S. Health Service, announces HTLV-III; Levy, USA announces ARV.
1985	CDC issues *Guidelines for AIDS in the Workplace.*
1986	Surgeon General issues report on AIDS.
1987	Presidential Commission on AIDS appointed.
1988	AIDS diagnoses in the U.S. surpass 60,000; 50 new cases added each working day; no cure or vaccine in sight.[12]
1989	AZT found to prolong the lives of those found as HIV positive; rate of infection is shifting, found to increase in IV drug users, women. Rate of infection among homosexual men is lessened.
1990	AIDS awareness and consciousness appears to be decreasing. There has been no government supported and educational materials distributed since the 1986 Surgeon General's report.

EPIDEMIOLOGY OF AIDS

Virtually every country except Antarctica has reported cases of AIDS to the World Health Organization (WHO). As of June 1, 1990, 263,051 cases of AIDS had been reported by about 150 countries to WHO. This figure, however, represents only a fraction of those afflicted. Experts say the more accurate estimate of those infected is closer to 500,000. Dr. Mann of the WHO, speaking at the WHO/Global Programme Management Committee Meeting in Geneva, December 1989,

estimated that the 1980s would produce five million new infections with HIV..., 600,000 cases of AIDS, and 300,000 deaths. He is convinced that the global strategy, where conscientiously applied, is beginning to show results. However, the pandemic is spreading while complacency increases. The threat of spread is particularly great in Asia, according to Dr. Mann. In Africa, Uganda alone, with about 800,000 seropositives, may have as many as 40,000 new AIDS cases in 1990. And the cumulative total of AIDS cases might reach as high as six million by the year 2000.[13]

There are three main geographic patterns of infection. The Pattern 1 is typical of largely industrialized countries such as the United States and Canada, Western Europe, Australia, New Zealand, and parts of South America. The two main groups afflicted are intravenous drug users (and their sexual partners) and homosexual men. Heterosexual transmission accounts for only a small percentage in these areas but that percentage is increasing. "There was transmission due to the transfusion of blood and blood products between the late 1970s and 1985, but that route has been virtually eliminated by convincing people in high-risk groups not to donate blood and by routine, effective testing of blood donors for antibodies against HIV."[14] The male to female sex ratio in this pattern ranges from 10:1, to 15:1. Because of the few women infected in these areas, perinatal transmission (transmission from mother to child) is not common.

Pattern 2 occurs in central, eastern, and southern Africa, the Caribbean, and, most recently, parts of South America. In these areas AIDS is reported to be transmitted primarily through heterosexual contact, with equal numbers of men and women afflicted. The lack of reporting of homosexual transmission stems from the denial of homosexual and bisexual activity in these areas. Therefore, homosexually and bisexually transmitted cases are being reported with the heterosexual figures. The prejudice against homosexuality also leads to a higher level of infection among women. Many men have not acknowledged their homosexuality and are still married and having relations with women. Because of the level of women infected, perinatal transmission is common. In central Africa transfusions of unscreened blood may still be a major source of transmission. AIDS now afflicts more than 8% of urban adults in central Africa.

Pattern 3, about which very little is known, covers Asia, the Soviet Union, Eastern Europe, the Middle East, North Africa, and most of the Pacific. In these areas, the virus has been reported as having arrived relatively late— in the mid 1980s. Most of the reported cases involve people who have had sexual contact with people from Pattern 1 or Pattern 2 or who have traveled to these areas. The lack of information about Pattern 3 is a result of the tendency of Pattern 3 nations to be dogmatic in their denial of addictions. They did not report having alcohol and drug problems until there were virtual epidemics. Because of this rigid attitude toward addictions, these countries are virtually blinded to the actual numbers of AIDS cases, especially those due to IV drug transmission.

AIDS IN THE UNITED STATES

As of June 30, 1990, 139,765 cases of full-blown AIDS have been reported in the United States. The total cases of AIDS in adults and adolescents were 137, 385. Of those with AIDS, 60% are male homosexuals, 21% are intravenous drug abusers, about 7% are both male homosexuals and intravenous drug abusers, 5% were infected by heterosexual transmission, 2% were infected by blood transfusions, 1–2% are hemophiliacs, and the remaining 3% are undetermined.

As of June 1990 the ten leading states for reported cases of AIDS were: New York, 30,798; California, 26,713; Florida, 12,041; Texas, 9,711; New Jersey, 9,143; Illinois, 4,113; Puerto Rico 4,039; Pennsylvania, 3,921; Georgia, 3,678; Massachusetts, 2,937. San Francisco and New York City have the highest rate of HIV infection among homosexual men. Otherwise, HIV presence in homosexual men varies geographically without major concentration in any one region.

The prevalence of HIV among intravenous drug users varies markedly by geographic region. In 90 studies, in 53 cities in 27 states or territories, rates range from 50% to 60% in New York City, northern New Jersey, and Puerto Rico to below 5% in most areas of the country other than the East Coast.

FUTURE PATH OF AIDS

The exact number of people who have contracted AIDS in the United States is unknown because there is no universal screening. According to the Public Health Service, nearly 1 million people in the United States are currently infected with the HIV virus and have some symptoms but not full-blown AIDS. As of 1993, the cumulative total of the disease is estimated to be between 390,000 and 480,000 reported cases with 285,000–340,000 deaths. In 1992 alone, 80,000 new cases are expected to be reported with 65,000 deaths.

It is next to impossible to calculate future worldwide projections for AIDS because of the information block in so many regions. It is especially hard to monitor and analyze the spread of the disease and its predominantly infected groups in most nonindustrialized countries because large segments of the population are not accessible to the health-care facilities where presence of the AIDS virus can be determined. In addition, many governments in underdeveloped countries are unwilling to officially acknowledge the existence of AIDS.

In addition, countries are underreporting not only because of lack of proper facilities but also because of the misdiagnosis of the disease. AIDS is often labeled as cancer or heart disease. Misdiagnoses are a consequence of the lack of information about the disease as well as prejudice. These countries are reluctant to report and identify the prevalence of homosexual and bisexual activity, and the prevalence of drug abuse. The total number of AIDS cases reported to the World Health Organization as of June 1, 1990, stands at approximately 263,051, and 139,765 of these are from the United States. These imbalanced figures demonstrate the misrepresentation of the disease rate in other countries.

Infection rates in some countries in Africa vastly exceed infection rates in the United States, prompting fears in those countries that their already inadequate medical systems will soon be totally overwhelmed. AIDS is a dramatically growing, world-wide medical crisis with no medical cure in sight. By the early 1990s it is likely that the AIDS epidemic will be the most deadly and costly epidemic of the twentieth century. AIDS deaths will exceed the cost of lives of the forty-year long polio epidemic and could approach the scale of the great influenza epidemic of 1918–1919, which took 400,000 lives in the United States alone, and caused millions of deaths world-wide. By the beginning of 1992, American deaths from the AIDS epidemic are expected to reach roughly three times the number of deaths of all American service personnel in the Vietnam War.[15]

At present the infection and disease rates of the predominantly infected groups in the United States are shifting dramatically. In the white homosexual male, the infection rate appears to have reached a plateau, but disease rate is on the increase. This change in the infection rate is largely a result of the change in the behavioral patterns of the white male homosexual population. Cohesive educational and monitoring efforts have produced a marked decrease, and so it is likely that in the future the infection rate will not have the rapid increase seen in the mid–1980s. However, what will become prevalent is the number of full-blown AIDS cases. These cases will emerge from the estimated 1–2 million people already infected before the widespread adoption of prevention patterns of behavior.

While the rate of new infections in homosexual men has sharply dropped since 1983, it is slowly but steadily rising among needle-using addicts, at the rate of 3% per year. This is a concern to public health experts, because intravenous drug users through their sexual contacts are viewed as the bridge to the general heterosexual population.[16]

To gauge the future of the epidemic, it is necessary to take geography into consideration. In order to prevent the spread of the disease it is crucial to know where people are getting infected and anticipate the health care needs of those already infected. In addition to focusing on changing high-risk behavior, it is necessary to focus on geographical problem areas in order to target high-risk regions. However, it is also important to remember that geography is not destiny. One can live in the highest risk area and not necessarily contract the disease. It is equally possible to live in a remote area but still contract the disease. In order for the disease to be thwarted, virtually everyone, everywhere, must change their behavior.

PREVALENCE OF HIV INFECTION IN SPECIAL GROUPS IN THE UNITED STATES

Children/Adolescents with AIDS

As of June 30, 1990, there were among children under 13 years of age 2,380 reported cases of pediatric AIDS and 541 among adolescents aged 13–19. Of the children under 13, 5% of the cases were hemophiliacs, 83% were from parents with/or at risk of AIDS, 10% from transfusions, and 2–3% undetermined. The nearly 2,500 cases among young children is almost double the amount reported a year earlier. The U.S. Public Health Service estimates that by 1991, 3,000 children will have suffered from the disease and virtually all will die. This number is undoubtedly an underestimate, as are all figures regarding AIDS cases to date. Unlike the path of the disease in adults, "the time at which the HIV infection of the fetus or infant occurs is not yet known; potential opportunities for transmission occur in utero, during labor and delivery, and postnatally through breast milk or other vehicles."[17]

"It has been found that congenitally acquired HIV infection may affect the infant's central nervous system and thus may lead to alterations in growth and development—signs and symptoms not previously identified with AIDS."[18] Children with AIDS are of special concern to the workplace because their families are living with the child's inevitable death, as well as trying to remain productive and efficient at work.

Teenagers are at very great risk for AIDS. They normally consider themselves invulnerable and have a devil-may-care attitude. Some 40% of runaway teens are seropositive.

Hemophiliacs and Blood Supply

The screening of blood and plasma did not become routine until 1985. Consequently, "there is a high prevalence of HIV infection among the estimated 15,500 persons with hemophilia in the United States. Overall, approximately 70% of tested persons with hemophilia A and 35% with hemophilia B are infected with HIV."[19]

There has been an unusually low diagnosis rate for hemophiliacs infected with HIV. This may be because of a longer incubation period of the AIDS virus due to the nature of the condition of hemophilia. However, although the outcome of this population is unknown, it is clear that the majority of hemophiliacs in the United States are HIV positive and therefore able to transmit the virus.

Before 1985 there was no screening of blood and plasma for transfusion patients. This means that anyone receiving a blood transfusion before 1985 could be at risk for HIV. About 2% of the patients diagnosed with AIDS contracted the virus from a blood transfusion.

Today in the U.S., the risk of getting AIDS from a blood transfusion has been greatly reduced. All donated blood and blood products are tested for the AIDS virus antibody, and donors are screened for risk factors. No one in the U.S. who really needs a blood transfusion should refuse it for fear of getting AIDS. The risk to health from refusing a blood transfusion is much greater than the very low risk of getting AIDS from the transfusion. Overseas blood supplies [however] do not necessarily undergo the same scrutiny. For workplaces sending employees overseas this is a serious question. There is a responsibility to know and inform employees of risks.

Each time blood is donated, a new sterile needle is used for each donor and then discarded. The need for blood is always great, and healthy people [in the U.S.] who are not at risk for AIDS should continue to donate as they have in the past. When scientists first learned that the AIDS virus could be spread through blood, they did not yet know what caused the disease. As a first step to improve safety, the Public Health Service urged that people with signs or symptoms of AIDS and members of groups known to be at increased risk not donate blood. Blood collection centers included questions about symptoms of AIDS to screen donors, and staff were taught to reject those with early signs and symptoms of the disease. Also, new heat and chemical procedures were developed to kill viruses in clotting factor concentrates manufactured for use in treating hemophilia. By spring of 1985, a test was developed and implemented at the nation's blood centers to screen all donating blood and plasma.[20]

The Military Population

As of October 1985 all persons involved with the military are screened for HIV infection as part of their routine medical examinations. These groups include active duty or reserve military service, the service academies, and the Reserve Officer Training Corps (ROTC)—a total of over 600,000 per year.

Military applicants are interviewed by recruiting officials about drug use and homosexual activity (both of which are grounds for exclusion from entry into military service) before referral for medical evaluation. Potential applicants are informed that they will be screened for HIV antibody. It is expected, therefore, that military applicants who are medically evaluated underrepresent IV drug users and homosexual and bisexual men, as well as persons with coagulation deficiencies.[21]

The military is still finding .03% of recruits HIV positive.

Prostitutes

Prostitutes are defined as women who exchange sex for money. (Male prostitutes, whose sexual exposure is predominately with other men, are included
in the data among homosexual and bisexual men.) This group is of particular
concern because of their risk for HIV infection and its implications for society. Female prostitutes are at a double risk of exposure to HIV infection. This
is because of the IV drug use common among prostitutes (the income provided from prostitution is a common and often necessary means of paying for
drugs), and because of multiple sexual encounters. In addition, they are a potential source of infection for their babies and their male clients.

The prevalence of HIV infection among U.S. prostitutes is three to four times higher
among prostitutes who acknowledge IV drug use than among those who do not.
HIV antibody prevalence tends to parallel the geographic pattern of AIDS cases for
women, and HIV antibody prevalence is over twice as high for black and Hispanic
prostitutes as for white and other prostitutes. Regardless of how prostitutes acquire
their infection, they represent a potential source for heterosexual transmission.[22]

BIOLOGICAL COMPOUND OF THE AIDS VIRUS

The Virus Alone

AIDS is the final stage of a disease with a very directed course. The HIV virus, the first element in this course, is a surprisingly weak microorganism that
requires a moist, temperature-controlled environment combined with genetic
material in which to survive. The only way the virus can enter the human
bloodstream is through the body's mucous membranes. The virus does not
exist well outside the body. Sunlight, common household products (such as
Lysol and bleach), and hot water are all easy killers of the virus when it is
found out of the body. The virus also cannot reproduce itself in an open environment. Therefore, the dismission of the myth that insect bites, toilet seats,
and further casual contact acting as a transmitter of the virus.

However, if the virus penetrates the human body through its transmission
methods—sexually or through the blood—it has the potential of incapaci-
tating our immune system and is extremely powerful and destructive to
human health.

The Path of the AIDS Virus Once Inside the Body

Inside the human bloodstream, this virus has the capability of identifying and at-
taching itself to a specific white blood cell known as a "T-Helper Cell Lymphocyte."
This particular kind of lymphocyte is a component of the immune system; it has a

major role in managing the response of the immune system whenever the human body is invaded by a disease. T-Helper Cell Lymphocytes help turn on and manage the immune response; their existence is essential to our health. There are millions of these cells as well as other types of lymphocytes in our bodies, each with a specialized function.

Once inside the circulatory system, the AIDS virus becomes one more part of the enormously extensive network in the bloodstream. It cannot control its own motion. It floats with the billions of other cells throughout the bloodstream. On the surface of the AIDS virus are antigens which allow the virus to attach itself to other cells with receptors which effectively match the design of the antigen of the AIDS virus. These antigens are a perfect match to the receptors on the surfaces of the T-Helper Cell Lymphocytes.

Once the virus attaches itself to the lymphocyte, it is capable of injecting its genetic material, or RNA, into the lymphocytes DNA, thus turning the lymphocyte into a manufacturer of the AIDS virus. The virus cannot reproduce alone, but can take control of the lymphocyte's genetic processes through the use of an enzyme called "reverse transcriptase." Once the virus has taken control of the lymphocyte's reproductive processes, it can remain dormant for extensive periods of time. Upon activating the genetic material of the lymphocyte, the virus can be reproduced hundreds, perhaps thousands of times.

When the reproduction process is activated the newly created viruses eventually break out of the lymphocyte's cell and independently are able to attach to other lymphocytes, thus repeating the process. As a consequence of all this reproduction, the original lymphocyte cell then dies.

Over time, more and more viruses are produced and more lymphocytes are destroyed. The human body does not manufacture unlimited quantities of new lymphocytes. They are among the longest living cells in the human body, and normally live about twenty five years. When the level of lymphocytes in the body becomes at a dangerously low level, the immune system can no longer properly function. The body then begins to become attacked by "opportunistic" diseases. These are diseases present in our environment, but which do not harm people with sound immune systems. Of the possible opportunistic diseases, the ones commonly associated with AIDS are pneumocystis [carinii] pneumonia, a lung disease caused by a protozoan, a small parasite, and a form of capillary cancer called Kaposi's sarcoma.[23]

SYMPTOMS

People who become infected with the AIDS virus may either have no symptoms or be affected by a variety of clinical conditions. People with less extreme complications (or AIDS Related Complex) may have tiredness, fever, loss of appetite and weight, diarrhea, night sweats, and swollen glands (lymph nodes), usually in the neck, armpits, or groin.

The patient in the final stages of AIDS has been afflicted with opportunistic infections. These infections, to a non-AIDS-infected patient, would not be fatal. However, these infections become fatal in the AIDS patient. Cancers such as Kaposi's sarcoma, and pneumocystis carinii pneumonia, are the most common opportunistic infections. Kaposi's sarcoma may be detected by the onset of multiple purplish blotches and bumps on the skin. In its final stages,

the AIDS virus may also attack the nervous system and cause delayed damage to the brain. This damage may take years to develop and the symptoms may show up as memory loss, indifference, loss of coordination, partial paralysis, or mental disorder. This is accompanied by extreme weight loss, to a virtual skeletal level near the final stages. These symptoms may occur alone, or with other symptoms mentioned earlier.[24]

An individual in the final stages of this disease, near death, is at the end of one of the most debilitating, regressive, and painful diseases in our society today.

PREVENTION

Prevention of the AIDS virus is best described by the *Surgeon General's Report on AIDS*. It is quoted extensively because of its applicability for the workplace:

Knowing the facts about AIDS can prevent the spread of the disease. Education of those who risk infecting themselves or infecting other people is the only way we can stop the spread of AIDS. People must be responsible about their sexual behavior and must avoid the use of illicit intravenous drugs and needle sharing. Described below will be the types of behavior that lead to infection by the AIDS virus and the personal measures that must be taken for effective protection. *Precautions must be taken.* The AIDS virus infects persons who expose themselves to known risk behavior, such as certain types of homosexual and heterosexual activities or sharing intravenous drug equipment.

Risks. Although the initial discovery was in the homosexual community, AIDS is not a disease only of homosexuals. AIDS is found in heterosexual people as well. AIDS is not a black or white disease. AIDS is not just a male disease. AIDS is found in women; it is found in children. In the future AIDS will probably increase and spread among people who are not homosexual or intravenous drug abusers in the same manner as other sexually transmitted diseases like syphilis and gonorrhea.

Sex Between Men. Men who have sexual relations with other men are especially at risk. About 70 percent of AIDS victims throughout the country are male homosexuals and bisexuals. This percentage probably will decline as heterosexual transmission increases. *Infection results from a sexual relationship with an infected person.*

Multiple Partners. The sexual revolution is over. The risk of infections increases according to the number of sexual partners one has, *male or female.* The more partners you have, the greater the risk of becoming infected with the AIDS virus.

How Exposed. Although the AIDS virus is found in several body fluids, a person acquires the virus during sexual contact with an infected person's blood or semen and possibly vaginal secretions. The virus then enters a person's blood stream through their rectum, vagina or penis.

Small (unseen by the naked eye) tears in the surface lining of the vagina or rectum may occur during insertion of the penis, fingers, or other objects, thus opening an avenue for entrance of the virus directly into the blood stream; therefore, the AIDS virus can be passed from penis to rectum and vagina and vice versa without a visible tear in the tissue or the presence of blood.

Prevention of Sexual Transmission—Know Your Partner. Couples who maintain mutually faithful monogamous relationships (only one continuing sexual partner) are protected from AIDS through sexual transmission. If you have been faithful for at least five years and your partner has been faithful too, neither one of you is at risk. If you have not been faithful, then you and your partner are at risk. If your partner has not been faithful, then your partner is at risk which also puts you at risk. This is true for both heterosexual and homosexual couples. Unless it is possible to know with *absolute certainty* that neither you nor your sexual partner is carrying the virus of AIDS, you must use protective behavior. *Absolute certainty* means not only that you and your partner have maintained a mutually faithful monogamous sexual relationship, but it means that neither you nor your partner had used illegal intravenous drugs.

Some personal measures are adequate to safely protect yourself and others from infection by the AIDS virus and its complications. Among these are:

- If you have been involved in any of the high risk sexual activities described above or have injected illicit intravenous drugs into your body you should have a blood test to see if you have been infected with the AIDS virus. [Note: It is extremely important to carefully appraise testing. Proper counseling *before* being tested is vital to be prepared for a possible positive result.]

- If your test is positive or if you engage in high risk activities and choose not to have a test, you should tell your sexual partner. If you jointly decide to have sex, you must protect your partner by always using a rubber (condom) during (start to finish) sexual intercourse (vagina or rectum).

- If your partner has a positive blood test showing that he/she has been infected with the AIDS virus or you suspect that he/she has been exposed by previous heterosexual or homosexual behavior or use of intravenous drugs with shared needles and syringes, a rubber (condom) should always be used during (start to finish) sexual intercourse (vagina or rectum).

- If you or your partner is at high risk, avoid mouth contact with the penis, vagina, or rectum.

- Avoid all sexual activities which could cause cuts or tears in the linings of the rectum, vagina, or penis.

- Single teen-age girls must be warned that pregnancy and contracting sexually transmitted diseases can be the result of only one act of sexual intercourse.... The same is true for teenage boys who should also not have rectal intercourse with other males. It may result in AIDS.

- Do not have sex with prostitutes. Infected male and female prostitutes are frequently also intravenous drug abusers; therefore, they may infect clients by sexual intercourse and other intravenous drug abusers by sharing their intravenous drug equipment. Female prostitutes also can infect their unborn babies.

Intravenous Drug Users. Drug abusers who inject drugs are another population group at high risk and with high rates of infection by the AIDS virus. Users of intravenous drugs make up 25 percent of the cases of AIDS throughout the country. The AIDS virus is carried in contaminated blood left in the needle, syringe, or other drug related implements and the virus is injected into the new victim by reusing dirty syringes and needles. Even the smallest amount of infected blood left in a used needle or syringe can contain live AIDS virus to be passed on to the next user of those dirty implements.

No one should shoot up drugs because addiction, poor health, family disruption, emotional disturbances and death could follow. However, many drug users are addicted to drugs and for one reason or another have not changed their behavior. For these people, the only way not to get AIDS is *to use a clean, previously unused* needle, syringe or any other implement necessary for the injection of the drug solution.

Hemophilia. Some persons with hemophilia (a blood clotting disorder that makes them subject to bleeding) have been infected with the AIDS virus either through blood transfusion or the use of blood products that help their blood clot. Now that we know how to prepare safe blood products to aid clotting, this is unlikely to happen. This group represents a very small percentage of the cases of AIDS throughout the country.

Blood Transfusion. Currently all blood donors are initially screened and blood is *not* accepted from high risk individuals. Blood that has been collected for use is tested for the presence of antibody to the AIDS virus. However, some people may have had a blood transfusion prior to March 1985 before we knew how to screen blood for safe transfusion and may have become infected with the AIDS virus. With routine testing of blood products, the blood supply for transfusion is now safer than it has ever been with regard to AIDS.

Persons who have engaged in homosexual activities or have shot street drugs within the last ten years should *never* donate blood.

Mother can infect newborn. If a woman is infected with the AIDS virus and becomes pregnant, she is more likely to develop ARC or classic AIDS, and she can pass the AIDS virus to her unborn child. Approximately one third of the babies born to AIDS-infected mothers will also be infected with the AIDS virus. Most of the infected babies will eventually develop the disease and die. Several of these babies have been born to wives of hemophiliac men infected with AIDS by way of contaminated blood products. Some babies have also been born to women who became infected with the AIDS virus by bisexual partners who had the virus. Almost all babies with AIDS have been born to women who were intravenous drug users or the sexual partners of intravenous drug users who were infected with the AIDS virus. More such babies can be expected.

Think carefully if you plan on becoming pregnant. If there is any chance that you may be in any high risk group or that you have had sex with someone in a high risk group, such as homosexual and bisexual males, drug abusers, and their sexual partners, see your doctor.

Summary. AIDS affects certain groups of the population. Homosexual and bisexual males who have had sexual contact with other homosexual or bisexual males as well as those who "shoot" street drugs are at greatest risk of exposure, infection and eventual death. Sexual partners of these high risk individuals are at risk, as well as any children born to women who carry the virus. Heterosexual persons are increasingly at risk.[25]

The global strategy as recommended by the World Health Organization in the prevention of AIDS worldwide "continues to depend on education, the use of condoms, and protection of the blood supply."[26]

CONDOMS AND STERILIZED NEEDLES

When discussing preventive measures and changing behavior, the subject of condoms and sterilization of needles is critical. One example of a state providing explicit education materials for prevention is Maryland. In its report about AIDS in the State of Maryland, the Department of Health and Hygiene included this information:

Using condoms every single time one has sex is absolutely crucial. The proper use of condoms will usually protect you effectively from other sexually transmitted diseases (STD or VD).... Safer sex means using condoms (rubbers) every time. Condoms can't protect you, however, if they break. Therefore, it is essential to learn how to use a condom BEFORE sexual contact. Learning to use a condom includes— how to choose a condom (rubber latex), finding the right kind of lubricant, putting on correctly, how to make them a part of your sex life and discussing with your partner the use of condoms.

The sharing of needles is also a form of transmittal of the AIDS virus. Thus, a clean, sterilized needle is essential every time before injecting the drug into the body. Running water through the needle, syringe, or works is not enough—it does not clean the needle or kill the HIV infection. Traces of infected blood are still left behind, even undetected by the naked eye.

If you are an IV drug user, use only your own works. If you do use someone else's, clean the needle and syringe with bleach straight from the bottle before injection. Pull the bleach into the needle and syringe, and push it out. Do this twice. Using bleach to clean needles and syringes is fast, easy, inexpensive, and may save your life.[27]

TREATMENT

The researchers in the field of AIDS are in the midst of a major effort to discover, develop, and test potential therapies for HIV infection and AIDS. "These efforts have focused on two major areas: (1) antiviral drugs with a direct effect against the causative agent, HIV, and (2) immunomodulators that act to reconstitute or enhance immune-system function in patients with HIV infection and AIDS."[28] In addition, progress is being made in the development of treatment for specific opportunistic infections and cancers that are associated with the disease.

Researchers attempting to discover and develop anti-HIV drugs are pursuing two approaches: screening large numbers of existing compounds for activity against HIV and targeting drug development with information gained about unique properties and critical functions of the virus to design agents that interfere with structural components of the life cycle of the virus.[29]

Clinical trials are the method employed to test the drugs that have the possibility of treating the AIDS virus. Clinical trials are carried out through a three-step process and involve progressively larger numbers of AIDS or HIV-positive diagnosed individuals. Drug sponsors arrange with physicians and hospitals to conduct these trials.

Phase I trials are concerned primarily with learning more about the safety of the drug, though they may also provide information about effectiveness. They provide information on: how the drug is absorbed, metabolized, and excreted; what effect it has on various organs and tissues; and what side effects it has as doses are increased.

Phase I testing is generally done on a small number of healthy volunteers. They are usually paid for their services, which essentially consists of submitting to a variety of tests to learn what happens to the drug in the human body. One of the chief causes of failure in this phase is evidence of toxicity at doses too small to produce any beneficial effect.

Phase II trials are designed to show whether the drug is effective in treating the condition for which it is intended. They also attempt to disclose short-term side effects and risks in people whose health is impaired.

Most Phase II trails are *randomized control studies*. Placebos are used when there is no historic or positive control available.

Phase III testing is geared to developing information that will allow the drug to be marketed and used safely. Optimum dose rates and schedules are determined and, hopefully, long-term side effects are revealed.[30]

Because of the frightening and increasing statistics on the rate of infection versus percentages of death from exposure to HIV, there has been mounting tension between the desire to provide potential treatment as quickly and widely as possible, and the necessity for accurate answers gained through carefully designed and monitored research. There has been much controversy surrounding the issue that the researchers are rigidly adhering to experimental traditions and rules that are not relevant to the AIDS crisis and that consequently impede progress to solutions desperately needed. Advocates of AIDS and HIV-positive patients feel that the structure and guidelines of the clinical trials are too complex and restrictive in their criteria for admission and execution. Consequently, there is mounting pressure on the scientific community to loosen its standards for drug evaluation and therefore to widely distribute the experimental treatments now because of the lethal results if experimental treatment is not accessible to currently infected patients.

DRUGS USED IN TREATMENT OF AIDS

The only drug currently licensed by the Food and Drug Administration (FDA) for the treatment for the HIV infection is AZT, a compound that interferes with virus replication. Carefully administered, it could significantly prolong life for certain individuals with AIDS. However, it does have considerable toxic side effects, including suppression of production of bone marrow.

A number of related antiviral compounds are also being investigated to see if they may be as effective as AZT, with less toxic side effects. Other drugs, alone and in conjunction with AZT, are also being explored in the hope of achieving greater results with reduced toxicities. AZT has recently been discovered to significantly prolong the length of life in asymptomatic or minimally symptomed HIV infected individuals.

VACCINE

The development of a vaccine against HIV infection is considered of utmost importance in the medical community. However, despite the intensive and costly research, as well as major scientific advances, a vaccine is still years away.

Developing a successful vaccine against HIV infection is difficult for several reasons. The first is because of the nature of the virus itself. "Many different strains of HIV exist, and even within one person's body, the virus can undergo mutations rapidly and easily. In addition, scientists still do not fully understand the nature of an effective immune response that can protect against initial infection of disease progression following infection."[31]

The second is a result of the inability to rely on past research methods. Progress made in the development of vaccines for past epidemics, such as polio and influenza, was gained due to the ability to research those epidemic sufferers who had recovered without treatment—using only their body's natural immune response. Because there have been no recovered patients from the AIDS virus, this critical method of research is nonexistent. Therefore, the task for the scientists has been further complicated.

Usually, vaccines that are potential successes are approved for distribution only after safety and immunogenicity are demonstrated in both laboratory and animal studies. However, because of the severity of the AIDS epidemic, active lobbying groups are demanding faster medical results and therefore the FDA has approved initial testing of several candidate vaccines.

SEARCH FOR A CURE

The wide scope of the AIDS epidemic and the urgency of developing treatments and a cure represent an enormous challenge for the medical profession.

Building upon a strong foundation of knowledge accumulated over several decades of research in such fields as immunology, microbiology, infectious diseases, molecular biology, and epidemiology, AIDS research efforts have moved forward swiftly and productively since this new disease was first recognized. Seldom has biomedical science progressed so rapidly, yet real solutions to the control and prevention of HIV infection remain elusive. Perhaps more than any other disease, AIDS has raised a host of complex questions, from the most fundamental nature of biological systems to the role of scientific research in society at large.[32]

COMMENTS

The dynamics of the AIDS virus are increasingly changing much of the medical field's methods of research and administration of treatment. As such research continues, new methodologies for treatment will be forthcoming. It is essential that the rest of society support this research and recognize the tremendous importance of the work being done in medical and research fields. The workplace will benefit enormously from all new medical findings. Therefore, it has a responsibility to support this effort financially as well as through education. Major funding will be necessary to support the treatment for the increasing number of persons with AIDS. It is time that the corporate social responsibility of U.S. business be called into action.

NOTES

1. *Surgeon General's Report on Acquired Immune Deficiency Syndrome*, U.S. Department of Health and Human Services and the American Red Cross, 1987, p. 21.

2. *Facts about AIDS*, U.S. Department of Health and Human Services, Public Health Control, Spring 1987, p. 1.

3. Sam B. Puckett and Alan R. Emery, *Managing AIDS in the Workplace* (Reading, MA: Addison-Wesley, 1988), pp. 1–2.

4. Robert C. Gallo and Luc Montagnier, "AIDS in 1988," *Scientific American*, October 1988, p. 41.

5. Robert E. Garry et al., "Documentation of an AIDS Virus Infection in the

United States in 1968," *Journal of the American Medical Association* 260, no. 14 (October 14, 1988): 2085.

6. Edited by Richard Golub and Eric Brus, prepared by World Information Systems, *The Almanac of Science and Technology: What's New and What's Known* (Orlando, FL: Harcourt Brace Jovanovich, 1990), p. 387.

7. Gallo and Montagnier, "AIDS in 1988," p. 47.

8. Max Essex and Phyllis J. Kanki, "The Origins of the AIDS Virus," *Scientific American*, October 1988, p. 66.

9. Thomas Bass, "Interview, Luc Montagnier," *Omni*, December 1988, p. 130.

10. Gallo and Montagnier, "AIDS in 1988," p. 41.

11. Bass, "Interview," p. 102.

12. Puckett and Emery, *Managing AIDS in the Workplace*, p. 4.

13. Anthony R. Measham, Chief, PHRHN, "Subject: World Health Organization/Global Programme on AIDS (WHO/GPA) Management Committee Meeting, Geneva, December 6–8, 1989," The World Bank/IFC/MIGA Office Memorandum, p. 1.

14. Jonathan M. Mann et al., "The International Epidemiology of AIDS," *Scientific American* October 1988, p. 84.

15. "Transmission of the AIDS Virus," *Science* 239, no. 4840 (February 5, 1988): 573–74.

16. Patricia Gadsby, "AIDS Watch," *Discover*, April 1988, p. 31.

17. "Transmission of the AIDS Virus," p. 575.

18. *Report of the Surgeon General's Workshop on Children with HIV Infection and Their Families*, U.S. Department of Health and Human Services, April 1987, pp. 3–4.

19. "Human Immunodeficiency Virus in the United States: A Review of Current Knowledge," *Morbidity and Mortality Weekly Report* 36, No. S–6, (U.S. Department of Health and Human Services, December 18, 1987), p. 3.

20. "AIDS and the Safety of the Nation's Blood Supply," American Red Cross, U.S. Public Health Service, pp. 2–3.

21. *Morbidity and Mortality Weekly Report*, p. 5.

22. Ibid., p. 8.

23. Puckett and Emery, "Managing AIDS in the Workplace," pp. 30–32.

24. *Surgeon General's Report on Acquired Immune Deficiency Syndrome*, p. 12.

25. Ibid., pp. 14–21.

26. Measham, "Subject: World Health Organization/Global Programme on AIDS," p. 2.

27. Maryland Department of Health and Hygiene, "Report on Acquired Immune Deficiency Syndrome," 1987, pp. 23–24.

28. Margaret A. Hamburg and Anthony S. Fauci, "AIDS: The Challenge to Biomedical Research," *Daedalus*, Winter 1989, pp. 28–29.

29. Ibid.

30. Presidential Commission on the Human Immunodeficiency Virus Epidemic, Chairman's Recommendations (Washington, DC, February 29, 1988), p. 56.

31. Hamburg and Fauci, "AIDS: The Challenge to Biomedical Research," pp. 34–35.

32. Ibid., p. 36.

CHAPTER 2

LEGAL ISSUES

INTRODUCTION

When an employer deals with a question of AIDS involving an employee or a job applicant, it is necessary to consider legal issues. The employer has to look beyond the scientific data and examine what the possible liability may be if negative action is taken against an applicant or employee with AIDS. Because expert medical opinion holds that AIDS can not be transmitted through casual contact, the legal trend has been to protect the applicant or employee with AIDS.

This chapter will examine the legal issues surrounding AIDS in the workplace. The discussion will begin with an overview of federal, state, and local statutes that have established precedents for how AIDS is dealt with in the workplace. Special attention will be given to the legal implications of the HIV antibody testing of employees and job applicants and the legal rights of both employers and employees. Insurance issues and laws that protect co-workers will be discussed, followed by a description of measures that employers can take to minimize the risks of litigation. It is important, however, to bear in mind that although the legal issues are important there are also basic ethical issues that each employer needs to consider.

ANTIDISCRIMINATION STATUTES

Federal Laws

To date, Congress has not enacted any legislation specifically addressing the issue of AIDS discrimination. Many persons with AIDS have, however,

sought protection from discrimination under the federal Vocational Rehabilitation Act of 1973, a model disability statute that was enacted before
AIDS was known. Section 503 of this act requires government contractors
and subcontractors with contracts of $2,500 or more to implement affirm-
ative action plans to employ qualified individuals with handicaps.[1] Most
federal courts that have considered the question have concluded that Section
503 does not give employees who have been discriminated against because
of handicap a private right of action against the employer, although there
is some judicial authority to the contrary. Under Section 503 (b), such
employees may file a complaint with the Department of Labor, which has
responsibility for investigating the complaint and taking appropriate action.[2]
Section 504 prohibits discrimination against "an otherwise qualified individual with handicaps" under any federal program or activity or any other
program or activity receiving federal financial assistance.[3] The act defines
a handicapped person as one who "(1) has a physical or mental impairment
which substantially limits one or more of such person's life activities, or (2)
has a record of such impairment, or (3) is regarded as having such an
impairment."[4]

The most recent antidiscrimination statute is the Americans With Disabilities Act of 1989. Based on sections 503 and 504 of the Rehabilitation
Act of 1973, the act clarifies the definitions of disability, a qualified person
with a disability, reasonable accommodation, and discrimination. More
importantly, the Americans With Disabilities Act mandates that employers
are prohibited from discriminating against individuals with disabilities, provides standards for addressing discrimination against individuals, and gives
the federal government the authority to act on behalf of individuals with
disabilities. Since AIDS clearly is a disability, this act supports the need for
employers to develop company policies before it becomes an issue at their
workplace.

In June 1986 the Office of Legal Counsel in the U.S. Department of Justice
issued an opinion regarding the applicability of the Vocational Rehabilitation Act to AIDS. In this controversial statement, the Justice Department
concluded that persons with AIDS are handicapped within the meaning of
the Vocational Rehabilitation Act but that Section 504 does not apply to
communicable diseases.[5] Under this view employers would not be barred
from discriminating against persons with AIDS when there is concern regarding the transmission of the disease in the workplace, even if this concern
is based solely on co-worker fears.[6]

The U.S. Supreme Court implicitly rejected the Justice Department's position in the context of tuberculosis in *School Board of Nassau County v.
Arline*.[7] Arline, a third-grade teacher, was fired from her job because of
reoccurring problems due to tuberculosis. Her lawsuit under Section 504
of the Vocational Rehabilitation Act was dismissed by the U.S. District
Court "which found it difficult . . . to conceive that Congress intended con-

tagious diseases to be included within the definition of a handicapped person."[8] The Court of Appeals reversed the decision and it was affirmed by the Supreme Court.[9] The Supreme Court held that people with contagious diseases, such as tuberculosis, are handicapped, as defined by the act.[10] The Supreme Court stated:

The fact that some persons who have contagious diseases may pose a serious health threat to others under certain circumstances does not justify excluding from the coverage of the Act all persons with actual or perceived contagious diseases. Such exclusion would mean that those accused of being contagious would never have the opportunity to have their condition evaluated in light of medical evidence and a determination made as to whether they were "otherwise qualified."[11]

Although the Supreme Court mentioned AIDS in its opinion, it explicitly refrained from expressing any view as to whether it constituted a "handicap" within the meaning of the statute. Most commentators believe, however, that the reasoning in Arline would apply to AIDS, and several lower federal courts have reached that conclusion.[12]

The Office of Federal Contract Compliance Programs (OFCCP), which has primary responsibility in the U.S. Department of Labor, has taken the position that AIDS does fit the Vocational Rehabilitation Act's definition of "handicap."[13] Because of the debilitating effects of AIDS, persons afflicted with the disease have been successful in obtaining relief from the Labor Department. Once it has been determined that a person is "handicapped" under the Vocational Rehabilitation Act, it is necessary to determine whether the individual is "otherwise qualified" for the position.[14] On December 23, 1988, the OFCCP issued a policy statement for complaint investigations under Section 503 of the Vocational Rehabilitation Act stating that all HIV-related conditions are considered handicaps under the act and the office will investigate all complaints of AIDS-based discrimination.[15]

Since AIDS is regarded as a handicap under federal law, employers are subject to federal laws that prohibit discrimination against the handicapped, and employees and job applicants are entitled to protection under these laws. Therefore, employers cannot discriminate against individuals who are known or suspected to be infected with HIV if the person is "otherwise qualified" to perform the job. Once the handicapping illness has progressed to the point where the employee can no longer perform his or her job, the employer may legally terminate the employee.[16] An employer must ensure, however, that he or she has provided reasonable accommodation for the handicapped employee, as required by the Vocational Rehabilitation Act, before termination. Reasonable accommodation requires flexibility by both the employer and employee. It may include adjusting job duties, changing the work area, and allowing flexible working hours. Under the law, an employer may also consult with the employee's physician to obtain assistance in making these accommodations.[17]

An employer may not move an HIV-infected worker from one position to another in order to deal with co-worker fears. Segregation, forced leave of absence, or termination without solid medical justification would violate the statute's prohibitions against discrimination on the basis of disability. For example, in the *Chalk* case,[18] the school board reassigned Chalk, an HIV-infected classroom teacher, to an administrative position. The District Court denied Chalk a preliminary injunction against the reassignment.[19] The U.S. Court of Appeals for the Ninth Circuit reversed the decision and granted an injunction placing Chalk back in the classroom. Starting with the determination that the Arline decision is applicable to AIDS, the court held that Chalk was "otherwise qualified" to perform his work in the absence of evidence that casual contact between a person infected with AIDS and children can transmit the disease.[20]

State Laws

To ensure that the protection loop for the handicapped is closed and that employers not subject to the federal Vocational Rehabilitation Act cannot discriminate against the handicapped, many states have enacted laws specifically addressing the issue of AIDS employment discrimination. Many states, like the federal government, have chosen to use existing discrimination laws to protect persons with AIDS.

As with the federal antidiscrimination statutes, such state legislation has generally been construed to prohibit discrimination against persons with an HIV infection as long as the individual is able to perform the job.[21] It is important for employers to find out if laws in their states are applicable either by express language or by interpretation to AIDS-related employment discrimination. Well over half the states have statutes protecting the handicapped, and since the trend in judicial interpretation suggests that AIDS will be regarded as a handicap, a large amount of litigation is anticipated.[22] Twenty-one states, including Washington, Michigan, Ohio, California, and Florida, have "formally classified AIDS as a handicap."[23] Some examples follow.

A New Jersey statute bars discrimination by state and private employers against qualified individuals with disabilities who are able to work with reasonable accommodation, and a court in that state has held AIDS to be a disability under the statute, albeit in the context of housing rather than employment discrimination.[24]

The California Fair Employment and Housing Act prohibits employers from discriminating against persons with a physical handicap or medical condition. In the case of *California Employment and Housing Commission v. Raytheon Company*, the California State Fair Housing and Employment

Commission determined that AIDS could be considered a handicap within the meaning of the statute. The Commission defined a physical handicap as "any physical condition of the body that has a disabling effect" and added that a handicap includes not only physical "conditions that disable in the present," but also "conditions . . . that may handicap in the future but have no present disabling effects." The Commission's decision was upheld by the court.[25]

In the case of *Shuttleworth v. Broward County Office of Budget and Management Policy*, a federal district court affirmed the decision of the Florida Commission on Human Relations that the firing of a person with AIDS violated the Florida Human Rights Act, which defines a "handicapped person" as an individual who "does not enjoy, in some manner, the full and normal use of his sensory, mental or physical facilities."[26] The Commission relied on medical evidence regarding the nature of the disease and the virtually nonexistent risk of transmission through casual contact.[27]

In a final example, a Massachusetts court supported the position of the Massachusetts Commission Against Discrimination that persons with AIDS are entitled to protection under the state handicap law, which is similar to the federal Vocational Rehabilitation Act of 1973. In *Cronin v. New England Telephone Company*, after the employee revealed to his supervisor that he was HIV infected the supervisor shared this information with his superiors who in turn informed other employees at several large group meetings. After receiving threats from co-workers, Cronin did not return to work for several months and his requests to return later were denied. After being diagnosed as having AIDS, he filed suit, claiming breach of privacy, violation of the state handicap statute, and violation of civil rights laws against the employer. The court rejected the defendant's contention that employers have a right to discriminate against persons with AIDS when there is a fear of transmission of the disease.[28]

Local Laws

Several cities have enacted laws that explicitly address the issue of AIDS discrimination in the workplace. These ordinances are similar to state and federal laws in that they prohibit discrimination against an "otherwise qualified" person with AIDS who is capable of performing his job responsibilities. Los Angeles, Sacramento, West Hollywood, and San Francisco have adopted such ordinances, and so has Austin, Texas.[29]

In Boston, an executive order prohibits discrimination against persons with AIDS in hiring, promotions, and employee benefits.[30] Both the San Francisco and Los Angeles employment discrimination laws allow claims for punitive damages.[31] New York City's Human Rights Commission has "pledged to prosecute any employer that discriminates against AIDS victims."[32]

Persons with AIDS who might not be protected under other laws may be protected under local ordinances. For example, the Federal Vocational Rehabilitation Act protects only those who work for federal contractors or subcontractors, or for programs that receive financial assistance. Employees of small businesses in a state that does not have antidiscrimination statutes who otherwise would not be protected might have protection against AIDS-related discrimination under a city ordinance.

Persons "Perceived" As Having AIDS

As the number of AIDS cases increases, employers are confronted with employees who have family members and friends who are infected with HIV or AIDS. Across the country, a variety of court cases have been heard as a result of persons "perceived" as having AIDS filing discrimination charges against their employers. In *Peterson v. Sperry Corporation* (Minnesota, 1987), an employee won a settlement for compensatory and punitive damages alleging that the company did not sufficiently respond to his allegation of harassment by co-workers who believed he had AIDS.

In *Leckelt v. Board of Commissioners*, Leckelt, a male licensed practical nurse at a county hospital in Louisiana, was fired for refusing to take an HIV antibody test after his roommate, who had AIDS, was admitted to and later died at the hospital where Leckelt worked.[33] Leckelt was asked by the hospital's infection control director, on behalf of the executive committee, to take a HIV antibody test. He refused to take the test or obtain the results of an anonymous test that he had chosen to take around the time of his roommate's death for fear that it might affect his job. After his termination, Leckelt brought suit against the hospital under Section 504 of the Vocational Rehabilitation Act and under the Louisiana handicap law on the basis that the hospital perceived him to be handicapped because of his alleged seropositivity. The hospital defended its decision by claiming it had a right to test an employee in order to effectively implement the prescribed CDC guidelines for the prevention of HIV transmission in the workplace. A federal district court declared that the hospital had a right to force disclosure of seropositivity to "fulfill its obligations to its employees and to the public concerning infection control and health and safety in general."[34] Leckelt was not found to be "otherwise qualified under Section 504 of the Vocational Rehabilitation Act." His attorneys plan to appeal the decision.[35]

Employer Defenses/Burden of Proof

Employers most frequently justify not hiring or employing persons with an AIDS-related condition based upon the following:

- the person is not "otherwise qualified"
- fear of contagion
- fear of loss of business, particularly in certain businesses such as restaurants and hotels
- increased costs and/or absenteeism.[36]

Generally, however, these rationales have not been accepted by the courts and agencies that adjudicate the cases.

An employer has the right under certain conditions to require a physical examination to determine if employment of a particular person would pose a risk or threat to others. However, it must be shown that the absence of HIV infection is a bona fide occupational qualification applicable to job performance. The medical examination should not be AIDS-specific since medical experts assert that AIDS is a health risk in the workplace only in special circumstances. Accordingly, if an employer wishes to require a physical examination, the requirement should be set forth in written company policies and should be applicable to all employees. In addition, written company policies should define the conditions under which leaves of absence will be permitted for illness and the circumstances under which employment will be available upon return from leave.[37] At a minimum, leave of absence should be available only in case of life-threatening illnesses. A policy should make it clear that part-time performance is not expected for a full-time position. In this connection, it is important that the employer be able to demonstrate that reasonable accommodation has otherwise been made to the employee's handicap. Employers have the right to expect their employees to report to work fit for duty.

In a suit for discrimination on account of disability, the plaintiff has the burden of proving that he or she is perceived as having a handicap, is able to perform the required job with reasonable accommodations, and was discriminated against because of his or her handicap.[38] The employer, or defendant, must prove that the employee's handicapping condition was not a factor in the decision or that persons with the disability in question are excluded from working because of justifiable business necessity.[39] Although most federal and state disability laws are similar, the burden of proof can vary from statute to statute and jurisdiction to jurisdiction.[40] Employers must also be aware of the requirements of executive orders and local ordinances that apply to their place of business.

LEGAL IMPLICATIONS OF HIV SCREENING

The most controversial issue concerning AIDS in the workplace is HIV screening. For the purposes of this discussion the author is addressing the subject from the perspective of the employer initiating the testing. With the development of new treatment drugs, employees may now request to be tested so that they may have access to these drugs if they test positive. This will raise a host of additional questions for employers that will not be legal issues alone. At the present time there are no federal statutes that prohibit private employers from testing applicants or employees. However, public employers at the federal, state, and local levels may be subject to constitutional limitations. For example, a U.S. district court for Nebraska held that a state agency's mandatory HIV antibody testing program for employees whose positions involved considerable client contact violated the Fourth Amendment guarantee against unreasonable searches and seizures.[41] Owing to the overwhelming medical evidence that AIDS is not spread through casual contact, the court concluded that, even though many of the agency's clients displayed violent or aggressive behavior, it was not reasonable for the state agency to require mandatory testing for the asserted purpose of protecting clients and providing a safe working environment.[42] This decision was affirmed by the U.S. Court of Appeals for the Eighth Circuit, which agreed that mandatory screening was a search or seizure, but concluded that it was unreasonable based on a balancing of the employees' privacy rights against the state's interest in the safety of its clients and personnel.[43]

Many state laws prohibit HIV antibody testing to screen applicants or employees. Florida, Wisconsin, Vermont, California, and the District of Columbia prohibit or restrict the use of HIV antibody test results for the purposes of employment decisions.[44] Moreover, California and Wisconsin prohibit the disclosure of test results, even where the tests are presumably for the protection of the person with the HIV infection.[45] A New Mexico statute enacted in 1989 prohibits employers from requiring individuals to disclose the result of an HIV antibody test as a condition of hiring, promotion, or continued employment, unless the absence of HIV infection is a bona fide occupational qualification. If so, then the employer must prove that the HIV antibody test is necessary to determine whether the individual is currently able to perform the job or whether there is a risk of transmitting the virus while performing the job duties.[46] San Francisco has a similar law.[47]

The Centers for Disease Control have suggested "there is no medical justification for employee screening in virtually any civilian workplace."[48] Simply stated, the test results are not indicators of the employee's ability to perform the job. If an applicant or employee tests positive for the presence of HIV antibodies, they would more than likely be considered handicapped under federal and state employment discrimination laws; therefore the employer may not take any adverse action against the individual unless he or she is not "otherwise qualified."

Employers must have reasonable cause to require an applicant to submit to an HIV antibody test. Acceptable reasons include justifiable concern about possible exposure of others to HIV through the employee's involvement in an accident or through performance of job duties. Current law does not prohibit employers from testing for the presence of HIV after careful analysis of the particular situation and for legitimate reasons.[49]

As with most tests for sexually transmitted diseases, the most commonly used AIDS test does not test for the presence of the virus but rather for the presence of antibodies, a substance produced by the body in response to infection by a foreign agent.[50] Once a person has become infected with HIV, it can take from a few weeks to, in some cases, up to a year for the antibody to be detected in the body. Currently, the most commonly used and least expensive test is the ELISA test. Because of its high sensitivity to the presence of HIV antibodies, there is increased chance of an accurate positive result if antibodies are present in the body.[51] Bearing in mind the nature of the AIDS virus and its sometimes lengthy incubation period, employers should not rely solely on the results of one ELISA test. It is recommended that a second ELISA test be performed, followed by the Western Blot test—the process of taking cultures of the virus from the blood to test for the presence of actual live virus—for confirmation. Although the Western Blot test is more complicated and more expensive than the ELISA, employers should not eliminate this step when implementing a responsible HIV antibody testing program.

When implementing an HIV antibody testing program, employers need to consider whether the sensitive information obtained as a result of these tests is worth the potential liability and the attention that would have to be devoted to producing accurate test results and ensuring that these results remain confidential.[52] At the present time HIV antibody test results are useless to employers when making personnel decisions. Employers should make the following considerations when contemplating whether to test job applicants or employees for AIDS:

1. Current tests only determine whether an individual has been exposed to AIDS and not whether the individual currently has, or will contract, the disease.

2. Current tests yield a significant percentage of "false positive" and "false negative" results.

3. It is unlikely that a person exposed to AIDS will be incapable of performing the duties of his or her job.

4. Disclosure of confidential medical records indicating an individual tested positive can expose an employer to liability.

5. Several states prohibit testing, or the use of tests, to deny employment or insurance coverage.[53]

The common law issues that place an employer at risk for liability in connection with testing include violation of the employee's right to privacy through breach of confidentiality, improper communication of medical records, and defamation.[54] Any employer who considers releasing the results of an employee's AIDS test should recognize that doing so places the company at risk for invasion of privacy claims under state laws or constitutional provisions, defamation claims arising from dissemination of test results, or claims for intentional or negligent infliction of emotional distress.[55] Because of the high probability that disclosure of an employee's positive HIV diagnosis will result in negative treatment by fellow workers, employers should conclude that the probability of losing a lawsuit is even higher if disclosure is made by the company. If the employer nevertheless regards some such disclosure as necessary, the employer, to attempt to provide some protection from such liability, should make an effort to obtain a written authorization from the employee.

A clear understanding of the legal issues regarding HIV antibody testing in the workplace will enable employers to anticipate problems and take preventive measures, such as adopting a comprehensive policy addressing life-threatening illnesses including AIDS. These preventive measures will not only minimize the risk of litigation but they will also improve employee relations. However, because the risks involved in testing outweigh the benefits, it is legally sound to refrain from HIV antibody testing in the absence of federal, state, or local statutory laws that protect employers from liability.

Employers should be aware that an increasing number of lawsuits are being filed by employees asserting breach of privacy or employment contract, infliction of emotional distress, and violation of good faith and fair dealing. The discharge or segregation of an employee with AIDS has often operated an invitation to the employee to bring suit.[56] Many such suits have been for alleged wrongful discharge, particularly in state courts. Until recently these cases were viewed unfavorably in some state courts. Now the courts are more receptive where the discharge (1) violates assurances of job security, (2) is contrary to the disciplinary procedures outlined in personnel manuals, or (3) undermines public policies based on state and federal laws.[57] A significant number of claims reportedly have been filed in California by persons with AIDS who were discharged in violation of personnel manual provisions or in an offensive manner. In these cases, many plaintiffs have been successful in obtaining sizable recoveries.[58]

The trend in recent cases indicates that employees have rights to privacy that can be violated by "intrusive" tests or disclosing information of a confidential nature.[59] Because of the panic surrounding AIDS, disclosure of information about an employee's AIDS-related diagnosis without prior permission substantially increases the risk of an AIDS-related claim. In the case of *Cronin v. New England Telephone Company*, which was described earlier in this chapter, a trial court supported the legal action for breach of confidentiality under a state statute on behalf of Cronin, the employee whose supervisor revealed information about his HIV positivity status.

Employers should proceed cautiously when taking any adverse action against an employee with an AIDS-related condition. To avoid potential litigation or negative publicity, it is advisable to consult with the legal counsel at the company. Employers should have substantial documentation of all misbehavior and poor performance before discharging the employee. A Montana statute protecting employees from discharge except for legitimate, work-related reasons could be the basis for similar statutes in other states. Employers should establish reasonable personnel decision making and documentation procedures before, not after, legislative developments occur in their state.[60]

INSURANCE

Federal Laws

The federal Employee Retirement Income Security Act of 1974 (ERISA) prohibits employers from discriminating against employees for the purpose of interfering with their right to claim benefits under an employee benefit plan.[61] ERISA applies to most employers in the private sector and includes pension and benefit plans—health, disability, or life insurance policies or programs.[62] Persons with AIDS can find protection under Section 510 of ERISA, which prohibits employers from discriminating against or firing an employee "for the purpose of interfering with the attainment of any right to which such participant may become entitled under the plan."[63]

As a result of this legislation, an employer may be liable for firing an employee with an AIDS-related condition because he has filed a claim for benefits to which he is entitled, to prevent him from filing a future claim, or to prevent him from achieving eligibility for benefits.[64] Although the health care costs associated with AIDS are predicted to be about $60,000 per individual diagnosed between 1988 and 1998, employers place themselves at risk for huge penalties if an employee is able to prove in court that the termination was for the purpose of avoiding costs connected to AIDS-related benefits.[65]

As a result of amendments to ERISA in 1986, employers have the added obligation of permitting employees who have been terminated for reasons other than gross misconduct to continue to participate in the employee group benefit plan for up to 18 months after termination. The employer may require the employee to pay a premium not to exceed 2% above the normal premium in order to remain on the group plan. In addition, the benefits must be the same as that provided to active employees.[66]

State Laws

Because insurance companies did not know about the AIDS virus until recently, they did not make provision for AIDS-related claims. Some companies have tried to eliminate coverage for claims related to or caused by AIDS.[67] If employers accept these provisions, employees with AIDS will not have the needed coverage, and subsequently may be denied hospital care or other health services.

Several state and local governments have enacted laws to protect persons with AIDS from discrimination by insurance companies. The District of Columbia, Massachusetts, and Wisconsin prohibit AIDS tests for applicants for life insurance policies.[68] According to Goldberg, in 1989 an administrative opinion was issued in Oregon to the effect that the exclusion of AIDS treatment from a company's self-insured health insurance programs constitutes sex discrimination because of its impact on males.[69]

Some insurance companies have been refusing to compensate for claims filed for medical costs related to AIDS on the grounds that AIDS was a "pre-existing condition."

As long as insurance companies continue to believe that AIDS is a disease that should be tested for like any other illness, it is likely that they will continue to challenge state and local laws, particularly those concerning the testing of applicants.[70] However, to ensure that test results are valid, insurance companies would have to administer two ELISA tests and one Western Blot test for confirmation. The legal trend in AIDS-related legislation is to protect the person with AIDS at all costs; but as the costs continue to rise steadily, states may begin to permit insurance companies to test under certain conditions.[71]

CO-WORKER CONCERNS

Occupational Health and Safety Act

Co-worker concern about the spread of AIDS has made it necessary for employers to take special precautionary steps to protect their workforces. If employers fail to do so, workers may seek protection under the Occupational Health and Safety Act, which requires employers to provide a workplace free from known harmful substances and prohibits an employer from taking adverse action or discriminating against employees who exercise their rights under this act, including the right to protest unsafe working conditions.[72]

Hospital workers have had the greatest concern over the spread of AIDS because of the large quantities of blood they are exposed to on a daily basis. In November 1987 the Occupational Safety and Health Administration (OSHA) published an advance notice of proposed rulemaking to protect workers against viruses that may cause Hepatitis B and AIDS. Currently, employers have a duty to provide a safe working environment and provide personal protective equipment.[73] On May 30, 1989, a proposed comprehensive, revised rule was published in the Federal Register (54 FR 23042) for comments.[74] This OSHA standard will cover all occupational exposures to blood-borne diseases, such as AIDS or hepatitis B, or potentially dangerous exposures to body fluids to reduce the risk of exposure. Workers in health care, law enforcement, fire and rescue, correctional facilities, research laboratories, blood banks, and the funeral industry will be covered by this rule.[75] The final rule is expected in early 1991.

Some workers believe that they have a right to know whether their health and safety are in jeopardy, and consequently that they have the right to know the HIV antibody status of co-workers, patients, and clients. If an employer establishes an objective policy about employees' rights and the organization's attitude about its functions and responsibilities to clients, this will assist in protecting the employer against liability. When establishing a policy, employers should consider the potential for exposure to the virus in the particular type of workplace involved.[76]

In most non-health-care settings, there is no need for a worker to know the HIV antibody status of co-workers since the risk of transmission through casual contact is virtually nonexistent. Most employers have chosen to deal with this issue through employee education and well-publicized company policies. When dealing with the issue of the right to know about patients or clients, employees need to identify the federal, state, or local confidentiality laws and regulations that address the disclosure of HIV antibody status in regard to who can be told the information and under what circumstances.[77]

In health-care settings, the issue of workers' right to know is more controversial because of the increased chance of discrimination against HIV-positive persons by the workers who are responsible for treating them. Some states have reacted to the latter problem by enacting laws to protect HIV-positive patients. For example, Florida passed legislation making it illegal to discriminate against or behave in a manner that would limit a health-care professional's ability to earn a living because he or she treats patients who are HIV-positive.[78] In general, it has been accepted that health-care workers do not need to know the HIV antibody status if the facility follows the OSHA guidelines and imposes universal precautions. Even in life-threatening situations, the responsibility of workers to provide care outweighs the need to know the HIV antibody status.[79]

The National Labor Relations Act and the Labor-Management Relations Act

An employee in a nonunion setting who refuses to work with a co-worker with AIDS may seek protection under section 7 of the National Labor Relations Act (NLRA). NLRA protects employees engaged in "concerted activity" related to wages, hours, and working conditions. "Concerted activity" is the action by two or more employees, without union initiative, activity, or involvement for the mutual aid or protection of employees.[80] Unionized employees find similar protection under Section 502 of the Labor-Management Relations Act (LMRA).

Workers may file a claim with the National Labor Relations Board based on the fear of contracting AIDS. Employers, who have to protect the HIV-positive worker under antidiscrimination statutes, could find themselves in a real dilemma. However, if employees refuse to work with an HIV-positive co-worker, employers can legally replace the workers in order to maintain their businesses. If the employer chooses to resolve the problem at the expense of the employee with AIDS, the refusal of employees to work will not serve as a defense to a charge of discrimination.[81]

The best solution for dealing with employees who refuse to work with an HIV-positive co-worker because of fear of contracting AIDS is to conduct employee education sessions. In terms of labor-management relations, it is not wise to discharge workers because they have a genuine fear of contracting a disease while at work. An AIDS education program can be included in an overall health and safety plan. It should be well thought out and presented in a manner that demonstrates genuine concern about feelings. It should present the facts about AIDS and teach employees sensitivity toward and how to safely work with a co-worker with AIDS. If employees are armed with the facts, their feelings of panic may subside and they may be more hesitant about refusing to work with a co-worker with AIDS.

Arbitration

Employers with unionized employees may be forced to submit AIDS-related issues to labor arbitration. If there is a collective bargaining agreement between the employer and the union, the terms of the agreement may determine the employer's response. Many collective bargaining agreements require "just cause" for discharge and procedural rules for handling issues such as disability leave, sick leave, and benefits entitlement. Although less than 20 percent of the workforce is covered by these agreements, they are in effect in companies in states with a high incidence of AIDS, such as New York and California.[82]

In the case of *Minnesota Department of Corrections v. A.F.S.C.M.E. Council 6*, a prison guard, who was discharged for refusing to conduct pat-down searches of prisoners without protective gloves because of fear of contracting AIDS, was reinstated after an arbitration proceeding. The guard was reinstated without back pay and the prison officials were found to be at fault for not providing an education program for the guards.[83]

In another case, a male United Airlines flight attendant with AIDS was placed on unpaid leave of absence. The flight attendant wanted to continue to work and filed a grievance against the airline with his union. The grievance was taken to arbitration and United Airlines, who argued that their decision was based on the health and safety of its passengers and other employees, was found to have violated its collective bargaining agreement. United Airlines insisted that the attendant complete a physical exam by a qualified physician to determine his fitness for duty and the danger to the health of co-workers before returning to work. This request was determined to be a violation of the collective bargaining agreement and the attendant was reinstated with back pay.[84]

The primary question in arbitration proceedings is whether or not the employer had "just cause" to treat the employee in an adverse manner. It is likely that arbitrators will require employers to prove that their decision to involuntarily terminate, transfer, or place an employee on leave is justified.[85] Other issues to consider in arbitration proceedings are the specific HIV diagnosis, documentation to support the risk of transmission in the workplace, and the grievant's length of service and past work record. The longer the length of service and the better the work record, the more likely the arbitrator will favor the grievant.[86]

The number of AIDS-related grievances is increasing. Unions can certainly be expected to take a grievance to arbitration rather than risk a failure to prosecute a claim from the upset member. As this occurs, unions can also be expected to protect the rights of their members. With the burden of proof resting so heavily on the shoulders of the employer, it would be wise to consider carefully any decision to involuntarily discharge or place an employee on leave of absence. Also, one must ensure that the decision is made within the provisions of the collective bargaining agreement, if one exists.

PREVENTING CLAIMS BY EMPLOYEES

Earlier in this chapter, some employer defenses in litigation were examined. These defenses are part of some general measures that employers can take to prevent AIDS-related claims and promote cooperation and harmony in the workplace. These include an antidiscrimination policy, reasonable accommodation, employee education, confidentiality, and precautionary measures.

The soundest piece of advice to give to employers is to develop a responsible company policy that applies to all life-threatening illnesses. This action would automatically include AIDS and provide managers, as well as employees, with a guide to appropriate personnel practice. If an employer has an established process that provides for consistent treatment, and a policy statement that supports all employees as long as they can meet acceptable standards, and medical evidence continues to indicate that persons with AIDS pose no threat to other employees, then this could be the greatest protection an employer has against AIDS litigation.

Reasonable accommodation has been discussed in detail throughout the chapter. This can sometimes be a difficult task for the employer because of the uncertainty of the illness. The employee may feel capable of performing his or her job for a period of time, then experiences a period of ill health, and later may return to a functional capacity once again. Although employers who must meet the requirements of the federal Vocational Rehabilitation Act must provide reasonable accommodation to employees with disabilities, they do not have to implement measures that would cause undue hardship, such as exorbitant costs, to the company.[87]

It has often been said that education is the key to the prevention of the transmission of AIDS. In the workplace, educating employees on the medical facts about AIDS is essential to reducing fears of working with a co-worker with an AIDS-related condition. Special emphasis should be placed on informing employees that AIDS can not be transmitted through casual contact, providing educational materials that employees can read at their leisure, and teaching employees how to make a co-worker with an AIDS-related condition feel welcomed at work. Chapter 5 will discuss this in detail.

Confidentiality is a critical issue because of the negative perceptions of AIDS. One aspect of this issue that is being discussed in great detail is the question of when confidentiality can be broken. Unfortunately, employers have not been able to determine an answer to this question. It is important that all personnel keep all oral and written information regarding an applicant or an employee with an AIDS-related condition confidential. Access to the personnel and medical files containing this data should be restricted to only those persons who absolutely need to have knowledge of the case.[88] Employers must realize that although they have an obligation to keep an employee's illness confidential, at some point in the course of the illness this may become difficult. In preparation for this possible occurrence, rules for breach of confidentiality should be established.[89]

A final measure that employers can take to prevent AIDS-related claims and promote cooperation within the workplace is to provide protective equipment. It is common practice for food handlers, dentists, and other health care professionals to wear gloves. If protective equipment is utilized, this should be stated in the company policy and used as general practice by the entire workforce. In addition, employers should apply the recommendations and guidelines issued by the Centers for Disease Control that pertain to their specific type of work or work environment.

CONCLUSION

The legal issues presented by AIDS in the workplace are complex and varied. From a legal standpoint, as more cases are brought before the courts, new precedents will be established. Meanwhile, it is necessary for employers to proceed on the basis of currently available information to adopt company policies for dealing with AIDS-related issues and, more importantly, for handling each case in a consistent manner.

NOTES

The author is indebted to Adin C. Goldberg, Esq., for his presentation in April 1989 before the American Management Association. The outline of his talk entitled "Acquired Immune Deficiency Syndrome: Workplace Issues" suggested the organization of this chapter.

1. Section 503 is codified at 29 U.S.C. Sec. 793.

2. 29 U.S.C. Sec. 793(b).

3. 29 U.S.C. Sec. 794.

4. Codified at 29 U.S.C. Sec. 706 (7)(b).

5. Michael Abramowitz, "Justice Limits Job Protection for AIDS Victims," *Washington Post*, June 24, 1986, p. A1.

6. A. Goldberg, "Acquired Immune Deficiency Syndrome: Workplace Issues," speech given at the American Management Association Executive Briefing of "AIDS on the Workplace" in New York, April 12, 1989.

7. 480 U.S. 281 (1987).

8. Ibid., p. 277.

9. 772 F. 2d 759 (11th Cir. 1985).

10. 480 U.S. 281.

11. Ibid., p. 285.

12. See *Chalk v. United States District Court Central District of California*, 840 F. 2d. 701 (9th Cir. 1988).

13. BNA Fed. Contracts Rep., March 27, 1989, p. 565.

14. Barry Sullivan, et al., *AIDS: The Legal Issues Discussion Draft of the American Bar Association AIDS Coordinating Committee* (Washington, DC: American Bar Association, August 1988), p. 57.

15. Buraff Publications, *AIDS Policy and Law* 4, no. 5 (March 22, 1989): 4.

16. Sullivan, *AIDS: The Legal Issues*, p. 163.

17. American Management Association, *AIDS: The New Workplace Issues— American Management Briefing* (New York: AMA Membership Publications Division, 1988), p. 42.

18. Note 13, supra.

19. *John Doe v. Orange County Department of Education* (D.Cal.1987), 44 BNA Fair Emp. Prac. Cases 1579 (1987).

20. Note 13, supra.

21. Sullivan, *AIDS: The Legal Issues*, p. 166.

22. William F. Banta, *AIDS in the Workplace: Legal Questions and Practical Answers* (Lexington, MA: D. C. Heath, 1988), p. 64.

23. Ibid.

24. *Poff v. Caro*, 228 N.J. Super. 378, 549 A. 2d 988 (1988).

25. *Raytheon v. California Fair Employment and Housing Commission*, 269 Cal. Rptr. 197 (1989).

26. Harry N. Turk, "AIDS in the Workplace," in J. Parry and D. Rapoport, eds., *Legal, Medical and Governmental Perspectives on AIDS as a Disability* (Washington, DC: American Bar Association Commission on the Mentally Disabled, 1987), p. 36.

27. *Ibid. Shuttleworth v. Broward County Office of Budget and Management Policy*, 639 F. Supp. 654 (S.D. Fla., 1986).

28. Turk, "AIDS in the Workplace," p. 36.

29. Arthur Leonard, "AIDS in the Workplace," in H. Dalton and S. Burris, eds., *AIDS and the Law: A Guide for the Public* (New Haven, CT: Yale University Press, 1987), p. 120.

30. Banta, *AIDS in the Workplace*, p. 71.

31. Ibid.

32. Ibid, p. 72.

33. Buraff Publications, *AIDS Policy and Law* 4, no. 6 (April 5, 1989): 11.

34. Ibid.

35. *Ibid*, p. 1.

36. Goldberg, AMA Briefing.

37. Stephen S. Mayer, "Legal Aspects of AIDS in the Workplace," in Richard Waldstein and Jo-Ann Heyer, eds., *AIDS in the Workplace: Here Are the Answers You Must Have* (Englewood Cliffs, NJ: Prentice Hall, 1988), p. 17.

38. Benjamin Schatz, "Employment Discrimination," in P. Albert, L. Graff, and B. Schatz, eds., *AIDS Practice Manual: A Legal and Educational Guide*, 2nd ed. (San Francisco: National Gay Rights Advocates and National Lawyers Guild AIDS Network, 1988), Chapter IV, pp. 3–4.

39. Ibid, p. 4.

40. Ibid, p. 3.

41. *Glover v. Eastern Nebraska Office of Retardation*, 686 F. Supp. 243 (1988).

42. Ibid.

43. *Glover v. Eastern Nebraska Office of Retardation*, 867 F. 2d 461 (1989).

44. Banta, *AIDS in the Workplace*, p. 63.

45. Ibid, p. 63.

46. Buraff Publications. *AIDS Policy and Law* 4, no. 8 (May 3, 1989): 1.

47. Irving J. Sloan, *AIDS Law: Implications for the Individual and Society* (New York: Oceana, 1988), p. 39.

48. Leonard, "AIDS in the Workplace," p. 117.

49. Banta, *AIDS in the Workplace*, p. 119.

50. AMA, *AIDS: The New Workplace Issues*, p. 129.

51. Ibid.

52. Ibid, p. 131.

53. David B. Ritter and Ronald Turner, "AIDS: Employer Legal Concerns and Employer Options," in Waldstein and Heyer, *AIDS in the Workplace*, p. 13.

54. Banta, *AIDS in the Workplace*, p. 64.

55. Goldberg, AMA Briefing.

56. Leonard, "AIDS in the Workplace," p. 117.

57. AMA, *AIDS: The New Workplace Issues*, p. 124.

58. Leonard, "AIDS in the Workplace," p. 121.

59. AMA, *AIDS: The New Workplace Issues*, p. 124.

60. Ibid.

61. Banta, *AIDS in the Workplace*, p. 49.

62. Leonard, "AIDS in the Workplace," p. 118.

63. Employee Retirement Income Security Act of 1974 (29 U.S.C. 1140).

64. Leonard, "AIDS in the Workplace," p. 118.

65. Buraff Publications. *AIDS Policy and Law* 4, no. 4 (March 8, 1989): 3.

66. Leonard, "AIDS in the Workplace," p. 119.

67. Banta, *AIDS in the Workplace*, p. 80.

68. Goldberg, AMA Briefing.

69. Ibid.

70. Ibid, p. 82.

71. Ibid.

72. Turk, "AIDS in the Workplace," p. 39.

73. Goldberg, AMA Briefing.

74. 54 F.R. 23042.

75. Buraff Publications. *AIDS Policy and Law* 4, no. 10 (May 31, 1989): 2.

76. Mona Rowe. "Workers' Rights to Know: Managing the Issues," *AIDS Workplace Update* 1, no. 6 (Greenvale, NY: Panel Publishers, January 1989), p. 1.

77. Ibid, p. 7.

78. Ibid.

79. Ibid.

80. Banta, *AIDS in the Workplace*, p. 50.

81. Leonard, "AIDS in the Workplace", p. 122.

82. Ibid, p. 120.

83. AMA, *AIDS: The New Workplace Issues*, p. 128.

84. Banta, *AIDS in the Workplace*, p. 87.

85. Ibid, p. 89.

86. Ibid.

87. Ritter and Turner, "AIDS: Employer Legal Concerns," p. 13.

88. Banta, *AIDS in the Workplace*, p. 141.

89. Ibid.

CHAPTER 3

POLICY DEVELOPMENT

INTRODUCTION

This chapter will discuss the overall philosophy and need for implementation of an AIDS policy; principles to consider before the policy strategizing begins; planning and defining of the goals of the policy; key questions that need to be considered when developing the company AIDS policy; various populations affected by AIDS and their need for a policy; and the approach when beginning the policy implementation. Pertinent and currently existing policies will be included for comparison and review.

Two policies are presented from the private sector and two from the public sector. They were selected because they are excellent as well as comprehensive. Even though there are similarities there are also differences with several options provided for companies to choose what best fits their policy needs. The populations from the sample companies differ in the following ways: IBM has primarily a white-collar workforce, and Emhart, blue-collar; the U.S. Department of Health and Human Services from the public sector is a federal agency, whereas the policy from the state of Wisconsin is that of a midwestern state.

PHILOSOPHY

According to the *Surgeon General's Report on AIDS*, "Offices, factories, and other work sites should have a plan in operation for education of the work force and accommodation of AIDS or ARC patients *before* the first such case appears at the work site. Employees with AIDS or ARC should be dealt with as are any workers with a chronic illness."[1]

When discussing AIDS transmission in the workplace, employees should also be made aware of the conclusion of the Centers for Disease Control that there are "no work-related cases associated with AIDS, no casual household transmittal, nor any transmittal to health care workers who have dealt with AIDS patients in all stages of the illness."[2]

The main philosophy of an AIDS policy in the workplace is fourfold. The policy should communicate to all employees that the employer will treat AIDS as any other chronic or life-threatening disease; will give support to enable these employees to continue working as long as possible; will emphasize to all employees in the company that there is no danger of transmission through normal workplace contact; and will provide education for all employees of the company about the disease, ways of transmission, and prevention. The policy enables the employer to set a standard of fair management, justice, and compassion.

There are distinct advantages to a company having an AIDS policy. A companywide AIDS policy sends an important message to employees, customers, and the community. This message emphasizes that the company is placing a special value on their employees by: providing human resources management of an important issue; helping to ensure the employer and the employee of a fair and equitable legal response; and hopefully, by stating a clear company position, employee fear and uncertainty will be reduced.

No policy is a policy: Companies that think it is not necessary to have a policy should consider that if they lack a policy, they are conveying a very distinct message to their employees. That message declares apathy and passivity in response to a worldwide health crisis.

NEED FOR IMPLEMENTATION

The potential effects of AIDS in the workplace can no longer be avoided. The predictions of the numbers of those afflicted with the virus brings the potential for work disruption, co-worker friction, a decrease in employee morale, discrimination suits, and incredible monetary costs for health care. AIDS has become a workplace issue that must be addressed. Ninety percent of AIDS patients, those with AIDS symptoms, and those who are HIV positive are working-age adults between the ages of 20 and 49. However, the workplace is not responding. "According to a recent survey of over 2,000 firms, only 10% of companies in the United States have a written policy on AIDS."[3] The naivete of some corporations is exemplified by the major automobile manufacturer who thought there was "no reason to believe that any of their 382,000 employees worldwide had AIDS."[4]

By the year 1991, just 10 years after the first reported cases of AIDS in the United States, an estimated 270,000 in the United States will have had AIDS. Of these, 179,000 will have died. AIDS will exceed automobile accidents as the leading cause of death. In addition, 1.5 million persons will be carriers, or show some symptoms but not have full cases of AIDS.

The costs of caring for persons with AIDS had been shown to be extremely high. Estimates from recent studies calculate the total hospital bill alone for AIDS patients in 1985 at $380 million, and economists project costs of greater than 8.5 billion for AIDS-related medical care by 1991. Financing of care for persons with AIDS-related medical care is complex, coming primarily from private insurance through the workplace, Medicaid, and other state, local and private monies.[5]

As previously stated, these figures are gross underestimates because of the underreporting and denial of the disease worldwide.

The New England Telephone Company offers an example of a company experiencing the disastrous effects of lacking a policy on AIDS. After being informed of an employee's diagnosis with AIDS, the company decided to fire the individual. An expensive legal battle ensued in which the employee was granted the right to return to work under the Rehabilitation Act and handicapped legislation. At the time, because the New England Telephone Company dealt with the issue solely as a legal one, and did not combine the legal decision with an organized employee communication and education program, some of the employees refused to work in the same facility with the AIDS-affected employee. Therefore, employees walked off the job while nightly television news cameras were rolling. The New England Telephone Company employee with AIDS eventually returned to work, but only in the wake of much avoidable chaos, confusion, and ill will between management and labor. The company endured costly litigation and bad publicity. The New England Telephone Company has used this problem to spearhead a progressive AIDS program and today is a leader in the Northeast in managing AIDS in the workplace.

Since AIDS tends to strike people in their economically most productive years, from twenty-five to forty-five, the people most likely to be diagnosed with AIDS in the future are generally employed somewhere in the workplace. AIDS has tended to strike people in certain recognizable "risk groups" and it is tempting to some people to ascertain that the "typical" American workforce will be unaffected as they do not belong to these "high risk groups." To the contrary, it is much more "atypical" that any workforce in America would consist entirely and exclusively of individuals in long-term monogamous relationships, people who for the past decade have had without exception only one sex partner, people who have never experimented with intravenous drugs, people who have never in the past decade had one homosexual experience. It is equally unlikely there exists a workforce in which no one is a hemophiliac or the sex partner of a hemophiliac, or that none of the workers have had a blood transfusion or had sex with someone with a blood transfusion.[6]

This "typical" workforce has become increasingly atypical as knowledge of the disease has progressed.

The company is responsible for educating all employees and for taking a leadership role in the public health needs of the community. The company may also play a role in "encouraging volunteer services for persons with AIDS as the epidemic expands within the community of IV drug abusers and minorities, which does not have its own internal support system as does the community of gay men."[7]

A discussion of the implementation of a company AIDS policy should include a review of the following summary list of key reasons for developing an AIDS policy:

a. To avoid retraining and hiring expenses by keeping experienced workers on the job, even if AIDS infected.

b. To reduce the possibility of slowed production or walkouts when co-workers oppose working with an AIDS-infected employee.

c. To gain employee respect with a companywide standard approach.

d. To provide support for employees with AIDS by a clearly stated policy.

e. To avoid a crisis by anticipating an actual case and being prepared to respond to questions.

f. To earn employee confidence that the company has fully studied the AIDS issue.

g. To review health insurance and benefits plans for adjustments that could control the costs of AIDS health care.

h. To establish policies that comply with legal constraints to avoid employee discrimination suits.

i. To promote a corporate public image that is responsible and caring.

j. To provide employee education programs to help prevent the spread of AIDS.[8]

OTHER EMPLOYEES AFFECTED BY AIDS

It is necessary for companies to develop policies for employees with AIDS. But it is equally important for a policy to include employees who are HIV positive or only showing minimal symptoms of HIV infection or AIDS. Once an individual has developed AIDS, the usual life expectancy is 18 to 24 months. During this time, the individual is in the final stages of an extremely debilitating disease. Remaining in the workforce is increasingly unrealistic and eventually impossible. However, individuals who test HIV positive or show minimal symptoms may not develop full-blown AIDS for several years. During those years the individuals will remain in the workplace. It is crucial that they remain as healthy and active as possible, as that reduces the likelihood of infections and various illnesses related to AIDS. As they live with the disease they will need medical and psychological support. Because the workplace is such an important element in these individuals' lives, it has been demonstrated to be life-lengthening for an employee to remain in familiar, supportive, and productive surroundings.

In conjunction with the company policy for the HIV-positive employee, the minimal-symptomed employee, or the employee with full-blown AIDS, companies must have a policy for the employees who have family members or loved ones diagnosed with HIV, showing symptoms, or having full-blown AIDS. These employees are in greater number and of equal need.

Persons with HIV infection, and their loved ones, suffer high levels of distress, depression, and anxiety due to the great degree of uncertainty associated with the diagnosis. There is an often overwhelming task of sorting through changing medical and scientific information in order to make accurate decisions regarding health care and life planning. Much anxiety is created by the many questions about HIV infection which remain unanswered.[9]

Family members of employees with HIV infection also need to be offered counseling and support to better assist the employee.

Before planning goals and strategizing the company policy, an employer should consider and include the following Ten Principles for the Workplace as developed by the Citizens Commission on AIDS for New York City and Northern New Jersey:

1. People with AIDS (PWAs) or HIV infection are entitled to the same rights and opportunities as people with other serious or life-threatening illnesses.

2. Employment policies must, at a minimum, comply with federal, state, and local laws and regulations.

3. Employment policies should be based on the scientific and epidemiological evidence that people with AIDS or HIV infection do not pose a risk of transmission of the virus to co-workers through ordinary workplace contact.

4. The highest levels of management and union leadership should unequivocally endorse nondiscriminatory employment practices and educational programs about AIDS.

5. Employers and unions should communicate their support of these policies to workers in simple, clear, and unambiguous terms.

6. Employers should provide employees with sensitive, accurate, and up-to-date education about risk reduction in their personal lives.

7. Employers have a duty to protect the confidentiality of employees' medical information.

8. To prevent work disruption and rejection of co-workers of any employee with AIDS or HIV infection, employers and unions should undertake education for all employees before such an incident occurs and as needed thereafter.

9. Employers should not require HIV screening as part of general pre-employment or workplace physical examinations.

10. In those special occupational settings where there may be a potential risk of exposure to HIV (for example, in health care, where workers may be exposed to blood or blood products), employers should provide specific, ongoing edu-

cation and training as well as the necessary equipment to reinforce appropriate infection control procedures and ensure that they are implemented.[10]

PLANNING AND GOALS OF THE COMPANY POLICY

When planning the company policy, consider the main objectives for having the policy. The purpose of an AIDS policy is

to reassure employees that AIDS is not spread through casual contact during normal work practices and to reduce unrealistic fears about contracting an AIDS-virus-related condition. The policy also would protect the legal rights of employees to work who have a diagnosis of an AIDS-virus-related condition and provide guidelines to manage employees or situations where infection with the AIDS virus is suspected.[11]

Before developing the actual AIDS policy, a company should take the following actions:

1. Define the company's goals and chart out a plan for reaching the goals. Consider the following elements for inclusion:

a. Comply with the law—to steer a safe, clear course through sometimes conflicting demands.

b. Maintain productivity—both on the part of the patients to the extent that they are able to work and desire to continue, and on the part of their fellow workers, whose legitimate concerns and ungrounded fears must not be neglected.

c. Manage costs—particularly those involving expensive medical care.

d. Retain trust—in the company's commitment to the health and safety of those whose lives the company or its products touch. This trust must be felt by employees, customers, and the public.

e. Show the company's caring for an employee who experiences the personal catastrophe imposed by the illness.

f. Demonstrate management competence and integrity in the handling of a sensitive issue.

g. Facilitate informed behavior on the part of all employees, especially those most directly associated with an afflicted fellow-worker.

h. Anticipate avoidable mistakes so that the potential for generalized catastrophic effects is contained.

i. Learn valuable lessons applicable to future experiences.[12]

2. Decide how, for whom, and under what circumstances there will be education about AIDS. Everyone should be educated. However, managers/supervisors are trained with more depth than the average employee population. In addition, the company must determine whether that education will be provided by an in-house resource person or contracted out. The education also must not be a one-time event. It is an on-going process,

changing as more information becomes available and medical facts and statistics are updated.

3. "Decide how the organization will respond to an AIDS crisis, now or in the future, and how the crisis will be resolved: (a) who will be called upon; (b) what will be done; (c) what resources are available currently and who will maintain the resource list; (d) how decisions will be made and carried out."[13]

4. An organization should know in advance what its approach to AIDS will be. "A minimum number of key people need to be expected to continually be responsible to understand the medical facts and keep themselves updated as new information is released, know the organizational viewpoint about AIDS should it occur in the workplace, and be equipped to educate others about the disease and the company's policy."[14] These individuals usually are based in the human resources department and work directly with the employee assistance program.

POLICY STRATEGY

Important ingredients of strategy development and implementation of the company AIDS policy include: the task force of key personnel, identification of medical/legal experts in the community, analysis of employee demographics, education and support of senior management, development of company educational standards, and evaluation of educational impact.

1. *Establish task force of key personnel.* In the implementation of the policy, the first step is to establish the task force of key personnel. Included in this task force would be members of such departments as human resources, legal, medical, employee assistance, public relations, training, employee communications, unions, and finally, and very importantly, senior management. "Leadership on the task force is crucial. Select a leader with the most knowledge about AIDS who also has the ability to organize and complete projects efficiently and thoroughly. One additional criterion for the leader is that this person be able to interact capably with senior management to communicate plans and progress."[15]

2. *Identify Community Medical/Legal Experts.* An actively maintained resource list in the office of human resources is necessary for any employees with questions and referral needs. This list should be updated and personally checked out by the human resource department in conjunction with the company's EAP. Many mental health professionals are not trained specifically in the issues surrounding the AIDS virus and its specialized needs. Therefore, all medical, psychological, and professional experts should specify their training and expertise in relation to the field of AIDS.

3. *Analyze Employee Demographics.* When conducting the analysis, consider the risks of the particular type of workplace and the geographical location of the worksite (see Chapter 6 on special workplace populations).

Based on the number of employees, ascertain the appropriate level of complexity of the educational package. For example, if the company has less than 100 employees, its needs are much different than the company with 30 regional offices and 10,000 employees. However, the AIDS policies of these companies should be similar. Regardless of the size of the company, every employer shares the same AIDS issues and risks.

4. *Educate and Gain Senior Management Support.* In all stages of the policy development and implementation, senior management support is crucial. If top management is not aware of policy decisions and development, then the policy is written and presented without endorsement from its key management role models. This could lead to mixed messages and diffused impact of the educational package and company AIDS policy.

AIDS and the new role for managers: Overseeing the consequences of an epidemic is not normally thought of as a management function. It is clearly a new role. It is unlikely that this topic could have been found in the curricula of the nation's graduate schools of business administration even a short time ago. It is unlikely that the men and women who manage the tens of thousands of organizations in our society—public or private sector—received any formal academic training in the management of epidemics. Nevertheless, to a large degree, management is the art of dealing effectively with the environment in which the organization finds itself. Many organizations over the past decade have found themselves suddenly coping with the specter of AIDS within their environment; many more organizations will be in the position of having to face some aspect of AIDS during the next decade. How well one manages this particular aspect of the organization's environment will considerably influence the organization's medical and legal costs, its public and employee relations, its efficiency and stability.[16]

5. *Develop and Implement a Company Educational Standard.* This is the responsibility of the human resource and EAP departments. The AIDS policy should be made clear to employees before a known AIDS case or problem arises. This will minimize crises and reduce employee fears, mistrust, and uncertainty. Possible dissemination methods include: special memo announcements, inclusion in employee and supervisor guides, inclusion in company newsletters/health columns, special meetings, and inclusion as part of new-employee orientation.

6. *Evaluate Educational Impact.* As with any policy and educational effort, the company needs outside evaluation for content, outreach efforts, and clarity. This will ensure that the company's efforts are in line with the tradition of the company philosophy.

ELEMENTS OF COMPANY AIDS POLICY

The company AIDS policy should include the following elements:

1. The commitment of the company to act responsibly in the face of this major public health crisis.

2. The commitment of the company to protect the health of all its employees.

3. The commitment to provide a safe work environment.

4. The commitment to treat AIDS like any other life-threatening illness; if the employee is medically fit and able to perform job duties, affected employees will be permitted to work.

5. The provision of reasonable accommodation and job modification for AIDS victims when appropriate.

6. An outline of the company position on AIDS testing, if any.

7. Procedures for supervisors to handle AIDS fairly, with compassion and understanding.

8. The commitment to keep the policy medically updated and provide employee education on AIDS and policy.

9. The commitment to maintain confidentiality of medical information.

10. A declaration stating that special transfer requests would not be accepted, unless medically indicated.[17]

11. The commitment to consider benefit plans that provide case management, hospice/home health care, and experimental treatment when applicable.

12. The commitment to provide referrals through the company's EAP or other departments to community resources and experts for consultation and treatment. There should also be an appointed team of appropriate employees to be held responsible specifically for communication dissemination—in particular, to assuage employee fear, possible threat of work stoppage, as well as customer complaints and other potential disruptive situations. This group should also have a representative to be the spokesperson on any matters to the company relating to the policy, program, and procedures regarding the company's position on AIDS. Team members should include such department representatives as senior management, personnel, EAP, unions, corporate communications, legal, medical, and public relations.

13. The statement of the role of the company in contributing to the community's efforts for development of treatment and support of research. This includes availability of company resources when appropriate.

SMALL BUSINESS AND THE EMPLOYEE AIDS POLICY

"There is an increasing number of worksite HIV/AIDS policy and program initiatives emerging on the scene. Most have occurred among large businesses at the corporate level and in varying degrees enjoy the support of both management and organized labor. Small business initiatives are less prevalent and perhaps less well known."[18]

In addressing the specific problem of small businesses (less than 500 employees) and the issues surrounding AIDS, one must consider that "the financial burden and negative impact on the business will be the greatest for the employer of 100 employees or less. These are the companies that can ill afford either the health care benefits cost increases that occur when an employee develops this disease, or the loss of reliability in the employee's productivity."[19]

It is also important for these employers to institute an AIDS policy and educational program. Their potential losses, although equal in severity to those of larger companies, may occur more quickly due to the dynamics of smaller business. These programs would be more likely to be developed with off-site EAP providers, and external educators such as the Red Cross, as well as other resources listed in Appendix A at the end of this book.

COMMUNICATING THE POLICY AND EDUCATION PROGRAM TO EMPLOYEES

When informing the company about the AIDS policy and the educational program, the first form of communication should come from top management, preferably the CEO or president. The communication should state why the company has decided to institute a formal policy and educational program and should include important facts about AIDS and the nontransmission through normal workplace activities. It should mention the specifics of the educational agenda.

The San Francisco Chamber of Commerce Model Approach

In 1987 the San Francisco Chamber of Commerce developed the highly recommended model approach to AIDS in the workplace. The following is reprinted in full from their "AIDS in the Workplace, Suggested Guidelines for the Business Community ":

Epidemics of disease present enormous dilemmas to our society, straining our human, financial and health resources. Like smallpox, cancer and polio before it, Acquired Immune Deficiency Syndrome (AIDS) and its related conditions are approaching pandemic proportions. The impact of AIDS is and will continue to be devastating. According to the Surgeon General of the United States:

By the end of 1991, an estimated 270,000 cases of AIDS will have occurred with 170,000 deaths within the decade since the disease was first recognized. In the year 1991, an estimated 145,000 patients with AIDS will need health and supportive services at a total cost between $8 and $16 billion. However, AIDS is preventable. ... It is the responsibility of every citizen to be informed about AIDS and to exercise the appropriate prevention measures.

If we are to overcome the obstacles presented by AIDS and its related conditions, it is imperative that we respond immediately as a unified society. A comprehensive and effective approach toward combatting the epidemic only can be realized through a national effort with the full support, understanding and informed decision-making of the business community. Any sensible and human response to the epidemic must be based on accurate information, not irrational fear and discrimination. There is an alarming tendency to label people as belonging to AIDS "risk groups." This is not only misleading, it is dangerous. AIDS is not confined to any single community. It is not caused by life-style or sexual orientation. It is caused by a virus—a virus that can be transmitted to anyone who engages in high-risk activity. Fortunately, by modifying these high-risk behaviors, we can stop virus transmission. Unlike many other life-threatening illnesses, AIDS can be prevented.

We are fighting a disease, not people. The business community in America can and must play a major role in creating policies and disseminating accurate information about AIDS and its related conditions.

Any employee with a life-threatening and/or catastrophic illness such as AIDS, cancer, or multiple sclerosis should be treated in conjunction with the principles outlined below. It is our desire that every business in America adopt and/or incorporate these principles into personnel policies and adhere to the content and spirit of the principles.

1. Employees with any life-threatening illness should be offered the right to continue working so long as they are able to continue to perform their job satisfactorily and so long as the best available medical evidence indicates that their continual employment does not present a health safety threat to themselves or others.

2. Employers and co-workers should treat all medical information obtained from employees with strict confidentiality. In the case of an employee with a life-threatening illness, confidentiality of employee medical records in accordance with existing legal, medical, ethical and management practices should be maintained.

3. Employees who are affected by any life-threatening illness should be treated with compassion and understanding in their personal crisis. Reasonable efforts should be made to accommodate seriously ill patients by providing flexible work areas, hours and assignments whenever possible or appropriate.

4. Employees should be asked to be sensitive to the needs of critically ill colleagues, and to recognize that continual employment for an employee with a life-threatening illness is often life sustaining and can be both physically and mentally beneficial.

5. In regard to the life-threatening disease of AIDS and its related conditions, a person carrying the AIDS virus is not a threat to co-workers since AIDS is not spread by common everyday contact. For this reason, the AIDS antibody and/or AIDS virus status of an employee is not relevant information in regard to the health and safety of his/her co-workers. Therefore, the AIDS antibody test and/or AIDS virus test should not be used as a prerequisite for employment or a condition for continued employment. Knowledge or

presumed knowledge of AIDS antibody and/or AIDS virus status should not be used to discriminate against an employee for any reason.

6. Given the irrational fear that AIDS, cancer and other life-threatening diseases often inspire, the most effective way to avoid necessary disruptions in the workplace is to prepare and educate both management and employees before any employee is affected by a life-threatening disease. To this end, employers should implement educational programs based on the best available medical knowledge to understand the disease; what services are locally available to help employees with any medical, psychological or financial hardships caused by the disease, and what policies the company has in place to cover employees with a life-threatening illness.[20]

EXISTING POLICIES AND COMMUNICATION FROM THE PUBLIC AND PRIVATE SECTORS

The following workplaces are very different not only in their businesses but also in their employee demographics. However, the policies are similar. The language is varied depending on the organization. However, the content is very much the same. All businesses, regardless of their size, location, or demographics should have a formal AIDS policy and educational package.

Private Sector: IBM

The following AIDS policy package[21] includes the letter of introduction from the director of Corporate Medical Programs of the IBM Corporation directed to all IBM employees; IBM Internal Communication on AIDS memo to all employees; and AIDS information distributed to all IBM Employees. The letter of introduction provided by the director of Corporate Medical Programs clearly and concisely introduces the AIDS issue to the IBM population. It includes a general policy overview, benefits information, and a reference to the surgeon general's report to be sent to all employees. If a company does not have a corporate medical director, then a similar letter from the CEO is appropriate.

Dear IBMer:

AIDS is a tragic affliction and a major public health threat throughout the world. IBM wants to ensure that employees affected by AIDS receive appropriate assistance and encourages employee awareness to help limit the spread of AIDS.

IBM medical departments and employee assistance programs are available to help employees with questions about AIDS. They will provide information, counseling, and referrals for testing as requested.

IBMers affected by AIDS will be encouraged to work as long as they are able, and their privacy will be respected. Of course, full benefits coverage will continue.

As part of the national effort on AIDS awareness and control, and our own internal education program, we are distributing to all IBM employees the enclosed brochure prepared by the United States Public Health Services. I urge you to read it and share it with others.

Sincerely,

Director, Corporate Medical Programs

As a follow-up to that introductory letter and brochure, IBM sent all employees an IBM Internal Communication on AIDS. In this memo, IBM summarized its policy on AIDS and its commitment to all employees (including those with the AIDS virus) to continuing education and to community outreach. These commitments are vital to a successful and effective policy and education program.

IBM INTERNAL COMMUNICATION ON AIDS

IBM's internal AIDS communication program is intended to provide employees information about the disease, the company's practice regarding those who have it, and about counseling programs that are available to them. Information has been provided in the following ways:

- Distribution of literature through IBM medical departments.
- Publication of an article in the company management newsletter.
- Offering a videotape through the employee video library for home and community use.
- Distributing to all employees a CDC brochure on AIDS with a cover letter from the director of corporate medical programs explaining the company's practice regarding those who have the disease.
- Bulletin board notices on the availability of the videotape and the mailing of the CDC brochure and cover letter.

Copies of the management newsletter article, the CDC brochure and cover letter, and the bulletin board notices are included with this package.

IBM's PRACTICE REGARDING PEOPLE WITH AIDS

IBM developed its practice regarding people with Acquired Immune Deficiency Syndrome (AIDS) in 1985 in response to the worldwide spread of the disease and the threat it poses to our employees and the communities in which they live and work. That practice provides that we treat employees with AIDS in the same manner that we treat employees with other chronic illnesses—giving guidance, support, and health benefits for persons with the disease, and education for employees.

Some elements of the practice are:

- IBM does not test applicants or employees for AIDS.
- As with other medical situations, IBM protects the confidentiality of employees with AIDS and will not disclose their identities, except at the employee's request.

- IBM provides information and education on AIDS, typically upon employee request, through medical departments, the Employee Assistance Program, brochures, and a video available through the IBM Employee Video Library. Also, IBM has mailed copies of an AIDS booklet to each employee and is providing ongoing management training.

- IBM attempts to keep employees with AIDS in the workforce as long as they are able. When possible, it makes accommodations to allow them to remain on the job.

- IBM makes available the full range of health benefits covered by employee health insurance to persons with AIDS, including long-term disability leave.

During the past two years, IBM and its employees also have provided support to education and research projects dealing with AIDS. Some examples are:

- Donated $100,000 to the Antenucci Laboratory, at Roosevelt Hospital in New York, to fund the development of an AIDS research center.

- Contributed $25,000 to the New York Blood Bank to help cover the costs of testing blood for AIDS.

- IBM employees are also actively supporting community-based education and research projects in several cities.

An update appeared in the IBM company newsletter. Following the Internal Communication on AIDS, it further demonstrated IBM's ongoing commitment to education and prevention.

AIDS INFORMATION DISTRIBUTED TO EMPLOYEES

A brochure about AIDS (Acquired Immune Deficiency Syndrome) will be sent to managers shortly for distribution to all employees. The brochure, prepared by the United States Public Health Service, is part of a national effort on AIDS awareness and control.

IBM encourages employee awareness to help limit the spread of AIDS. For this reason, IBM medical departments and employee assistance programs are available to help with questions about AIDS. They will provide information, counseling, and referrals for testing as requested. IBM medical departments also can provide additional copies of the brochure.

In addition, employees are reminded that an AIDS videotape is available for viewing through the IBM Employee Video Library. the 18–minute tape includes frank and open discussion about how AIDS is caused, transmitted, and prevented.

The tape is intended for viewing by parents and students of at least ninth-grade level. Since it contains candid material about a sensitive subject, parents should preview the tape before showing it to children.

The tape may be ordered by————. All costs will be prepaid by IBM.

By recommending the ages and audience of the videotape and other materials available, the AIDS issue in the IBM community has penetrated the wall of fear and opened the topic for discussion and education. Informality is necessary when addressing communication to employees to set a tone of ease that must be present in order for the issue to be discussed openly.

Private Sector: Emhart Corporation

The following policy is reprinted in full from the Emhart Corporation (now part of Black and Decker).

Emhart Corporation believes that:

- All employees are entitled to a safe working environment.
- All employees should be free from any discrimination in employment that may result from medical conditions from which they suffer.
- A life-threatening illness such as AIDS should not affect the entitlement to a safe working environment and discrimination-free employment.
- Individuals who are suffering from AIDS should be free to continue to engage in all regular employment activities, provided their doctor concurs and so long as they are able to perform their job requirements in a fully satisfactory manner, without significant risk or harm to themselves or to others.

In recognition of these beliefs, and the complex legal and social issues surrounding AIDS, the following guidelines should be followed by supervisors within all divisions of the Corporation in the U.S. and Canada:

1. Supervisors aware of an individual with AIDS should immediately contact their human resources department in order to coordinate the effective handling of the matter.

- The employee's illness and treatment is to be kept private and confidential.
- Do not send any employee with or suspected of having AIDS home without the prior consent of the local human resources department head.
- Do not inform co-workers of any employee's medical condition or its potential communicability without the prior consent of the local human resources head.
- Local human resources representatives should contact the Corporate Manager Benefit Analysis and Communication to discuss what actions, if any, are appropriate.

2. Employee over-reaction to the effects of casual contact with an employee suffering from AIDS can occur as a result of misinformation. The Corporate Manager Benefit Analysis and Communication shall be responsible for the dissemination of available accurate information regarding AIDS, and the local human resources function should immediately contact the Corporate Manager Benefit Analysis and Communication for the same.

- Group educational or informational meetings should be planned and coordinated by the local human resources department, with advice of the Corporate Manager Benefit Analysis and Communication, when co-workers are, or may become, concerned about an employee with AIDS.

- No employee should be terminated for refusing to work because of a co-worker who is known to have or is suspected of having AIDS prior to his receiving appropriate information and counseling regarding the illness.
- In the remote event that co-workers should refuse to work, they should be sent immediately to the local human resources department for discussions regarding AIDS, its effects on work-place safety, and its contagiousness.

3. Employees with AIDS and their co-workers should have complete access to the local human resources department at their location to discuss their concerns on a confidential basis.

- Direct any employee to the local human resources department for information pertaining to AIDS.

4. Employees with AIDS should not be treated differently than employees not suffering from AIDS as long as they are able to perform their job requirements in a fully satisfactory manner without significant risk of harm to themselves or to others.

- No employee should be requested to release medical reports or to submit to independent medical evaluation without prior consent of the local human resources department head, who will consult with the Corporate Manager Benefit Analysis and Communication.
- Testing for the AIDS antibody in employees or prospective employees shall not be required. There is no evidence that AIDS is transmitted through casual work-place contacts, so AIDS antibody people are of no risk to co-workers.
- Supervisors who suspect that an employee with AIDS cannot perform the full requirements of his or her job in a satisfactory manner, should contact the local human resources department head. The local human resources department head, in consultation with the Corporate Manager Benefit Analysis and Communication, would determine what reports should be requested to determine whether an employee can continue working and any reasonable accommodations to be made.
- Disability leaves for those suffering from AIDS should be granted on the same basis as those suffering from other illnesses or injuries.
- Personal leaves should be considered when requested by employees with AIDS consistent with the illness and business considerations.

5. Reasonable accommodations will be made for employees with AIDS consistent with that condition, its communicability and potential risk of harm to themselves or others, except where business necessity prevents accommodation.

- Supervisors who know of any employee needing special accommodations should contact their local human resources department for approval of proposed changes.

• Local human resources shall be responsible for coordinating any accommodations deemed appropriate and consistent with the business needs of the division, in consultation with the Corporate Manager Benefit Analysis and Communication.

6. Consistent with the business needs of the division, reasonable accommodations may be made at the discretion of management for co-workers of employees with AIDS.

• Co-workers requesting special accommodations should be referred to the local human resources department head.

Public Sector: U.S. Department of Health and Human Services

The following memorandum and AIDS policy (reprinted in full) are from Dr. Otis R. Bowen, secretary of the U.S. Department of Health and Human Services (HHS) in 1986. The HHS policy outline has separate sections for management, employees, and personnel departments that clearly delineate the responsibilities and roles of the Health and Human Services employee with regard to the AIDS issue. The more particular and defined the policy and expectations of the employees are presented, the easier the scope of the AIDS issue becomes, which consequently reduces fear. When the AIDS issue is left vague and tenuous there is most likely to be chaos and disorder within the company. This policy was a model policy for the federal government and has been used throughout the various offices.

MEMORANDUM TO: ALL HHS EMPLOYEES
SUBJECT: Concern About the Transmission of Acquired Immune Deficiency Syndrome (AIDS)

Because there has been some concern about the transmission of AIDS in the workplace, I wish to assure you that medical evidence provides no basis for employees to fear contracting AIDS through casual contacts in the workplace. The most recent medical information on this subject was published by our Centers for Disease Control in the *MMWR [(Morbidity and Mortality Weekly Report)* of November 15, 1985, Vol. 34, No. 45]. I have asked the Assistant Secretary for Personnel Administration to assure that copies of the *MMWR* are available to you through our Personnel and Employee Counseling Services Program staffs who also can provide additional information and counseling services.

As the *MMWR* indicates, AIDS is a sexually transmitted disease. Because it is bloodborne, it may also be transmitted by the use of contaminated hypodermic needles, contaminated blood and blood products, or by perinatal transmission from infected mother to child. There is no evidence that it is airborne, foodborne, waterborne, or transmitted by the kind of nonsexual person-to-person contact as generally occurs in the workplace (for example, by sharing the same work environment, handshaking, interviewing persons who have AIDS, touching papers or other objects previously touched by persons who have AIDS, preparing and serving food and beverages, or using common washroom facilities).

Employees who have AIDS are entitled to request and receive the same consideration and employee benefits as any other employees who have other debilitating illnesses. Employees who have AIDS or who have concerns about contracting AIDS in the workplace should confer with their supervisors or their organization's designated counseling staff who can provide competent information and referral services.

Most importantly, fear based upon misinformation is both unfortunate and unnecessary. I am confident that our employees will carry out their duties in an intelligent and responsible manner consistent with the leadership mission of this Department in health matters.

792–4–40 POLICY

The General Policy stated in the FPM Bulletin is quoted below: Guidelines issued by the Public Health Service's Centers for Disease Control (CDC) dealing with AIDS in the workplace state that "the kind of nonsexual person-to-person contact that generally occurs among workers and clients or consumers in the workplace does not pose a risk for transmission of (AIDS)." Therefore, HIV-infected employees should be allowed to continue working as long as they are able to maintain acceptable performance and do not pose a safety or health threat to themselves or others in the workplace. If performance or safety problems arise, agencies are encouraged to address them by applying existing Federal and agency personnel policies and practices. . . .

HIV infection can result in medical conditions which impair the employee's health and ability to perform safely and effectively. In these cases, agencies should treat HIV-infected employees in the same manner as employees who suffer from other serious illnesses. This means, for example, that employees may be granted sick leave or leave without pay when they are incapable of performing their duties or when they have medical appointments. In this regard, agencies are encouraged to consider accommodation of employees' AIDS-related conditions in the same manner as they would other conditions which warrant such consideration.

Also, there is no medical basis for employees refusing to work with such fellow employees or agency clients who are HIV-infected. Nevertheless, the concerns of these employees should be taken seriously and should be addressed with appropriate information and counseling. In addition, employees such as health care personnel, who may come into direct contact with the body fluids of persons having the AIDS virus, should be provided appropriate information and equipment to minimize the risks of such contact.

GENERAL MANAGEMENT RESPONSIBILITIES

Management responsibilities include:

A. Making the Departmental policy on and programs and services concerning AIDS in the workplace known to all managers and employees.

B. Making AIDS information, education, and counseling available to all employees.

C. Providing training and guidance for managers and supervisors on AIDS in the workplace.

D. Maintaining a safe and healthy workplace environment for all employees.

E. Providing reasonable accommodation in employment matters to persons who, because they have AIDS or AIDS-related conditions, are qualified handicapped persons within the meaning of Section 501 of the Rehabilitation Act of 1973.

F. Maintaining the confidentiality of medical information in accordance with applicable law and regulations.

G. Addressing other personnel and management issues within the framework of existing procedures, guidance, statutes, case law, and regulations.

RESPONSIBILITIES OF SERVICING PERSONNEL OFFICES AND EMPLOYEE COUNSELING SERVICES UNITS

Servicing Personnel Offices are responsible for advising both managers and employees on personnel programs (e.g., leave administration, insurance, disability retirement, reasonable accommodation, discipline, and performance management), as they pertain to AIDS. The Employee Counseling Services Program provides a combination of services to employees with problems caused by or associated with AIDS, to their supervisors or managers, and to their co-workers, including information, counseling, referral to community resources, and on-going support and advocacy for coping with workplace issues.

EMPLOYEE RESPONSIBILITIES

Employee responsibilities include:

A. Becoming knowledgeable about the Departmental policy on AIDS in the workplace

B. Seeking competent counseling about concerns pertaining to AIDS in the workplace

C. Carrying out their duties in an intelligent and responsible manner consistent with this Instruction and the leadership mission of this Department in health matters.

PRIVACY AND CONFIDENTIALITY

Medical documentation of AIDS received by Department officials and employees that is for the purpose of an employment decision and is made part of the file pertaining to that decision is a "record" protected by the Privacy Act and, generally, may not be disclosed without the consent of the subject of the record. Any official or employee who has access to the record is required to maintain the confidentiality of that record. In addition, supervisors, managers, and others included in making and implementing personnel management decisions involving employees with AIDS should strictly observe applicable privacy and confidentiality requirements.

Public Sector: State of Wisconsin

The following excerpt from the State of Wisconsin's Communicable Diseases and Life Threatening Medical Conditions Policy is introduced by the documentation of the State of Wisconsin's responsibility to its employees. This documentation provided as a prelude to Wisconsin's policy on AIDS is another example of a different approach in communicating to all employees of a company the issue of AIDS and the company's philosophy and plan.

Background: The State of Wisconsin is committed to employment practices which encourage people with disabilities, regardless of the nature of the disability, to maintain productive status in the state workforce.

The State of Wisconsin recognizes that it is important for employees with life-threatening medical conditions including but not limited to cancer, heart disease, hepatitis and AIDS/HIV to continue to participate in as many of their normal activities as their condition will allow, including work.

The State of Wisconsin recognizes that employment may be therapeutically important in the remission or recovery process and may help to prolong and improve the quality of the employee's lives. As long as employees meet acceptable performance standards, and medical evidence indicates their conditions pose no risk to themselves or others in the workplace, managers shall be sensitive to their conditions and ensure that they are treated with dignity and respect consistent with the treatment of other state employees.

The State of Wisconsin is obligated to provide a safe work environment for its employees and the public it serves. The State of Wisconsin will ensure to the best of its ability that an employee's health condition does not present a significant health and/or safety risk to other employees or the public.

The State of Wisconsin recognizes the need to maintain an open and informed environment for its employees, and employees shall have access to education resources on health issues to eliminate prejudice and unwarranted fear about diseases in the workplace.

The State of Wisconsin further recognizes that an employee's medical condition is personal and confidential and not subject to disclosure to others without the affected employee's consent unless otherwise provided by law. It assures employees of complete confidentiality when seeking counseling or medical referral assistance.

Employees' rights to confidentiality are subject to the employer's responsibility to protect other employees and the public from contracting or being exposed to a contagious disease.

State law prohibits AIDS testing as a condition of employment.

The Secretary of the Department of Employment Relations, pursuant to Sec. 230.04 Stats., is charged with the responsibility of ensuring that employees who have communicable diseases and/or life-threatening medical conditions do not suffer discrimination in employment.

NOTES

1. *Surgeon General's Report on Acquired Immune Deficiency Syndrome*, U.S. Department of Health and Human Services and the American Red Cross, 1987, p. 32.

2. Dale A. Masi, "AIDS in the Workplace, What Can Be Done?" American Management Association, Periodicals Division (1987), p. 58.

3. *Fortune Magazine* and Allstate Insurance (1988) "Business Response to AIDS: A National Survey of U.S. Companies," in Kathleen C. Brown and Joan G. Turner, *AIDS, Policies and Programs for the Workplace* (New York: Van Nostrand Reinhold, 1989), p. 39.

4. Masi, "AIDS in the Workplace, What Can Be Done?" p. 57.

5. Presidential Commission on the Human Immunodeficiency Virus Epidemic, Chairman's Recommendations (Washington, DC, February 29, 1988), p. 23.

6. Sam B. Puckett and Alan R. Emery, *Managing AIDS in the Workplace* (Reading, MA: Addison-Wesley, 1988), p. 14.

7. Thomas E. Backer, "AIDS/HIV Infection and the Workplace: Emerging Issues," unpublished notes from NIDA-sponsored conference on AIDS/HIV Infection, November 17, 1989, p. 2.

8. Brown and Turner "AIDS, Policies and Programs for the Workplace," p. 43.

9. Presidential Commission on the Human Immunodeficiency Virus Epidemic, p. 28.

10. American Foundation for AIDS Research, *AIDS Education: A Business Guide*, 1988, p. 4.

11. Bryan Lawton, "How to Develop a Successful AIDS Policy That Can Help Both the Company and Its Employees," Personnel Manager's Letter, February 1, 1988, p. 8.

12. Maryland Center for Business Management, Inc., "AIDS in the Workplace and other catastrophic diseases," joint presentation by the Maryland Center for

Business Management, Inc., and M. Rosenberg and Co., The Johns Hopkins University School of Hygiene and Public Health, and The Educational Center of Sheppard Pratt, Division of Employee Assistance Programs, October 22, 1987, p. 4.

13. Puckett and Emery, *Managing AIDS in the Workplace*, p. 65.

14. Ibid., p. 66.

15. Brown and Turner, "AIDS, Policies and Programs for the Workplace," p. 44.

16. Puckett and Emery, *Managing AIDS in the Workplace*, p. 3.

17. Allstate Forum on Public Issues, "Corporate America Responds" (Allstate, 1987), pp. 6–7.

18. Daniel M. Merrigan, "NIDA Meeting: HIV/AIDS in the Workplace," unpublished presentation at NIDA-sponsored conference on AIDS/HIV Infection, November 17, 1989, p. 1.

19. Bryan Lawton, in ibid.

20. San Francisco Chamber of Commerce, "AIDS in the Workplace: Suggested Guidelines for the Business Community," June 1987.

21. IBM corporate policy materials on AIDS, from Glenn E. Haughie, MD, Director of Corporate Medical Programs, November 1987.

CHAPTER 4

THE ROLE OF EMPLOYEE ASSISTANCE PROGRAMS/CASE MANAGEMENT

INTRODUCTION

In discussing Employee Assistance Programs and their role in addressing AIDS in the workplace, this chapter will define an EAP and explain the EAP's relationship to AIDS. The history of EAPs and their various models will be described, including discussion of the in-house and out-of-house EAP models, followed by the actual design of an EAP and the essential ingredients of a successful program. The EAP's specific application to AIDS will follow, with issues for the EAP professional and appropriate guidelines for them.

The chapter will also address employee benefits and case management, the definition and goals of the case manager, and the role of the EAP practitioner as case manager. The discussion will cover the various populations that will be able to utilize the EAP and the unique skills the EAP practitioner can bring to this workplace issue. The chapter will present recent developments in issues surrounding AIDS and their relationship to the EAP profession. Concluding the chapter will be the author's comments on the challenges this issue brings to the EAP profession as well as the present shortcomings of the EAPs and their lack of attention to AIDS.

DEFINITION OF EAP AND ITS ROLE WITH AIDS-AFFECTED EMPLOYEES

Any comprehensive plan for addressing the issue of AIDS in the workplace must include plans for counseling and support. Over the past several decades, Employee Assistance Programs have been developed to deal with employee problems that may affect workplace performance. Specifically,

EAPs are a professional assessment/referral and/or short-term counseling service offered to employees with alcohol, drug, or mental health problems that may be affecting the workers' jobs. Because AIDS affects people who are in the workforce, whether the person with AIDS is the actual employee or the employee's loved one, the EAP is the umbrella under which the issue of AIDS in the workplace will fall. Employees are either self-referred to the company's EAP or referred by supervisors. EAP services also include managerial/supervisory consultations and training and employee education.

EAPs can have a significant impact on the employee dealing with AIDS or HIV-positive status, whether directly or through a loved one. Millions of employees diagnosed as HIV positive will be living with a time bomb inside them. Helping the employee to cope with anxiety, fear, and other emotions is clearly an EAP mandate. EAP staff can work as team members with the personnel and medical staff of the organization. EAP personnel can also provide support services to unions for its members who are dealing with AIDS.

A company's EAP can become a calming voice amid reactions and overreactions to AIDS-related incidents. The EAP can serve as a valuable resource in developing an AIDS policy, and it can help allay employee anxieties and fears as the company develops its philosophy and policy. An EAP is in a unique position to offer this kind of support for several reasons. EAPs have expertise in working with drug abusers. Therefore, they have a particular responsibility to their current clients who are IV drug users, and a responsibility to reach out to other drug-addicted employees and provide the necessary information related to HIV infection and drug abuse.

EAP professionals, especially social workers, have traditionally worked in hospitals where they have offered the support to terminally ill persons. This experience makes them particularly well suited to work with persons with AIDS and their families. Their professional objectivity should enable them to operate as advocates for the person with AIDS while maintaining a perspective that allows them to remain sensitive to the anxieties of co-workers. EAP personnel need to focus their efforts in two directions: providing appropriate support and referral services for persons with AIDS and HIV-positive status, and providing educational information for all workers to continually remind them of the importance of prevention.

EAP professionals have been trained to work with community resources and are knowledgeable regarding those services. They should be able to assist in making contact with appropriate community programs. Employees with AIDS and their family members will need such support services to face the terminal illness, to make appropriate plans, and to achieve adequate medical care. Counseling from the EAP could give them the help they need to deal with other employees, supervisors, and the workplace in general. Family members as well as persons with AIDS will experience denial, anger, bewilderment, and even shame. They will need assistance as they face their own loss and try to cope with helping their loved ones.

The EAP can also help companies in the interpretation and implementation of legislation pertinent to persons with AIDS. The Rehabilitation Act of 1973, which declared persons with certain illnesses to be handicapped, has been interpreted as extending specifically to persons with AIDS. The EAP staff is already familiar with this law as it pertains to persons with other handicapping conditions. This will be an invaluable aid in understanding its ramifications for employees who have AIDS, as issues arise concerning disability benefits and termination on medical grounds.

HISTORY OF EAPs

Employee Assistance Programs developed out of the concept of Occupational Alcoholism Programs (OAPs), which began in the 1940s. OAPs were developed through the efforts of recovering alcoholics. They were based on the premise that the troubled employee should be confronted while still on the job; the employer should not try to cover up the problem. In this way the addiction could be treated and the job could be saved. These early programs dealt solely with alcoholic employees.

During the 1970s there was a shift in the OAP field. It was becoming increasingly difficult to justify turning away employees who needed assistance with problem areas other than alcoholism. This began the evolution of a broader-based program called Employee Assistance Programs. Unlike OAPs, EAPs deal with other addictions besides alcoholism, along with emotional, family, and marital problems. EAPs train supervisors to focus on and confront employees with decreases in job performance and not to try to diagnose what the problem may be.

By building and maintaining a strong EAP, an organization reaps several kinds of benefits. It significantly reduces the many costs, financial and otherwise, that would have been incurred because of employees' personal problems. There is no way to measure the true savings in relief from anxieties, fears, and distress, but this savings clearly has a positive effect on overall morale, team spirit, loyalty to the organization, and public image.

EAPs: ESSENTIAL INGREDIENTS

Establishing an EAP requires careful planning and forethought, whether it is an internal program or contracted out. The problems and requirements of the company must be closely examined, and a clear policy is essential. Once a company has decided to start an EAP it must decide on the type of delivery model. An in-house model is one in which the entire EAP staff is employed by the company. In an out-of-house model, a firm is contracted to provide the EAP staff. However, variations and combinations of the two models are possible. For example, a company may use in-house staff to oversee the program, to evaluate and train the supervisors, and to educate the employees. The contractor would then provide the actual referrals, assessments, and short-term counseling. Location of the program may be on or off the company premises, be it in-house or a contractor model.

When determining the best approach for the organization, it is best to ascertain the complexity of the program, and the company's commitment to it. Many companies prefer the contractual approach because the commitment need not be long-term. If evaluation deems the EAP ineffective, it is easier to terminate a contract than to terminate members of the company's staff. Once the approach has been decided, the designing of the program begins.

12 ESSENTIAL INGREDIENTS OF AN EAP

To design an EAP, a company should include 12 essential ingredients: program support, program plan, policy statement, information assessment and referral system (and/or short-term counseling), staffing, record-keeping, a community referral network, location, funding, training of union and management personnel, program evaluation and employee education, and outreach.[1] Regardless of the chosen plan for the company's EAP, it is necessary for the company to monitor its EAP carefully and to evaluate its performance as a separate, functioning department of the entire company.

1. Program Support. Top-level management support for the EAP must be assured from its inception. This will act as an endorsement to the employees from the highest level of management. Financial support is also vital. The company must be willing and able to fund the EAP at an adequate level from the beginning. Therefore, it is optimal to have the company's top management team accept responsibility for the program from its inception. Adequate funding translates into approximately one full-time EAP staff member for every 3,000–4,000 employees. That estimate includes services for family members. Small companies have the option of hiring part-time staff or contracting.

2. A Program Plan. A projected plan (a minimum of three years) for the EAPs growth and development is also essential. This can be a fluid outline, changing as the EAP grows and as the company redefines its needs. However, the plan must still consistently delineate values, assumptions, goals, and strategies for achieving the EAP's goals. This program plan should be updated annually.

3. A Policy Statement. This is the most critical part in the development of an EAP. A written policy statement must precede implementation of any EAP. This statement should contain input from those important to the program, including top management and, if appropriate, union officials. It must address several crucial questions concerning the direction and responsibilities of the EAP: location of the EAP offices, family member inclusion, maximum age of dependent children, and so on.

4. *An Information Assessment and Referral System and/or Short-Term Counseling.* During the information assessment and referral component of the EAP, the counselor assesses the particular problem(s) and needs of the client and makes a recommendation or diagnosis. The counselor must possess the specialized professional skills requisite for an informed referral or diagnosis. In the case of AIDS, the counselor now consults with the employee's physician and family members and provides whatever coordination, case management, and support are necessary.

5. *Staffing.* An EAP providing mental health counseling assessment should be staffed by trained, licensed professionals. This means individuals educated in and practicing psychology, social work, psychiatry, or psychiatric nursing—the core mental health professions. It is necessary that these staff members be clinically licensed and have at least two years of alcoholism and drug-abuse training and/or experience. Since drug-abusing persons are the fastest growing group with AIDS, this particular familiarity with the drug treatment community will be helpful. The use of trained, licensed professionals protects the EAP from the legal problems surrounding malpractice, because unlicensed persons make an employer vulnerable to legal suit. In addition, these professionals must have previously demonstrated the ability and flexibility to work with managers, supervisors, employees, and unions. Because of the difficult combination of the counseling and administrative components, many EAPs separate the EAP's administrative role from counseling.

If the company has less than 2,500 employees in a given location, the EAP may use a qualified affiliate or subcontractor. These subcontractors are located within the company's community, so they are accessible to the employees. Subcontractors are used when an internal EAP program is too complex for small companies, or for smaller branches of larger companies located in distant cities and states. It is important that the subcontractor have the same qualifications as would a regular EAP staff in a larger company.

6. *Confidential Record-Keeping System.* The implementation of a confidential record-keeping system must be closely examined, as it involves many more factors than are frequently apparent. Employers are regulated by a host of laws, including the rehabilitation acts, alcoholism and drug regulations, drug-free workplace legislation, handicapped legislation, and OSHA guidelines. Because of privacy laws and sensitivity surrounding AIDS, it is vital that records are maintained and stored confidentially.

7. *A Community Resource Referral Network.* One of the EAPs responsibilities is to evaluate community resources for appropriate employee re-

ferrals. For example, in the case of the AIDS-afflicted employee, support groups for the employee and family would be appropriate. This service may be available through the community hospital. The referral system should be constantly updated. Diversity is crucial so that all the mental health professionals and agencies in the community can be tapped as resources.

Attention to community resources has been neglected and misused. Too often, company officials and supervisors naively suggest an employee go to a referral source from a resource list. This is inappropriate and also has liability potential. Referral sources must be researched and monitored. This must be done through the expertise of an EAP practitioner. Often companies have considered the compilation of a "list" of referral agencies to be a sufficient company EAP, which it clearly is not.

8. *Appropriate Location of the EAP.* If the EAP is within the organization it should be under the auspices of the company's human resource or personnel department. Physically, the EAP design should take into consideration the following: accessibility to the handicapped; a location inconspicuous enough to increase confidentiality; and well-furnished and -maintained surroundings to demonstrate the company's commitment to the EAP. If the EAP is located off-site there also should be an office on the premises, where supervisors and clients can meet with the EAP counselor.

9. *Funding.* The basic funding approaches involve two options. In option one, the company maintains an in-house staff. In option two, the company contracts out all functions on a per capita basis. The fees, regardless of the option used by the company, range from $22–30 per employee, per year, depending on the location of the company. This fee is based on the total number of employees in the company, regardless of how many use the program and how much they use it. This fee structure runs contrary to the traditional fee-for-service mental health medical model. It is more cost-effective because fee-for-service often results in unnecessarily longer treatment, as it provides no motivation to move treatment toward a goal and eventual completion.

10. *Training of Union and Management Personnel.* The training and education of union and management personnel is covered extensively in Chapter 5.

11. *Program Evaluation.* This element is necessary to ascertain whether the EAP is reaching its objectives and performing successfully and cost-effectively. Masi Research Consultants, Inc. is an example of EAP evaluation firms. Masi specializes in EAP evaluation, aiding client companies in designing and later evaluating appropriate and successful EAPs. The comprehensive, qualitative evaluation begins with a "peer panel review." Nationally recognized experts in the fields of psychiatry, psychology, and social work examine a significant number of individual case records using a copyrighted evaluation instrument of 60 items for a complete review. All evaluations are confidential.

This peer review method has precedents in the medical profession, as represented by the American Medical Association and the psychiatric profession. The process has four major components: a general orientation session, a review of case records, direct dialogue with company vendors (optional), and a company debriefing with a final written report. The individual review of case reports includes a protocol instrument that reviews cases for questions about assessment of problem outside referrals, quality of counseling, and a full discussion of the employee's options. Another instrument rates the individual counselor by reviewing the resume and verifying a current license to assure training and experience.

Examining the cost-effectiveness of the EAP, another evaluation used by Masi, involves comparing the EAP clients' absence and attendance records, health insurance claims, worker's compensation, and disability claims before and after utilizing the EAP. This is then compared with the aggregate population.

12. Employee Education and Outreach. To make the EAP effective, employees must be informed of its availability and possibilities. Memos, posters, and programs, including slide shows or films, can all be used to inform the employee of the EAP's existence. These should be offered regularly— several times a year. In addition, the EAP should provide separate educational material on updated relevant medical research.

EAP APPLICATION TO AIDS

The EAP can perform very specific functions for the employee dealing with AIDS or HIV-positive status: employee education, counseling for the AIDS or HIV-positive employee, counseling for the employee who is a family member of a person with AIDS or HIV-positive status, counseling for the family members of the employee with AIDS or HIV-positive status, and developing community resources and health-care alternatives.

Issues of AIDS in the workplace have only recently emerged and many EAP practitioners will not have received any specific instruction on this issue during their formal education and training. As a result, factual information may be lacking and certain critical skills not well-developed. Therefore, the following, paraphrased from the *EAP Digest*, May/June 1988, are guidelines that provide an extensive overview for the EAP professional to adhere to and maintain when dealing with employees affected by AIDS. In addition, professional EAP associations such as the American Management Association often sponsor workshops and training sessions on the topic.

1. EAP professionals should carefully examine their own attitudes and beliefs about HIV disease. Personal feelings about people infected with the HIV virus and behaviors that increase the risk of infection should be explored. Self-examination, awareness, and emotional readiness are crucial when an EAP professional prepares to respond to HIV-disease-related needs.

2. EAP professionals should stay informed and seek training about HIV disease in the following areas:

a. medical aspects—epidemiology, symptoms, transmission, risk reduction and treatment; of particular importance is knowledge about HIV-disease-related symptoms that may be present in the worksite, such as AIDS dementia; and the unpredictable, cyclical nature of the disease, which makes supervision of workers with HIV disease especially problematic

b. legal aspects—AIDS screening, compulsory testing, current litigation, confidentiality, and state and federal antidiscrimination laws, including a thorough understanding of the Federal Rehabilitation Act of 1973

c. psychological aspects—reactions to learning one's HIV status or becoming ill; behavior problems associated with AIDS dementia; acceptance and denial issues; grief and loss; crisis intervention and risk-reduction counseling; the effects of catastrophic illness on HIV-disease-affected individuals, their families, friends, and co-workers

d. community aspects—public and private services available in the local community, including medical and self-help support groups; opportunities for philanthropy and in-kind service donations/support

e. organizational aspects—training programs and media for AIDS education in the workplace, development of policies and programs in given areas of work and geography, resources for management, supervisory and worker program development

3. EAP professionals should be interested in and willing to talk about AIDS. They need to respond emphatically to the fear, anger, hurt, frustration, or shame that a person associates with being HIV positive, having the HIV disease, or having a loved one with the disease. The reactions of supervisors and managers are often laden with fear and irrational emotion as well. These can be diffused by discussions with EAP staff, with resulting improvements in how an organization handles AIDS cases.

4. The EAP professional should explore how much an employee and his/her co-workers and family know about the disease. Is the person in denial, or is he/she willing to talk about the disease? What are the individual's plans for informing others about his/her AIDS-related problems? An individual employee's specific concerns may center around lovers, family members, friends, supervisors, or peers at work. The counselor may use a combination of empathic listening, cognitive or emotional anticipation, and behavioral rehearsal via role playing to help a person with HIV disease prepare to disclose the illness to others.

5. EAP professionals should treat the news about an employee's test for HIV antibodies seriously, regardless of the employee's attitude. Of particular concern are the emotional and social implications of HIV testing, the need for follow-up counseling, and the offhand, casual ways some test results are given.

6. EAP professionals need to develop good assessment and referral services for persons with HIV disease. Extra effort may be required to find AIDS peer support groups, support for affected loved ones, HIV-positive support groups, physicians, lawyers, financial consultants, psychotherapists, or substance abuse treatment programs and counselors who are both willing and specifically trained to work with HIV illness. Such referral services need to link these people and others with HIV-disease-related concerns to support groups as well, though such support groups may be few or nonexistent outside the gay community. When these resources are lacking, they should collaborate with other employers and community groups to help develop these resources where possible.

7. EAP professionals should help persons with AIDS anticipate and constructively deal with others who fear and/or act out toward persons with AIDS because of irrational beliefs. Exploring alternative scenarios and developing strategies for dealing with each one may be of special value.

8. EAP professionals also have an obligation to empathetically and knowledgeably address the needs of any employee who is anxious, angry, or scared about living, working, or associating with persons with AIDS. After creating a trustful climate in which the person can express his/her feelings, it may be possible to overcome irrational beliefs or ignorance of the facts about HIV disease (through both internal and external education referrals) that may be fueling an emotional response, and to begin building consideration for the rights of the person with AIDS.

9. EAP professionals should advocate for a consistent, clearly stated AIDS policy regarding employee and employer rights and responsibilities. The policy should be made available to all workers and supported by the company.

10. EAP professionals should promote or conduct specific educational programs related to AIDS for both supervisors and employees in the workplace. Collaboration with human resources, medical, legal, benefits, and training departments may be helpful in this regard.

11. EAP professionals should be alert to their own signs of emotional burn-out in their dealing with HIV-affected individuals. EAP staff should seek peer support and recognize their own limitations in dealing with death and dying issues over time.[2]

RECENT DEVELOPMENTS FOR EAPs AND ISSUES OF AIDS

As the issues and developments surrounding AIDS are constantly changing, employers should consider the growing scope of the disease.

People with AIDS are living much longer now than in the earlier years of the epidemic. ... Five years ago, 80% of the people with AIDS died within two years of diagnosis, sometimes within six months. Now, with advances in treatment such as AZT and aerosol pentamidine, those with access to good medical care often live three years or more.... Many will die eventually. Nevertheless, AIDS is taking on the dimensions of a chronic disease as well as a fatal one—with profound implications for treatment, services, counseling, living and health care financing, according to social workers involved in AIDS programs.... There needs to be a growth in chronic care.... We need to develop services for people who are sick for a very long time and their families. We need to look at ongoing interventions to support the persons' and families' independence.... An increasing number of people with AIDS are able to work after being diagnosed or leaving the hospital, making education and adaptation in the workplace important.... Job sharing, flexible hours, and retraining of productive employees who cannot perform all of their former duties need to be considered.[3]

As recent medical findings have been developed, the

medical management of HIV disease is improving and changing in the direction of aggressive, earlier intervention in HIV persons who are asymptomatic. Because of treatments like AZT and DDI, patients will live longer and follow a zig-zag course of recoveries and relapses, instead of a straight downhill path. This will pose new obstacles in the workplace and medical management of HIV. The Human Resources departments, management, supervisors and employees need to be educated as to the understanding and importance of workplace support for persons who are HIV positive. Issues around potential discrimination, confidentiality, workplace disruption, grief, and reasonable accommodation require strategic planning, and preventative education.[4]

The challenge of honoring the confidentiality of persons with AIDS, while satisfying the co-workers' "right to know," has become a major issue in the workplace. To date courts have consistently ruled in favor of the AIDS patient involving cases of confidentiality. However, in California, a workers' compensation board recently awarded $5,000 to a co-worker who filed for emotional stress compensation due to working alongside an AIDS patient.

The ethical principle of violating the confidence between physician and patient is about to be redefined, especially in California and New York. The issue is that there is a responsibility for the physician involved to let the sexual partner know if the partner is positive. Counselors are offering to be with the parties when they are told. The author would support informing the partner, in conjunction with the company's EAP practitioner. As more and more decisions are supporting the rights of AIDS patients, it is in the context of the duty of a medical professional to warn the appropriate parties who may be in a life-threatening situation.

Counseling Employees about Experimental Drug Programs

EAP practitioners should be responsible for keeping informed about experimental drug treatment programs for AIDS. These programs or "clinical trials" are federally funded voluntary programs conducted in major medical centers throughout the country. The programs offer access to drugs in the research phase, which are not yet approved by the Food and Drug Administration. They can be a major tool in the AIDS patient's prolonged life span, as well as assisting in the research toward a cure.

Although there have been no documented cases of anyone recovering from AIDS, some patients do survive longer than others. This is partially because of the participation of AIDS-afflicted individuals in one of the dozens of experimental drug programs offered throughout the country. In the past, only people with full-blown AIDS took drugs. Now with the discovery of the life-lengthening advantages of AZT and other drugs, more people are taking drugs at earlier stages of the infection. Most of the individuals who are eligible for participation in these programs are in the workforce, and therefore information regarding these programs should be available from the company EAP and human resources department. In order to assist these employees in making the best choice, EAPs must know all the facets of participation in an experimental drug program.

AIDS patients thinking about taking experimental drugs should know the following information. It is up to the EAP and the corporate medical director (if applicable) to help employees find the answers.

- What is the evidence that the drug may have a positive effect?
- What qualifications do the scientists in charge have?
- What are the known side effects of the drug?
- How will taking this drug interfere with my work schedule?
- If the drug works, how long will the licensing process take?
- Are there patients I can talk to who have been in the program or who have taken the drug?
- What are the medical consequences if I withdrew from the program?
- Is there provision for psychological support during the course of the programs, or is it strictly medical?

Kinds of Drugs

There are several categories of drug treatment options available:

- Antiviral drugs fight HIV at some stages of its reproduction. Some researchers theorize that taking more than one antiviral at a time may increase a patient's chances of fighting off the virus. However, some drugs are antagonistic to one another; that is, one cancels out the effect of the other. For instance, AZT and ribavirin should not be taken simultaneously.
- Immune stimulants are designed to rebuild what the AIDS virus has destroyed. Although many such drugs are under investigation, they are surrounded by controversy because some doctors believe that stimulating the immune system may also stimulate the cellular machinery that encourages reproduction of the virus.

There is also debate about the quality of new immune system cells that are produced and their ability to fight the virus. Many physicians believe that antivirals should be used before starting treatment with immune stimulants.

- Prophylactic (preventive) treatment for opportunistic infections is designed to head off infection before it strikes. Two of the most widely used drugs are pentamidine for pneumocystis pneumonia and clofazimine for mycobacterium infections.[5]

The patient participating in the program must understand the use of controls in research. There is an equal chance of receiving a placebo (no drug) as the one being tested. Known as a "double blind study," in this procedure neither the patient nor the researcher knows who is receiving which drug. This procedure must be in place in order to test the experimental drug. Many participants become unwilling to risk taking only a placebo and therefore should not participate in such a program.

The participant must agree to follow the rules of the research project. Although they differ from program to program, they usually include the stipulation that the participant must not take any other drugs without the researchers' assent. Participants are sometimes unwilling to lose a chance for other types of treatment. Again, these individuals should not participate in the program.

The employee should be made aware of the advantages and disadvantages from the onset. Among the advantages: the disease may slow its course; a sense of control and of doing something about the disease; and the positive ramifications of participating in something that will further the development of research for others afflicted with the disease. The disadvantages include: being subject to the harmful toxic side effects of many of the drugs; the loss of hope if a treatment is found ineffective; and wasting time and energy on treatments that are ineffective.

The decision to participate in an experimental drug program is met with important emotional and physical considerations that the EAP counselor must be aware of in order to ensure that employees are making an informed decision.

AIDS and Insurance Benefits

The way insurance companies deal with AIDS is another area of concern for both employers and employees. The cost of treating individuals who are currently exposed could come to billions of dollars. In addition, because of recent advances in treatment, the lives of AIDS patients are being prolonged; hence their treatment period is prolonged as well. Caring for a person with AIDS costs money, and insurers are trying to find ways to protect themselves from the risk of making enormous outlays for this treatment. Treatment for AIDS runs approximately $50,000 to $75,000 per patient. Private insurance companies are currently absorbing most of these costs, as well as Medicaid.

At this time insurers are prohibited from excluding AIDS coverage in their policies. Some insurers, however, are requiring the applicant to take a test as a prerequisite for some types of personal and life insurance. This testing has been criticized as discriminatory by leaders in the gay community, and some cities and states have banned the practice completely.

The only reason a company would require the test is to deny coverage to those who test positive or to exclude AIDS-related health problems, which is only shifting the financial burden onto the taxpayer. Furthermore, there is no guarantee that confidentiality will be protected, which means those who test positive may face discrimination in other areas such as housing or employment. Many insurance companies fail to use confirmatory tests and therefore have high rates of false positives; little concern is shown for the way in which individuals are informed of positive test results. In addition, denying coverage on the basis of geographic or occupational stereotypes (e.g., not accepting an unmarried male designer living in particular areas of San Francisco) is seen as discriminatory. Companies who agree that such screening is inappropriate, including Blue Cross/Blue Shield, say they will treat AIDS like any other long-term illness. Workers with AIDS have a right to affordable, quality, and accessible health care. Employer and insurance company concerns about potentially high health care costs for AIDS patients should not result in benefit cutbacks. Rather, innovative, alternative programs which contain costs and maintain benefits should be pursued.[6]

In another approach, some insurance companies have denied coverage to whole companies that they consider to be possibly employing "high-risk" individuals. Industries that have been named as having possible concentrations of these high-risk employees include: hair salons, restaurants, clothing designers, nonprofit organizations, the entertainment and arts industries, funeral parlors, hotels, and motels. At this time, this practice is legal.

In most cases, it is virtually impossible for an individual diagnosed as having AIDS to obtain medical and/or life insurance. Because of this, some companies are allowing employees with AIDS to retain their benefits as long as possible after leaving employment. However, this gesture does not come inexpensively.

In the past, health-care benefits accounted for 1–2% of a company's overhead. Today, they threaten to exceed 10%, with a large portion going to the long-term care of patients with catastrophic or chronic conditions— a category that now includes AIDS. Because insurance policies so often put constraints on the treatment of certain injuries and/or illnesses, the health care implemented often is costly but not as effective as it could be.

In 1988, the CDC reported that employers had spent $4.1 billion on AIDS. This included $832 million for health care and $3.26 billion attributed to lost productivity and premature deaths of workers. By the end of 1992, projections for health and support services are toward $5–13 billion. Because the majority of persons with AIDS are either in the workplace or of working age (102,000 out of 105,000), this becomes a critical issue for the workplace.

THE EAP AND CASE MANAGEMENT

AIDS has been responsible for the acceleration of a relatively new and atypical approach to health care known as case management. Case management is a system of assessing and monitoring client needs throughout the treatment continuum. Its elements include assessment of the patient's needs, referral to the appropriate resources, follow-up, and consultation. Extended follow-up is necessary because of the chronic nature of the disease and the potential for varying stages of psychological and physical stresses. Case management is a process specifically designed to customize care for individual patients with catastrophic illnesses. The patient is assigned a coordinator, an experienced health-care professional, to provide psychological and sociological support for the patient and the patient's family. The EAP counselor can perform this role effectively. The coordinator also acts as a liaison between the person with AIDS, the physician, and the family and helps plan details of medical care and finances. Case managers also strive for a timely discharge from hospitals and utilize atypical health-care venues, such as hospices or home-care settings. For example, the estimated average daily cost for home health care and hospices is estimated to be $100–300 per day. The average daily cost of hospitalization stands at $880–1000 per day. Ironically, only 50% of the nation's insurers cover home health care, and only 30% cover hospices.

Clearly, the high cost of health insurance is one of the most difficult and vital problems facing employers dealing with AIDS in their workplace. Therefore, it is the role of the EAP practitioner to find alternative resources to supplement those offered in the traditional health-care benefits package. By acting as a case manager for the employees with AIDS or HIV-positive status, the EAP worker will assist in providing "cost-effective, appropriate, and more compassionate care by matching the patients' and families' needs with the most appropriate alternative."[7]

This approach has two obvious advantages. It allows the AIDS patients to achieve their optimum recovery faster, and it greatly reduces the number of unnecessary hospital days. However, not many insurance companies have the mechanisms in place to offer case management. Therefore, it is up to the employer to exert pressure on insurers to change language and/or policies so that case management can be implemented.

In their roles as case managers for the employee, EAP practitioners should reach out to the following groups to make their status known: family members, managers/supervisors, employees, medical department, and senior management. The EAP practitioner would coordinate with the insurance company, physicians, and psychological experts and act as an advocate for the employee.

ALTERNATIVES IN EMPLOYEE WORK SCHEDULES AND BENEFITS

In the coming decade employees affected by AIDS will remain much longer in the workforce. This is due to the earlier testing for the virus and new treatment options being developed. Therefore, companies must be ready to be as creative as possible to allow their employees to handle the disease. This includes allowing for change in work schedules; allowing for the opportunity for employees to bring work and company equipment (if applicable) home; and being conscious of the necessity for varied sick leave due to numerous physician appointments. Employers must keep in mind that this flexibility must also apply to the employee who is the caretaker of a loved one with AIDS, as well as the AIDS-affected employee.

It is also necessary for companies to continue their willingness to investigate all aspects of their employee benefits packages to allow for a more comprehensive program for employees with AIDS and employees with family members with AIDS. This is especially true for smaller companies and those companies that traditionally employ younger workers. These companies especially must be willing to expand their benefits packages because of the higher percentage of younger workers being afflicted with AIDS.

As more employees became sick with AIDS, employers realized that their benefits plans were poorly suited to provide for long-term illness, especially the lack of provision for income benefits during the waiting period until a long-term disability policy took effect. Some employers have added or enhanced a self-funded short-term disability plan, and others create a sick leave pool. The pool works this way: earned sick leave accruals are reduced from 10 to 12 days a year to 6 or 7 days, and the unused balance can be used by employees who have exhausted their sick and annual leave.[8]

KEY ROLE OF EAPs FOR REFERRALS

EAP practitioners must develop reliable assessment and referral services for employees and family members with AIDS. As with many issues that have emerged in the past, the AIDS tragedy will spawn many professionals who profess expertise in the treatment of AIDS patients. The EAP practitioner must find physicians, lawyers, dentists, financial consultants, psychotherapists, AIDS policy and education consultants, and substance abuse counselors who are qualified to work with AIDS-related problems. Identifying and evaluating professionals who are skilled in working with AIDS patients and family members is a vital task for the EAP practitioner.

Because of the significant discrimination that often occurs concerning AIDS, EAP practitioners may often assume the role of advocate, ensuring that services are provided and employees' needs are met.

AIDS-affected employees may also need help in drafting wills, planning child custody, and assigning medical or durable power of attorney to a close friend or significant other to make medical or other important decisions should they become incapable of doing so.[9]

In addition to providing help for the employee dealing with AIDS or HIV, the EAP practitioner can be a valuable resource for managers by providing guidance, support, and information to enable them to cope with their own feelings, as well as ensuring that the AIDS-affected employee remains in the workplace for as long as possible with limited workplace complications.

EAPs AND AIDS: THE NEW CHALLENGE FOR THE EAP PROFESSION

HIV infection and the employed drug user or employees who are sexual partners of drug users present challenges to the definition of the Employee Assistance Program. For discussion purposes, consider the following case report of an employed woman who sought assistance for an HIV problem related to intravenous drug abuse. This was presented at a recent meeting the author attended that was hosted by NIDA (National Institute of Drug Abuse).[10]

Ms. A is now a 34 year old woman who is employed as a clerical worker by a large public utility company. She began to snort cocaine at age 25 years and first used cocaine intravenously at age 28 years. She considered herself addicted to cocaine at age 31. Although her supervisor and co-workers had not noted any changes in her behavior, the spouse had become increasingly concerned regarding her drug use and insisted that she seek treatment or he would leave her.

Ms. A sought outpatient treatment at age 32 years in a publicly funded outpatient drug treatment program. She participated in 12 weeks of twice weekly counseling and urine testing and became abstinent by Week 4. After completing the 12–week program she was seen monthly in outpatient follow up and attended Cocaine Anonymous meetings regularly.

At no time were her supervisor and co-workers aware of her addiction or treatment. When asked why she did not seek assistance from her EAP, she stated that she did not trust the program, which she perceived to be an extension of her employer and not particularly useful other than obtaining a list of mental health or substance abuse treatment programs. She chose not to use her medical insurance for drug abuse treatment because of concerns regarding confidentiality.

During the evaluation for drug abuse treatment, she underwent HIV counseling and antibody testing and tested HIV-antibody positive. Although she and her husband were counseled regarding the need for precautions during sexual intercourse in order to avoid infecting her husband, the spouse refused to wear a condom.

Ms. A diagnosed as being pregnant six months after she entered drug abuse treatment. Her obstetrician and internist recommended that she terminate the 6 weeks old pregnancy because of reports that pregnancy accelerated the progression of HIV infection to AIDS and there was a 50% chance that her fetus would be HIV-infected. Ms. A agreed with the recommendations. However, although there were documented recommendations of pregnancy termination from her obstetrician, internist, and drug abuse counselor, Ms. A's insurer refused to pay for pregnancy termination because the pregnancy was not associated with a life-threatening condition. At this point Ms. A contacted her EAP office for assistance. She was told that the EAP staff could not help her because her addictive disorder was in remission and the office handled only insurance matters which were associated with mental health or substance abuse treatment. The pregnancy was not terminated.

Ms. A began to abuse cocaine during the fourth month of pregnancy but again was undetected at work. She delivered a small infant six weeks prematurely.

The infant was hospitalized for 6 weeks for respiratory distress. The baby tested positive for HIV infection and died of AIDS at age 18 months. During the child's illness, Ms. A missed approximately 6 months from work caring for her child. Total medical expenses for the child were over $300,000.

As the foregoing case shows, the EAP was completely out of line when it refused assistance. It is inconceivable that an EAP would not see the urgency of the problem and not only provide assistance to the employee but become her clear advocate. Unfortunately this is an example of what an EAP should not do.

COMMENTS

Unfortunately, although there is a vital role for EAPs in an AIDS-at-work program, it is increasingly discouraging that the EAP field has failed to take more initiative in the leadership role in developing appropriate programs for AIDS in the workplace. Too often, human resource directors have been left to develop programs and sort their way through the maze of material that is available. As late as October 1989, the Employee Assistance Profession Association's (formerly ALMACA) annual conference featured only one program on AIDS, with only two presenters. The EAP profession has not addressed its feelings about PWAs and has chosen to ignore and deny the issue. However, there remains a heavy professional responsibility for EAPs to act. Their inactivity cannot continue and EAP counselors need to initiate activity even if EAP program managers are not doing so.

Because the EAP field is a new profession, there is no accrediting of programs. As a result, there is wide diversity in delivery of services. Some programs have clinically licensed personnel, and others have employee relations people wearing an EAP hat without any human resource training. Because of this it is difficult to generalize on the appropriate role of the EAP. However, there is no doubt that as an emerging profession it still has a responsibility to assume a major role in the workplace in this area. It is incumbent upon corporate management to see that their EAP people are trained appropriately to deal with this sensitive subject.

NOTES

1. Dale A. Masi, *Designing Employee Assistance Programs* (New York: AMA-COM, 1984), p. 23.

2. *EAP Digest*, May/June 1988, with permission of Performance Resource Press, Inc., 2145 Crooks Road, Suite 103, Troy, Michigan 48084. Paraphrased by Bryan Lawton, Thomas E. Backer, and Kirk B. O'Hara, "AIDS Handbook for Employee Assistance Professionals in the Entertainment Industry" (Los Angeles: Human Interaction Research Institute, June 1989), pp. 9–11.

3. John Hiratsuka, "AIDS Being Treated as a Chronic Disease," *NASW News*, October 1989, p. 4.

4. Yvonne Ellison-Sandler, "AIDS/HIV Infection and the Workplace Workgroup," unpublished notes from NIDA-sponsored conference on AIDS/HIV Infection, November 17, 1989, p. 1.

5. Margot J. Fromer, "Counseling Employees About Experimental Drugs," AIDS Workplace Update (Greenvale, NY: Panel Publishers, March 1989), p. 1.

6. Service Employees International Union, AFL-CIO, CLC, *The AIDS Book: Information for Workers* (Washington, DC, April 1988), pp. 17–18.

7. Beverly J. Anderson and Edward A. Lemerise, "The Role of the EAP Practitioner in Managing AIDS," AIDS Workplace Update (Greenvale, NY: Panel Publishers, October 1988), p. 4.

8. Cliff Balkam, "New HR Policies," AIDS Workplace Update (Greenvale, NY: Panel Publishers, February 1989), p. 7.

9. Anderson and Lemerise, "The Role of the EAP Practitioner," p. 5.

10. William W. Weddington, "Summary," unpublished notes from NIDA-sponsored conference on AIDS/HIV Infection, November 1989, pp. 1–2.

CHAPTER 5

AIDS EDUCATION AT THE WORKSITE

INTRODUCTION

When dealing with the subject of AIDS, the most provocative elements are fear and ignorance. People are afraid of future contraction of the virus or that they have already been exposed to the virus. Because there is no vaccine or cure as yet, the most effective weapon to combat such fear and ignorance is education. This means education by all systems in our society—businesses, schools, churches, and community organizations.

This chapter will cover issues pertaining to specific educational programs in the workplace. A discussion of the philosophy behind establishing an AIDS education program for all employees will be followed by a look at specific arguments commonly presented by management and employees who do not want the education. To assist companies in defining the education program best suited for them, the goals of an education program will be presented. A specific and defined educational program will be outlined with an adaptation that is easily applied to suit every company. The chapter will cover the selection of the material to be used in the program, the content that material must provide, and other related issues. The discussion will look at what a company should do when an employee is diagnosed with AIDS. The language of AIDS and sensible workplace precautions will be described. The chapter will conclude with an explanation of an evaluation of the company AIDS education program and results of a survey on attitudes toward AIDS in the workplace.

PHILOSOPHY

AIDS information and education programs, as with any company policy, are most effective if they begin before a problem situation arises relative toAIDS and employee concerns. Experience in the private sector has demonstrated that employees' level of receptivity to accurate information will be higher when management has a policy of open communication and when educational efforts are initiated before an incident.

Education and information should be of an ongoing nature. Management must not get complacent about the necessity to update and maintain employee education. According to Dr. Constance Wofsy

it takes five go-rounds before the educational effort is completely heard. . . . During the first go-round there is fear and denial; the second is accepting that this is information that you have to hear but you don't want to really listen; the third is intellectual curiosity. After all, it is an interesting topic; the fourth is real interest and wonder; and finally in the fifth go-round the individual is able to be concerned about people other than themselves and exhibit the appropriate responses necessary when dealing with the topic.[1]

Many businesses are hesitant in their willingness to respond to AIDS issues in the workplace. Some typical rationales presented by businesses not to develop an AIDS policy and education program include:

- The wish to deal with only "business" and "business issues."
- The inability to see how the company would be affected.
- The desire not to want to promote fear and disrupt work.
- Some businesses feel if they promote an AIDS policy, negative publicity will follow with the assumption that the company is employing and catering to homosexuals.
- The businesses do not want to appear as tolerant/sympathetic of homosexual lifestyle—it may attract high-risk individuals to the company resulting in increased health costs.
- The businesses are not convinced of the employees' wish for the policy and educational program.
- There is fear of customer reaction.

These rationales represent management's unwillingness to see AIDS for what it really is: a public health crisis. In some form it will eventually affect much of the workplace population—either by affecting the employees themselves or by affecting employees' families or loved ones. Efficient management deals with issues before they reach crisis proportions; and with AIDS, management must face the challenge of battling much fear and ignorance.

There are many reasons to educate employees about AIDS. AIDS education

- helps save lives
- avoids work disruption problems

- maintains employee morale
- demonstrates corporate responsibility
- avoids unnecessary litigation
- avoids customer complaints
- avoids negative publicity
- helps contain health costs
- helps affected employees to receive compassion and understanding—especially if they return to work
- helps employees deal with issues surrounding this disease and death and feelings of helplessness toward affected employees/loved ones.[2]

By employing periodic, updated educational approaches, employees will be reassured of management's commitment to open communication about AIDS. By providing AIDS information to all employees, companies will enhance employee understanding about the nature and transmission of the disease.

GOALS OF AN EMPLOYEE EDUCATION PROGRAM

Before designing the employee education program, the company should address the goals of the program. A company AIDS education program should involve these goals: changing behavior so that the epidemic is slowed; increasing awareness about the issues pertaining to AIDS; dispelling myths; lessening the fear surrounding the disease; and preparing the company and its employees to handle a case of AIDS with care, compassion, and minimal disruption.

The goals of the employee education program should be determined prior to implementation and the impact evaluated periodically in order to make any changes to the education program necessary. Knowledge change is easiest to achieve, followed by attitude change, with behavior change being the most difficult. Therefore, in order for educational efforts to be most effective they must be credible, targeted for the special high-risk behavior change and, consequently, a decrease in the spread of AIDS. Employers should also recognize the value of broadening the audience, to include the employees' families and loved ones.

When discussing and defining goals of the educational program, consider

who is to benefit from a workplace HIV/AIDS program? . . . Will this program exist for individuals with HIV disease, those who are HIV+, all who are at potential risk for HIV, those who must work with such individuals, for the "good" of the business or for society-at-large? Assumptions about WHO will benefit by WHAT by HOW MUCH or by WHEN are rarely made explicit. Without such considerations the potential for evaluation of educational impact of program outcomes is limited.[3]

STRUCTURE AND MODEL OF AN AIDS EDUCATIONAL PROGRAM

History has demonstrated that fear and denial lead only to panic and irrationality. Education always has been the best weapon against situations that seem chaotic and frightening. Historically, the workplace has taken a leadership role in combatting other employee welfare concerns, such as alcohol and drug abuse, smoking reduction, and physical fitness. The same positive results can be achieved with the issues surrounding AIDS. Workplace-based educational programs can provide information to achieve this knowledge and assuage fear. The following are steps to follow when developing an employee educational program for AIDS in the workplace:

1. Inform and gain the support of top management. Without their knowledge and approval any education program will be ineffective. This support should be communicated to all employees when the program is announced. The remainder of the staff is educated with each manager helping to facilitate the education of their staff.

2. Establish a resource/education committee composed of managers and employees. This increases the sense of ownership and acceptance for any program developed. Composition of the committee should include representatives from human resources, legal, medical, labor, management, communications, EAP, and special interest groups. Once selected, these representatives need to be educated about the issues surrounding AIDS, the company's policies, and the availability of community resources. Once trained, this committee can work together to design the company's AIDS educational program, respond to employee questions and concerns, and promote a positive attitude about AIDS.[4]

3. The AIDS education program must be an ongoing effort. Companies that have already employed an AIDS education awareness program state that employees' awareness of AIDS was only increased over a period of time with repeated approaches through a variety of dissemination methods. Consequently, an AIDS education program must plan for a time frame that is long enough to promote behavioral change and alleviate fear. This program must also include a commitment to revising the educational program if change is not induced.

4. Educational material should be presented. As new information becomes available, it must be disseminated. Dissemination methods include brochures, videos, posters, and seminars. Appendix A at the end of this book provides a listing of national organizations with free publications and material available for a variety of populations covering all aspects of AIDS. Small businesses will have a different approach than large, multinational corporations. AIDS education should be consistent with other employee education programs. Consider the special needs of special work populations

(for example, non-English-speaking/reading, parents, etc.) within the general employee population (see Chapter 6 on "Special Work Populations").

When choosing the material either to distribute to employees or to assist the educator, consider that the United States is a visual society. Material loaded with statistics, tables, and medical jargon will only alienate the audience. The *Surgeon General's Report on AIDS* brochure is excellent and should be mailed out to all employees or distributed within the office. Videotapes should not be racist, sexist, homophobic, condescending, or preachy. Many are informative, conversational, and educational. Consider that these materials will remain with the employees and represent the company's philosophy. Therefore, careful research and thought should go into their selection.

5. Appointing one person within the company, who is usually from the human resource department, to act as the reference point within the organization is an important component. This individual should be responsible for answering questions about the company's AIDS policy, benefits, and other personnel issues related to AIDS. By designating one person, a company can be assured of confidentiality for the individual employee as well as dissemination of correct information to the employees at large.

6. In-house educational workshops are an effective method for training employees about AIDS. Employees may feel more comfortable and trusting of an in-house workshop rather than outside resource organizations. They are relatively easy to conduct and are effective in reaching employees. Members of the resource/education committee, human resource department, and the EAP should contribute to the meeting.

The type of person who presents the workshop and his or her knowledge and sensitivity about AIDS must be evaluated beforehand. One of the author's clients set the subject of AIDS in the workplace back for a year by assuming their EAP person could provide AIDS education. The company's EAP arranged for an outside speaker who showed slides that were inappropriate for the workplace and many employees were offended and frightened. The whole point of the educational effort was lost. If the company education program is done in-house, the Red Cross, the State Department of Health, and the resources in Appendix A can provide information and guidelines for conducting an in-house AIDS education seminar.

7. Consider the information to be presented in the educational program. Information directly related to the workplace should include transmission/nontransmission of AIDS at the worksite, the company's policy on dealing with employees who have AIDS, and what to do when a co-worker has AIDS.

When presenting the specific characteristics of the disease include the following:

- origin and epidemiology of the disease in the United States, the world, and the particular state
- death rates in the United States, the world, and the particular state
- infection rate versus death rate of disease
- projections for the spread of AIDS
- AIDS testing: explanation of the company policy
- AIDS testing: accuracy and who should be tested
- economic impact of the disease
- treatment, vaccine, up-to-date research

The medical material to be presented should include:

- general discussion about AIDS
- transmission of the virus
- high-risk behaviors
- use of condoms and clean needles
- definition of related terms (AIDS, HIV, PWA)

One of the most controversial areas in AIDS education is the subject of safe sex. The workplace, in the author's opinion, would be hypocritical not to include this as a major area of its education program. Unless the subject is addressed directly, mixed messages will be given that might result in employees thinking the use of condoms does not pertain to them.

Prevention is the only true weapon to fight the spread of the disease. The basics of AIDS prevention should be incorporated in the employee educational package. Distribution and discussion of the information to family and friends should be emphasized. When discussing prevention consider the following:

1. AIDS is hard to get. Casual contact is safe. So is hugging, swimming, and eating in restaurants. If it wasn't safe, there would be millions more cases of AIDS.

2. AIDS is spread by sex; by blood transfusions; by the sharing of already used needles or works; and from infected mother to infant. These are the only ways AIDS can be spread.

3. Anyone who has sex or shares needles with an HIV infected person takes a big chance and risks becoming infected. Condoms and clean needles are the tools necessary to help to protect against infection with an already infected person.

4. Healthy people are spreading AIDS. Most people infected with HIV don't know it—so how could they possibly tell anyone?

5. If one's sex partner has ever used needles to shoot drugs, he or she may be infected, and can give you the virus during sex. (Almost every drug user who has used needles has also shared needles.)

6. Every time one has sex with someone who he or she is not absolutely sure is not carrying the virus, and a condom is not used, one is taking a chance of getting infected.

7. The virus that causes AIDS lives in white blood cells in semen (cum) and blood. All it takes to stay safe is keeping someone else's blood or semen outside of one's body.

8. Using a condom the right way makes most any kind of sex safer.

9. Share the facts about AIDS with people. One may save lives.[5]

In addition to the outline for an AIDS workplace education program, the program should address other issues. All employees should be educated. Often employees self-diagnose themselves as not needing to be educated about AIDS or are fearful that their attendance may be misinterpreted. As a result voluntary attendance is often limited. Mandatory or required attendance for all manager/supervisors and all employees is crucial if the educational program is to complete its goal of comprehension, clarity, and consistency. Education provided on company time is more likely to be favorably received and increases management's credibility.

The number of employees per education group should not exceed 30. This will ensure a more effective presentation. By having a smaller number, employees are less likely to feel embarrassed and more likely to ask questions. In addition, the education should be conducted in such a way as to protect any PWAs that are within the company.

AIDS education programs should update the employees as new scientific evidence is reported, and should be repeated periodically. Because the media is the main source of dissemination of new information from the scientific community regarding AIDS, the information is often presented in a confused, abbreviated, and contradictory manner. It is important that employees be continually educated to all new relevant information and be given a chance to clarify any area that is unclear.

ISSUES RELEVANT IN PARTICULAR TO MANAGERS/ SUPERVISORS

In training managers and supervisors to deal with AIDS, issues such as confidentiality, legal obligations, and co-worker stress come into focus. Some common concerns of managers/supervisors who have had to deal with AIDS in their departments include:

• What should I do if someone in my department is suspected of having AIDS?

• How do I handle a rumor that someone in my work group is suspected of having AIDS?

- Can I insist that an employee take the AIDS antibody test?
- How do I handle the issue of confidentiality if an employee who has AIDS wishes to remain anonymous?
- What are my legal obligations to an employee with AIDS?
- What are my obligations to co-workers who must work with an employee who has AIDS?
- What benefits are employees with AIDS entitled to?
- What should I do if employees react with a sudden outburst of panic because of a co-worker who has AIDS?
- Is there counseling available for employees with AIDS or employees with any life-threatening illnesses?[6]

Managers/supervisors should be prepared to deal with employee concerns and other issues related to AIDS in the workplace. Companies should consider, therefore, conducting ongoing training and education programs on AIDS for their managers/supervisors on the medical and personnel management dimensions of AIDS. These programs can be used to educate managers/supervisors on the latest research on AIDS in the workplace, to provide advice on how to recognize and handle situations which arise in their organizations, and to convey the importance of maintaining the confidentiality of any medical and other information about employees' health status. In addition, managers/supervisors should be given a point of contact within the company where they can call to obtain further information or to discuss situations which arise in their work departments. Companies should attempt to initiate training and guidance activities before problems occur.[7]

In presenting the topic of AIDS, managers often assume that the modes of communication necessary are entirely different from discussing other management issues. The communication methods employed by a company are exactly the ones to employ when communicating about AIDS. Properly explained in nonmedical terms, AIDS can be more easily understood by both managers and employees.

Clearly, education must be targeted to the specific group of employees. The managers/supervisors have some different issues than the average line worker. Consider the varying employee populations in the company when designing an effective, comprehensive employee AIDS education program.

THE TRAINER AND THE AIDS RESOURCE PERSON

Properly training the trainer is an important component of an effective program. Because of the relatively new issues surrounding AIDS, as well as the continual new information pertaining to the disease, the trainer leading the education program should be a specialist in AIDS. Generally, no one person can cover all the medical, legal, and human resource aspects of AIDS in the workplace. It is best to bring in outside resource persons to conduct such training. In addition, EAP and medical personnel should seek further education to remain fully informed of all the issues surrounding AIDS.

The most essential skill needed for the AIDS resource person is the ability to assist people in discussing their fears and to guide them towards authoritative sources for answers to their questions. Resource people also have to have already dealt with their own issues about AIDS, sex or drugs so that their personal biases will not affect their interactions with employees. Resource people need to understand and deal with the occasional hostile reaction; they need to be patient people. Finally, they need to serve as role models at work for employee responses to the AIDS issue.[8]

While training employees to be sensitive to the issues surrounding the AIDS virus in the workplace, it should also be noted that

families are not taking the responsibility to educate teens (13 +) on HIV. There will be an ever increasing number of teenagers developing HIV, using drugs, and placing themselves at risk for teen pregnancy. The workplace should be a model for change in managing HIV. Teach employees in the workplace about HIV. Teach them to be an agent of change in their family system, school system, community, religious community, etc. Give families the tools to talk about sexuality, drug abuse, and HIV with their children.[9]

This will be beneficial to the society as a whole.

WHEN AN EMPLOYEE IS DIAGNOSED WITH AIDS

When a company is faced with its first case of AIDS at the worksite, and as the employee's AIDS status becomes revealed throughout the company, co-workers and even supervisors may become fearful and hesitant to work alongside the employee. This happens most frequently and acutely when there have been no prior education and policy programs implemented regarding AIDS-related issues. Employee Assistance Practitioners are often the catalyst for information in these situations. Group sessions (with or without an AIDS expert) are held to discuss areas of fear and concern with the affected employees, co-workers, and managers. The discussion of legal and public relations consequences of certain actions held either in private sessions with managers or employees as well as sessions with the affected employee are a variety of scenarios that have proven effective.

At times, special meetings may be held with employees to openly share that a co-worker has AIDS. These meetings, held with the affected employee's knowledge, cooperation and written consent, are particularly effective and warranted when a key staff member is diagnosed—especially if the employee is well known and liked or has worked with a significant number of other employees. The goal of this meeting is to head off unnecessary rumors, to dispel myths and fears and to give co-workers an opportunity to deal with their sense of sadness and loss that an AIDS diagnosis usually generates. An outside expert, together with an EAP and other human resources personnel can help co-workers process these feelings while giving them a chance to ask questions about transmission, prognosis, course of illness and concerns about the affected employee's intentions to return to work. Handled properly, these sessions can be extremely positive and cathartic for all concerned.[10]

When educating employees how to treat their co-worker with AIDS, there are some specific points to assist them.

Even well intentioned friends and co-workers may feel inadequate or helpless when confronted with the illness. To help, a New York based AIDS support group offers several suggestions on dealing with a co-worker who has AIDS:

• Don't avoid him or her. Be there—it instills hope.

• Touch him or her. A simple squeeze of the hand or a hug lets the person know you care. (Don't be afraid . . . you cannot contract AIDS by simply touching.)

• Don't be reluctant to talk about the illness. Find out if he or she needs to talk about the condition by asking.

• Don't permit him or her to accept blame for the illness. People don't cause diseases, germs do.

• Talk about the future—tomorrow, next week, next year. Hope is important.

• Bring a positive attitude. It's catching.[11]

Workers who are diagnosed as HIV positive must deal with some particularly difficult issues, including

fear of family rejection due to AIDS; work performance issues associated with symptoms of HIV, or with the sometimes crippling anxiety associated with learning of one's own HIV status; fear of rejection by co-workers; substance abuse relapse associated with learning of one's HIV status; continuing high-risk behaviors after learning of one's HIV status; and finally, financial assistance to meet the high costs of HIV treatment, especially since many alternative therapies are not currently covered by most health insurance policies.[12]

Conducting employee meetings regarding the co-worker diagnosed with AIDS augments the effectiveness of the existing educational program to help diminish the stress and anxiety placed on the HIV-positive employee.

LANGUAGE OF AIDS

When conducting an effective employee education program, frank discussions about sexual orientation are necessary. To prevent the spread of the virus, the education program will also need to include candid discussions about intravenous drug transmittal and proper cleaning of drug paraphernalia ("works"). Most of the heterosexual, non-IV-drug-related cases of AIDS are among women, and many of the women are minorities. Most pediatric cases involve minority children. The workplace program must be sensitive to these populations.

The success of the educational effort depends in large part on how the educator presents reactions to an audience's fear, prejudices, and questions.

Sensitivity to terminology is also important. [Persons] with AIDS (PWA's) or AIDS related complex (ARC) do not want to be called "victims." The term has a negative effect on people, and for PWA's in particular it is crucial that good psychological health translates into fewer bouts with infection and a longer life. These people thus regard themselves as "survivors," an attitude which allows them to accept their illness and get on with their lives.[13]

It is important to keep in mind that there is no such thing as one virus that results in AIDS. The term "AIDS" refers to a complex series of illnesses and infections that occur in individuals infected with the HIV virus. The antibody for the HIV virus is the forerunner of the disease. When one tests positive to the HIV antibody one is "HIV positive."

Grouping AIDS with other "catastrophic illnesses" such as cancer and heart disease enables workers to view AIDS more easily. The company must present the AIDS topic neutrally, without making moral judgments.

If someone got lung cancer, one would not say "Well, it's his/her fault because they smoked for years," nor if someone were to have heart disease would they say "It's his/her fault because they were overweight or drank too much or didn't exercise enough." All employees should be treated with respect and be accommodated to continue working.[14]

SENSIBLE PRECAUTIONS IN THE WORKPLACE

Although there is no medical evidence of any transmission of the HIV antibody through casual workplace contact, some work situations could lead to blood-to-blood contact. The Centers for Disease Control have developed a list of recommendations for dealing with blood-to-blood contact. These guidelines should be posted on employee bulletin boards, in the medical office, in the human resources department, and elsewhere in the workplace.

1. In case of an accident where there is a lot of blood, clean up any spilled blood immediately. A freshly prepared solution of water and household bleach, ten parts to one, is a very effective disinfectant and a good way to clean up spilled blood. Individuals cleaning up such spills should wear disposable rubber gloves and wash their hands thoroughly and immediately with soap and water afterward. These precautions should be followed regardless of whether the person involved is known to be infected with the HIV virus.

2. Sharp items (needles, knives, machinery blades) should be handled with extreme

care to prevent accidental drawing of blood. When the possibility of exposure to blood exists (handling of blood-soaked towels, garments, or sharp instruments, etc.), be sure to wear gloves. Wash hands with soap and water after removing the gloves.

3. Disposable sharp items (blades, needles, and other sharp instruments) should be placed in puncture-proof containers located as close as practical to the area in which they are used. The containers should be disposed of in a manner consistent with local regulations on solid waste disposal.

4. Take the time to renew understanding of basic hygiene. Soap and water can go a long way toward stemming the spread of all kinds of infections, and soap and water can kill the AIDS virus. To avoid the transmission of any infectious diseases, keep the work area clean. Make sure that spilled chemicals, food, and other substances are cleaned up right away.

5. Make sure that one thoroughly understands the safety procedures required at the workplace. Be sure that everyone understands and practices those safety procedures as well. If someone is not familiar with the safety procedures for your work area, ask the supervisor to make them clear.[15]

RESISTANCE TO ACCEPTANCE OF INFORMATION ABOUT AIDS

When presenting AIDS information to employees, it is important to remember the fear generated by this and other catastrophic illnesses: the fear of death. Because at present AIDS is incurable, thinking about AIDS forces one to face one's own mortality. Thus different individuals process AIDS information differently according to their own attitudes about life and death. For some individuals, this is an initial reaction that passes quickly. For others, the reaction will be more acute and last longer. When considering the presentation of material to all individuals, the presenter must be sensitive and patient. Continuing educational efforts of the facts will usually calm these reactions. However, some employees may require individual counseling to help them deal with the anxiety created by AIDS.

EVALAUTION OF THE EDUCATIONAL PROGRAM

A confidential evaluation by the employees is necessary after the initial educational effort is complete. This evaluation should rate the presentation of material and personnel policy, the videotape, the educator, and the written material; there should be space to write any additional questions about the disease. These questions should be addressed with the assurance that they will be answered confidentially and in the near future.

Another tool to evaluate the success of an AIDS education program is to note what has not occurred since the program's inception. Companies that have enstated a policy note such nonevents as: people are not refusing to work with employees who are diagnosed with AIDS; the companies are not getting criticism about the uncertainty of the company's stand on AIDS;

and, most importantly, there are no outbreaks of panic. However, it must be made clear that by having a company AIDS educational program is not a guarantee that there will not be any work disruption. There is the employees' reaction to the information that is the unpredictable factor. However, it is important to keep in mind the positive indicators that companies with an education program have enjoyed. For example, the employees may express appreciation for the information, and there can be a renewed respect for the company as it is demonstrating its stand on this sensitive issue and taking some control of the problems that can arise.

EMPLOYEES' REACTIONS TO AIDS IN THE WORKPLACE

Dr. David M. Herold, with the Georgia Institute of Technology, conducted research concerning employees' attitudes and behavior about AIDS in the workplace. This survey is the only one of its kind and is relevant when discussing the need for educational programs surrounding AIDS issues in the workplace. Dr. Herold kindly gave permission to reprint in full the following material.[16]

Background

In order to better understand the nature of workers' beliefs and attitudes about AIDS, a national probability sample of American households was used to conduct telephone interviews with over 2,000 workers who were at least 18 years old, worked full-time, were civilian employees, and were not self-employed. Interviewees were assured that their responses will be treated with complete confidentiality and reported only as part of a nationwide sample. For a sample of this size, the chances are 95 in 100 (0.95 confidence level) that survey results differ by no more than $+/-3\%$ from the similarly defined U.S. worker population.

The survey focused on four areas of particular interst: (1) the extent and types of fears people have concerning contact with AIDS patients, (2) people's willingness to accommodate workers who have AIDS, (3) people's beliefs about issues thought to be central to their attitudes towards AIDS, and (4) the extent to which people in the workforce have personal knowledge of people with AIDS. The questions and results are reported below.

Findings

Fears concerning contact with employees known to have AIDS—"If a person were known to have AIDS":

1. Would you be concerned about using the same bathroom?—66% yes, 34% no
2. Would you be concerned about eating in the same cafeteria?—40% yes, 60% no

3. Would you be willing to share tools or equipment with the individual?—
63% yes, 37% no

Comments—As can be seen here, substantial portions of the work population expressed concerns or fears about sharing facilities and/or tools with people who have AIDS. The percentages of people fearful of using bathrooms and cafeterias suggest possible disruptions of day-to-day activities in organizations. The fact that over one third of the sample would be unwilling to share tools or equipment could have severe implications for those jobs where such contact or sharing is essential....

Willingness to accommodate—"If a person were known to have AIDS":

1. Would you favor making special work arrangements for the individual if his or her health deteriorated?—75% yes, 25% no
2. Would you be willing to help the individual perform aspects of the job with which he or she was having difficulty?—81% yes, 19% no

Comments—In contrast to the rather negative views expressed in the last set of items, this set indicates a strong degree of sympathy for the AIDS-afflicted co-worker. A strong majority of workers favor making special arrangements to accommodate the AIDS patients, with an overwhelming proportion offering to provide assistance....

Associated beliefs:

1. What are the chances that people who are thought to have various illnesses are really covering up the fact that they have AIDS?—22% unlikely, 36% unsure, 42% likely
2. Do you believe the reported evidence that AIDS can only be transmitted by sexual contact or blood contamination?—65% yes, 35% no

Comments—This set of items offers interesting insights into the fears and concerns expressed in the first set of items. Namely, over one third of the workers in the sample do not believe the bulk of the information which has been offered by government agencies such as the CDC, and the medical profession, concerning how AIDS is transmitted. If the alternative personal hypothesis is that causal contact may lead to the transmittal of the disease, then it is easy to see why such contact would be feared. The finding concerning beliefs that people are covering up the fact that they have AIDS is a potentially important issue, since it suggests a certain level of hysteria, as illnesses which have similar symptoms (e.g., pneumonia, leukemia, skin cancer) are rumored by workers to be AIDS. This would probably be especially true if the affected worker belongs to one of the so-called "high risk" groups.

Personal knowledge:

1. Do you personally know anyone who has the disease AIDS or who has died from it?—14% yes, 86% no

Comments—This last item was intended to assess the penetration of AIDS into the lives of the general population. . . .

Recommendations

The data suggest two general areas in which considerable work needs to be done by organizations. First, major educational agendas need to be addressed if the workplace is to impact those workers' beliefs and attitudes which may form the basis for future problematical behaviors. Second, organizations need to realize that corporate denial, or pat answers and solutions are not likely to address the problems which are likely to be encountered. A proactive and integrated approach must be taken.

Education—There is no question but that any corporate response to AIDS in the workplace will need to have a strong educational component. The data from the present survey reveal a strong need for education. Furthermore, the data point out that different messages may be needed for different audiences, and, perhaps more importantly, that some messages may be heard but not believed.

COMMENTS

AIDS education by all segments of our society is vital. The workplace cannot rely on the media, schools, or churches to provide the necessary education of AIDS to its employees. It is too vast and complex an issue and therefore demands that all institutions in our society work in unison to educate the entire population. It is in the best interests of the workplaces to educate their employees. This is because of the alternate negative consequences of not educating employees, such as the drain on employee emotions; the overwhelming potential for a chaotic and disruptive work environment; and the real dollar expense in medical benefits and loss of productivity. The economic impact of these factors will far outweigh the cost of any employee AIDS education program.

NOTES

1. Levi Strauss and Co., "Talk About AIDS," videotape distributed by the San Francisco AIDS Foundation, 1987.

2. Bryan Lawton, "Personnel Directive on AIDS," AIDS, The Crisis for American Business Conference, November 2–3, 1987, p. 10.

3. Daniel M. Merrigan, "AIDS/HIV Infection and the Workplace Workgroup," unpublished notes from NIDA-sponsored conference on AIDS/HIV Infection, November 17, 1989, p. 1.

4. American Foundation for AIDS Research, *AIDS Education: A Business Guide*, 1988, p. 3.

5. The Maryland Department of Health and Mental Hygiene, "AIDS, Teaching/ Learning Module," p. 34.

6. Allstate Forum on Public Issues, "Corporate America Responds," October 1987, p. 10.

7. Office of Personnel Management, "AIDS in the Workplace, Guidelines for AIDS Information and Education and for Personnel Management Issues," March 1988, p. 2.

8. Sam B. Puckett and Alan R. Emery, *Managing AIDS in the Workplace* (Reading, MA: Addison-Wesley, 1988), p. 108.

9. Yvonne Ellison-Sandler, "AIDS/HIV Infection and the Workplace Workgroup," unpublished notes from NIDA-sponsored conference on AIDS/HIV Infection, November 1989, p. 2.

10. Caitlin Ryan and Ellen Ratner, "EAPs and AIDS: Meeting the Challenge," in Elizabeth Danto and Robert McConaghy, eds., *New Concepts in Employee Assistance Programs: Designing Today's EAP* (Englewood Cliffs, NJ: Prentice-Hall, 1989), p. 5.

11. UAW-FM Human Resource Center, AIDS Information Network, "Dealing with AIDS," 1988, p. 18.

12. Bryan Lawton, Thomas E. Backer, and Kirk B. O'Hara, "AIDS Handbook for EAP Professional in the Entertainment Industry," (Los Angeles: Human Interaction Research Institute, June 1989), p. 10.

13. UAW-FM Human Resources Center, p. 16.

14. American Foundation for AIDS Research, p. 14.

15. Department of Health and Human Services, Public Health Service, "Update: Universal Precautions for Prevention of Transmission of Human Immunodeficiency Virus, Hepatitis B Virus, and Other Bloodborne Pathogens in Health-Care Settings," *MMWR*, June 24, 1988.

16. David M. Herold, "Employees' Reactions to AIDS in the Workplace," Center for Work Performance Problems, College of Management, Georgia Institute of Technology, February 1988, pp. 4–10.

CHAPTER 6

SPECIAL WORK POPULATIONS

INTRODUCTION

This chapter will discuss the specific work populations that could be at risk for transmission of the AIDS virus through normal workplace contact. The chapter will discuss different classifications of work populations and guidelines for how to ascertain the level of risk for the workplace. Specific populations at risk as determined by the Occupational Safety and Health Administration will be presented as well as OSHA guidelines and enforcement information for each workplace. The chapter will outline specific guidelines for the special work populations at risk, including food handlers, personal service workers, corrective service and mental institution employees, emergency and medical personnel, and employees overseas.

The discussion of health-care workers will be presented in detail, because they are the work population placed at the most risk. The chapter will discuss the prevalence of HIV, likelihood of risk, and universal precautionary procedures as recommended by the Centers for Disease Control. The chapter will consider the responsibilities of employers of health-care workers to establish policies, education, and support elements. The segment on health-care workers has a discussion of the management of the HIV-infected health-care worker.

In discussing the special workplace population of the overseas employee, the chapter will feature excerpts from the United Nations medical director's circulars on AIDS. This will demonstrate the level of complexity of communication necessary when sending employees to foreign countries.

ANALYSIS OF WORK POPULATIONS AT RISK

People do not contract AIDS by doing things they are paid to do in the workplace.

All research indicates that there is no need to take special precautions or establish any new procedures or standard to prevent the spread of AIDS in the office, factory or commercial center.... There are particular occupations, however, that because of the nature of the job, raise questions about job safety and AIDS. These positions include food handlers, personal service workers, police, firefighters, other rescue personnel, and medical and dental personnel.[1]

Although it seems clear that most employers want to provide a safe working environment for their employees, it is now federal law that U.S. workplaces must comply with regulations and guidelines for a safe working environment for all their employees. Although most applicable for health-care workplaces, these guidelines provide a thoroughly scientific and uniform set of regulations and guidelines for preventing transmission of the AIDS virus in any workplace.

OSHA'S RECOMMENDED PRACTICES FOR PROTECTION AGAINST OCCUPATIONAL EXPOSURE TO AIDS AND HBV

With advice from health care professionals, OSHA has made recommendations to protect workers from HIV and HBV (hepatitis B). These precautions should be practiced routinely; they are aimed at preventing the transmission of these viruses and other blood-borne-type infections. These guidelines are for *all* workplaces, not just those at increased risk for HIV transmission. (See Appendixes E and F for the complete OSHA guidelines and communication by the Department of Labor.) The following recommendations are from OSHA's guidelines:

Personal Protective Equipment

- Use gloves where blood, blood products, or body fluids will be handled.
- Use gowns, masks, and eye protectors for procedures that could involve more extensive splashing of blood or body fluids.
- Use pocket masks, resuscitation bags, or other ventilation devices to resuscitate a patient to minimize exposure that may occur during emergency mouth-to-mouth resuscitation. Employers should place these devices where the need for resuscitation is likely.

Workplace Practices

- Wash hands thoroughly after removing gloves, and immediately after contact with blood or body fluids.
- Use disposable needles and syringes whenever possible. Do not recap, bend, or cut needles. Place sharp instruments in a specially designated puncture-resistant container located as close as practical to the area where they are used. Handle and dispose of them with extraordinary care to prevent accidental injury.

- Follow general guidelines for sterilization, disinfection, housekeeping, and waste disposal. Use appropriate protective equipment. Place potentially infective waste in impervious bags and dispose of them as local regulations require.

- Clean up blood spills immediately with detergent and water. Use a solution of 5.25 percent sodium hypochlorite (household bleach) diluted at 2–10 parts water for disinfection, or other suitable disinfectant.

- Treat all blood and body fluids as potentially infectious.

Education

- Know the modes of transmission and prevention of these infections.

Enforcement of OSHA standards

- Various OSHA standards apply to exposure both HIV and HBV. These standards cover personal protective equipment, sanitation, and waste disposal.[2]

In addition, the General Duty Clause of the OSHA Guidelines Act requires employers to provide "a place of employment which is free from recognized hazards." Employers must comply with either the federal OSHA standards and the General Duty Clause or with state standards. States with approved plans to operate their own occupational safety and health program enforce standards comparable to the federal standards and are encouraged to enforce state counterparts to the General Duty Clause. State standards, unlike federal standards, apply to state, county, and municipal workers as well as to private employers.

Workers whose employers will not correct hazardous situations may complain to federal OSHA or to their own state's OSHA program. Complainants' identities will not be revealed to employers. OSHA also investigates employee complaints of discriminatory actions by employers against employees who have exercised safety and health rights. (For further information see Appendixes A, E, and F.)

CLASSIFICATION OF RISK BY WORKPLACE TASKS

OSHA guidelines recommend that when determining the actual risk of exposure for each specific workplace, each employer must evaluate all working conditions and the specific tasks that workers are expected to encounter as a consequence of employment.

All jobs should be classified in one of the following categories:

1. Jobs requiring protective equipment to be worn during the occupational task, e.g., medical personnel performing tests on and working in close contact with bodily fluids, blood, or tissues.

2. An intermediate group that generally would not require protective equipment but whose

jobs inherently include tasks that might require some protection on short notice, e.g., policemen and firefighters called upon to conduct first aid, etc.

3. Tasks requiring no protective equipment, e.g., normal office work, even if it requires handling or cleaning shared implements, utensils, bathroom facilities, telephones, and personal contact like handshaking.[3]

The guidelines emphasize that these classifications apply "to tasks rather than individuals, and that work practices and protective equipment should be selected after careful consideration for each specific situation, or the overall risk associated with the task."[4]

SPECIFIC WORK POPULATIONS AT RISK FOR HIV INFECTION

Job Classification #1: Highest Risk for Transmission

Workers at risk of blood, body fluid, or needle stick exposures face the highest risk of infection. These employees include, but are not limited to, nurses, physicians, dentists and other dental workers, podiatrists, laboratory and blood bank technologists and technicians, phlebotomists, dialysis personnel, medical technicians, medical examiners, morticians, housekeepers, laundry workers, and others whose work involves contact with blood or other body fluids, or with corpses. Other personnel at risk include paramedics, emergency medical technicians, law enforcement personnel, firefighters, lifeguards, and others whose jobs might require first-response medical care and potential contact with blood or body fluids.

Health-Care Workers

According to the CDC, health-care workers are defined as "persons, including students and trainees, whose activities involve contact with patients or with blood or other body fluids from patients in a health-care setting."[5] Health-care workers are the most vulnerable work population at risk for infection with HIV. As of January 1990, the total number of health-care workers infected with AIDS in a health-care setting is 26. To place that figure in context, 6.8 million persons, representing 5.6 percent of the U.S. labor force, were employed in health services. On the other hand, "as of July, 1987, . . . 5.8% of the total AIDS cases reported to the CDC reported being employed in a health-care or clinical laboratory setting. Of the health-care workers with AIDS, 95% have been reported to exhibit high risk behavior."[6]

The hepatitis B virus (HBV) is transmitted in the same way as the AIDS virus, but HBV infection is much more common among healthcare workers than HIV infection. For example, the risk of getting hepatitis B after being stuck with an HBV-contaminated needle is estimated to range from 6% to 30%, far greater than the risk of HIV infection under similar circumstances (estimated to be less than 1%).

Many healthcare workers are afraid of AIDS, some excessively so, because of the publicity, etc., and meanwhile hepatitis B, which is rarely in the news, strikes 12,000–15,000 healthcare and dental workers, hospitalizing 500–600 and killing over 200 each year. Although a safe and effective vaccine to prevent hepatitis B has been available since 1982, only 30%–40% of healthcare workers in high-risk settings have been vaccinated to date. This is not to downplay the very real risk of acquiring HIV infection in the workplace, but it is important to view this risk in its proper perspective, and not let AIDS hysteria cause other occupational health hazards to be overlooked.[7]

The U.S. Department of Health and Human Services has established universal precaution recommendations regarding the prevalence of the HIV antibody in health-care settings:

HIV has been isolated from blood, semen, vaginal secretions, saliva, tears, breast milk, cerebrospinal fluid, amniotic fluid, and urine and is likely to be isolated from other body fluids, secretions, and excretions. However, epidemiologic evidence has implicated only blood, semen, vaginal secretions, and possibly breast milk in transmission....

The increasing prevalence of HIV increases the risk that health-care workers will be exposed to blood from patients infected with HIV, especially when blood and body fluid precautions are not followed for all patients. Therefore, it is the recommendation of the CDC to emphasize the need for health-care workers to consider ALL patients as potentially infected with HIV and/or blood-borne pathogens and to adhere rigorously to infection-control precautions for minimizing the risk of exposure to blood and body fluids of all patients.... Since medical history and examination cannot reliably identify all patients infected with HIV or other blood-borne pathogens, blood and body-fluid precautions should be consistently used for ALL patients. This approach is referred to as the "universal blood and body-fluid precautions" or "universal precautions," and should be used in the care of ALL patients, especially including those in emergency-care settings in which the risk of blood exposure is increased and the infection status of the patient is usually unknown.[8]

Responsibilities of Employers of Health-Care Workers

1. POLICY. Employers of health-care workers should ensure that policies exist for:

a. Initial orientation and continuing education and training of all health-care workers—including students and trainees—on the epidemiology, modes of transmission, and prevention of HIV and other blood-borne infections and the need for routine use of universal blood and body-fluid precautions for ALL patients.

b. Provision of equipment and supplies necessary to minimize the risk of infection with HIV and other blood-borne pathogens.

c. Monitoring adherence to recommended protective measures. When monitoring reveals a failure to follow recommended precautions, counseling, education, and/ or re-training should be provided, and, if necessary, appropriate disciplinary action should be considered.

Professional associations and labor organizations, through continuing education efforts, should emphasize the need for health-care workers to follow recommended precautions.[9]

When developing or revising employment policies regarding AIDS in the health-care settings,

employers should develop employment policies that cover (1) what to do when an employee claims to have been exposed to HIV on the job, (2) who is allowed access to such information, (3) what to tell other employees about an infected co-worker, (4) what support should be provided to an HIV-positive employee. In addition, employers should develop a policy for reporting needle-stick and other exposure-related incidents.[10]

2. EDUCATION. Employers of health-care workers "also need to think about educating people not directly in their employ: physicians, therapists, volunteers, and those hired on a contract basis, such as some emergency room personnel and nurses."[11]

The following is excerpted from "A Prospective AIDS Education Program," from the CDC's Management of HTLV-III/LAV Infection in the Hospital:

The hospital should recognize that the admission of an AIDS or other HTLV-III/LAV infected patient may cause substantial anxiety among some staff members and patients who are concerned about their personal safety. Moreover, an AIDS patient is also anxious, having to cope with a serious disease. AIDS or other HTLV-III/LAV infected patients have sometimes been shunned or abandoned by family or close friends, and they may feel similarly neglected or abused by hospital personnel unless special supportive steps are taken by hospital staff members. These nonmedical needs of both patients and staff may become so pressing that medical care of AIDS and other patients may be compromised.

Hospitals that have developed aggressive education and intervention programs for their staff, including the medical staff, have been successful in minimizing anxiety and disruption. Intensive efforts at education and crisis intervention by skilled, knowledgeable, and respected hospital personnel are perhaps the most useful activities to ensure that a hospital continues to function adequately when an AIDS or HTLV-III/LAV infected patient is present. Several hospitals have developed special teams of personnel who are readily available to answer medical questions about AIDS and HTLV-III/LAV infection, advise about appropriate practices, and provide support to personnel and patients. These teams usually include an infection control practitioner, a psychiatric social worker, a psychiatrist, a chaplain, a nursing administrator, a patient representative, and often an infectious disease specialist. Some hospitals may wish to include the public relations coordinator, also.

Widespread and open discussion of the issues raised by treating patients with AIDS or HTLV-III/LAV infection appears to be beneficial, especially when that discussion occurs before such a patient is actually admitted. Some hospitals have made special efforts to involve persons from support services, such as housekeeping, engineering, dietary, laboratory, and radiology departments, in these discussions. Some hospitals have also found it useful to include hospital labor union representatives. When a broad-based group of hospital employees participates in discussions of what is known and not known, they are likely to respond appropriately when given the opportunity to care for a patient with AIDS or HTLV-III/LAV infection.

The advisory committee recommends, therefore, that hospitals consider the formation of a special AIDS coordinating group, which would have broad educational and support responsibilities within the hospital setting. The group should be broadly representative of the hospital community, and should not be limited to "experts" or to ranking administrative personnel. The group must have visible and aggressive support from both administration and experts. In small hospitals, the group might consist of only two or three individuals.

The coordinating group should develop education programs directed toward all levels of hospital personnel, and the program should, if possible, be implemented before an AIDS or HTLV-III/LAV infected patient is admitted. Representatives from the employee or staff groups to be educated should be involved in determining the content of the educational program. This program should be reviewed regularly for accuracy and timeliness and presented periodically to update the staff.

Occasionally, physicians caring for patients with AIDS or HTLV-III/LAV infection may wish to employ extraordinary or overly stringent precautions. Such instances have been disruptive to patient care as well as demoralizing, both to the patient and to hospital personnel. It is particularly harmful when a physician uses extraordinary precautions since that unnecessarily raises anxiety on the part of patients and other hospital personnel. The AIDS coordinating group is encouraged to educate the medical staff about the epidemiology of AIDS and to work with them to ensure uniform and consistent application throughout the hospital of recommended AIDS or HTLV-III/LAV precautions.[12]

3. SUPPORT. There are unique and difficult challenges for the health-care professionals who are dealing with the medical and psychological needs of patients with AIDS. They must learn to assist and care for patients with a disease that is still relatively new and unknown. Most of these patients are dealing with incredible suffering and imminent death. The remainder of AIDS patients with little or no symptoms, however, require treatments, information, as well as sometimes exhaustive comfort. In addition, health-care workers must provide this care while simultaneously managing their own fears about the disease, as well as the stress of working with patients whose outcome is bleak or uncertain. Compounding these challenges is the necessity to be cautious and conscious to provide this care with the respect due these individuals who may be considered social outcasts.

Cancer and other diseases associated with fatal outcomes have taught mental health professionals much of what they know about caring for people with AIDS and other types of HTLV-III/LAV infection. As with cancer, health care providers need the opportunity to discuss feelings about the vulnerability of their patients. They typically experience anticipatory grief for patients they expect to die, actual grief when patients do die, frustration over their inability to change the course of the illness, and anger over the negative reactions of others.

. . . Fears about the transmission of HTLV-III/LAV infection still exist among some health care staff. Meetings give staff an opportunity to discuss fears about personal safety, as well as to raise concerns about other issues, such as the drain on insti-tutional resources, organization of AIDS services and the burden on staff. Support groups for health care workers treating AIDS patients have been found helpful in some settings.

. . . Institutions caring for people with AIDS should keep an updated file of AIDS information—mode of transmission, cause, and treatment. The information then can be regularly passed on to staff members, who should also attend local AIDS update courses and request rounds on AIDS at their medical center. The staff is then able, in turn, to keep patients informed of new developments, especially those likely to offer hope.[13]

It is important to recognize our medical and health-care professionals and the support they need. They are not used to having young patients die. The burn-out rate for professionals working with AIDS patients runs very high and must be monitored.

HIV-Infected Health-Care Workers

It must be determined on an individual basis whether workers infected with HIV—especially those who perform invasive procedures—can ade-quately and safely be allowed to perform patient-care duties or whether their work assignments should be changed. These decisions should be made by the health-care worker's personal physician in conjunction with the med-ical directors and personnel health service staff of the employing institution.

Consider the case of a health-care worker, Veronica Prego, M.D., who sued her workplace for $175 million for negligence. Dr. Prego claims that she was pricked with a needle due to negligence. This is the first case of a health-care worker bringing suit for negligence to their workplace. "The case will be watched closely from hospital administrators, staff and unions concerned with determining a hospital's obligation to protect its workers from accidental exposure to AIDS."[14] As of March 8, 1990, this case was reported as being settled for a $1.35 million cash payment.

Job Classification #2: Intermediate Group

Personal Service Workers

The Red Cross has concluded that cosmetologists, acupuncturists, beauticians, and barbers face a very low risk of spreading AIDS from normal personal service, and such individuals already observe sanitation procedures that protect from infections. However, the Red Cross notes that

1. All instruments such as razors and cuticle scissors and all instruments that penetrate the skin, e.g., earpiercing devices, should be discarded after use or disinfected between uses with chemical germicides.
2. All personal service workers with open sores or weeping sores should refrain from direct client contact until the sores are healed, or wear protective gloves and other clothes.[15]

The British government's Department of Health and Social Security has established a set of recommendations for specific personal care workers:

General Guidelines:

Disposal of "Sharps"—If you have used sharp or pointed instruments be careful when throwing them away. Put them in a secure container such as a plastic bottle or commercial box first so that they cannot accidentally injure anyone.

Sterilization—The best way to sterilize needles and instruments is in an autoclave [a closed vessel similar to a pressure cooker]. The autoclave you should choose should be fully automatic, so that all you need to do is [fill] it up with water, close it and press a button [and the steam will sterilize it].

Skin Preparation—Do not use sharp or pointed instruments on or near areas of a client's skin that are obviously diseased or inflamed.

Specific Procedures for:

Electrolysists:

a. Do not test needles on yourself. Test the needles on a damp piece of cotton wool held between forceps.
b. Use soothing creams from a tube, not a jar. The cream should be applied to the skin on a piece of fresh gauze, and not directly with your fingers.

c. Disposable needles are recommended. They should be used only once and then discarded safetly.

d. If you have to use re-usable needles, they must be sterilized before use on another client.

e. It is not safe to keep needles for one client for more than one session.

f. If the skin bruises or bleeds after the insertion of a needle, a small pad of dry cotton wool should be used to cover the area until the bleeding has stopped.

Tattooists:

a. Use fresh colours for each customer.

b. Dispose of pigment containers after each customer.

c. Use only disposable razors.

d. Use vaseline or jelly from a tube, not from a jar. It should be applied to the skin on a piece of fresh gauze or disposable wooden spatula, and not directly with your fingers.

e. After tattooing, cover the area treated with sterile non-stick dressing.

f. Never test needles on your own skin.

g. All other instruments—whether needles, needle bars, tubes, forceps or any other— must be sterilized after being used on each client.[16]

Emergency Medical Services Personnel

Emergency medical services personnel may be exposed to body fluids or blood in a variety of ways. This can occur without any medical knowledge of the patient involved. At the scene of an accident, blood contact may occur because the accident victim is infectious. The universal precautions discussed in the section for health-care workers should be in place for emergency medical services personnel as well.

In addition: mechanical ventilators should ordinarily be carried in ambulances, eliminating the need for mouth-to-mouth resuscitation. Should these not be available, ambubags or disposable devices should be used to perform mouth-to-mouth resuscitation.

Masks, goggles, and gloves should be worn by emergency workers when suctioning an incubated patient.

Accidental splashes of blood to the face should be gently rinsed with soap and water to minimize the risk of infection through the mucous membranes of the eyes and mouth.[17]

Corrective Services and Mental Health Institution Workers

Because of the high rate of AIDS cases among prisoners, the workers in these institutions must consider taking special precautions to protect themselves from contracting AIDS. In addition, the workers at mental health institutions are an at-risk workplace group.

Corrective services and mental health institution workers may also be exposed to blood and body fluids by being bitten or through parenteral exposure to a needle, knife, or other sharp instruments, contaminated with the blood of an infected person. Staffing levels in such institutions have a profound influence on whether individual workers are successfully able to avoid this type of exposure.

With regard to bites, there are no known cases of AIDS being transmitted through a bite, although the AIDS virus has been found in saliva in extremely small amounts. Transmission of the AIDS virus requires a higher concentration of the virus and more direct contact with the recipient's bloodstream than a typical bite provides.[18]

The country's federal, state, county, and city prisons and jails face major problems in dealing with HIV infection.

Incarcerated settings are disproportionately composed of members of racial and ethnic minorities, which themselves have also been disproportionately impacted by HIV infection and AIDS; AIDS education of prison, detention center, and jail administrators, staffs and inmates is of vital importance to containing the AIDS epidemic and promoting the welfare of incarcerated persons and correctional staff; funding for AIDS education for incarcerated populations is inadequate in terms of quality; inmates who are known (or assumed) to be HIV-positive are being segregated, stigmatized, denied access to programs and services, and subjected to harassment and violence in many prisons, jails and court systems; racism, sexism, homophobia, and AIDS-phobia are barriers to the provision of effective education and services to incarcerated populations; and finally, the consenting sexual activities and sharing of drug paraphernalia and tatoo instruments occur in prisons, detention centers, and jails.[19]

Job Classification #3: Lowest Risk for Transmission

Most work populations fall into this category. In this environment, there is no evidence of transmission of the AIDS virus through normal workplace contact. This group includes offices, factories, restaurants, hotels, commercial centers, and so on.

Food Handlers

This workplace population presents an especially delicate issue because of the customers involved. Restaurants have been forced to close because waiters have been homosexual and carry the AIDS virus. Although research shows that HIV cannot be transmitted through food or drink, the general public is largely ignorant of that information.

Food handlers, such as cooks, waiters, bartenders, airline attendants, need not take precautions other than normal personal hygiene and sanitary food-handling procedures because the AIDS virus is not transmitted in food or through casual contact.

Even food handlers infected with the AIDS virus need not be restricted from work,although they should take special care to avoid hand injuries and follow sanitation guidelines that require throwing away any food contaminated with blood. Further, if a food service worker with AIDS has open sores, skin lesions, or another illness that would prohibit food handling, that individual must be restricted from food handling.[20]

Resolution in this issue must depend on the facts of the individual cases. An employee who publicizes his HIV-positive status or illness to co-workers or customers may be less deserving of solicitude (in a job with public contact) than one who makes an effort to accommodate the reasonable business needs of the employer. If the publicity is traceable to the employer, it would seem unfair to make the employee suffer the consequences.[21]

SPECIAL GROUPS

The Arts Community

One of the hardest hit work populations regarding incidence of AIDS is the field of the arts. These professions include the design industry and visual, performing, and musical arts. Companies that employ individuals in the arts area (for example, retailers, museums, galleries, dance and musical companies) must be particularly sensitized to specific issues of this group and consider these when assessing the educational and policy needs of the company.

Overseas Population

A particularly vulnerable and yet undereducated population in the work-force is the population of U.S. workers in the private sector who travel or are assigned overseas on business. The employer in the United States has an obligation to protect these employees, given that the medical conditions in many other countries are far less advanced than in the United States. Companies should create policies specific to this important workplace group to spell out concerns such as blood supply, needles, and emergency situation procedures. Each country to which the employer sends its employees should be thoroughly investigated by the company's medical department, and proper precautions and education should be directed to each individual employee for each specific country to which he or she is traveling.

The following are excerpts from circulars sent by Dr. Michael Irwin, medical director for the United Nations, to United Nations personnel.[22] The private sector should study and include them in any policy that might include the overseas population of multinational corporations. Dr. Irwin continually specifies precautions and preventions for the United Nations population.

To: All UN Development Program (UNDP) Resident Representatives and UNICEF Representatives
Subject: AIDS
August 1987

... By now, I expect most people in your office are aware that the AIDS virus can be spread by sexual contact, contaminated needles and syringes, or less commonly, through transfused blood or its components. Also, it may be transmitted from an infected mother to her infant during pregnancy or birth. ...

The risk of infection is increased by having multiple sexual partners, either homosexual or heterosexual, and sharing needles among those using illicit drugs. If sexual fidelity is not followed, the use of condoms will reduce the possibility of spreading the virus, although they are not always effective, especially if one indulges in activities that may tear body tissues such as in anal intercourse.

I consider it your responsibility to see that the staff in your office (and indirectly or directly, their families) are properly informed about the known methods of transmission of the AIDS virus—you should involve the WHO (World Health Organization) Programme Coordinator, the UN Examining Physicians and the nurse in the UNDP-sponsored dispensary, if one exists at your duty station, in this important educational activity.

My major concerns about UNDP and UNICEF staff, and their families, relate to the transmission of the virus through contaminated blood transfusions and by the use of unclean syringes and needles (such as when someone has to have an injection of a medication, a blood test, or when some immunization is necessary).

As I noted in my February [1987] circular, in many countries, where it is still unfortunately impossible to properly test blood for the presence of the AIDS antibodies, transfusions should not be given except in life-threatening situations. Whenever this kind of emergency arises, I hope that other staff members, in the "UN Community," would volunteer to give blood for their colleagues—after all, we are all "walking" blood banks. At several duty stations, members of the UN Community have already prepared lists of individuals' blood groups. It might also be possible to involve others in the local diplomatic community in this kind of endeavor. Obviously, you must keep in close touch with the WHO Programme Coordinator and the local UN Examining Physicians regarding the safety of the blood supply at your duty station, and also keep your UNDP and UNICEF colleagues fully informed.

All internationally-recruited staff should ensure that immunizations needed by themselves and their families are given when they are on home leave or in places where no problems about sterilization techniques arise.

In some developing countries, staff members can buy their own clean disposable syringes and needles to be used whenever they or their dependents need the injection of some medication, or have to have blood taken for some laboratory test. In other places, where a UNDP-sponsored dispensary exists, there should be a stock of disposable syringes and needles there which can be given for specific individual use.

However, in countries where such disposable items cannot be purchased easily, or where there is no dispensary, and there is a risk of AIDS, I hope that all UNDP and UNICEF Offices now have their own supply of sterile syringes and needles, as I suggested last February.... A record must be kept of who gets these, and, after being used, all syringes and needles must be destroyed.

I have seen little reference to the possibility of dental treatment being a factor in the transmission of the AIDS virus. But, dental instruments can sometimes draw blood and these should be properly sterilized after each patient....

During the past year, several medical evacuations have been necessary either because someone needed a blood transfusion (and there was concern about the safety of the local blood supply, as a test for AIDS antibodies could not be properly done) or because it was suspected an individual might have AIDS, and specific investigations could not be made at the duty station.

The decentralized procedure introduced in 1985 for the evacuation of UNDP and UNICEF internationally-recruited personnel in Africa (except for the few countries on the Mediterranean), by which the prior approval of Headquarters was not routinely required, has worked well, with very few unnecessary evacuations happening. The main reasons for having this procedure are the difficulties of communications between some African duty stations and New York, and the problems of air transportation which occur from many places. This procedure remains in effect....

December 1987

... When New York staff members are travelling now to developing countries, and have come to the Medical Service to receive anti-malarial medication or immunizations, each nurse and physician is prepared to talk to the traveller about the prevention of AIDS. One specific action we do is to inquire (along with other questions) whether an individual might be "in a high-risk group for AIDS?" Because, if someone is a carrier of this virus, there could be a risk in taking anti-malarials or receiving certain immunizations (such as yellow fever). Also, when UN, UNDP, and UNICEF staff members travel to Africa now, we give them a disposable syringe and 2 needles which can be used if any injections must be given during the trip or if blood has to be taken for a laboratory investigation.

Frankly, our main concern now about AIDS, is the increasing problems about this disease to be found at certain duty stations in the developing countries, where staff are naturally worried about the danger of contaminated blood, and about unsterilized syringes and needles being used by physicians, nurses and laboratory technicians. Supplies of syringes are being given to some UNDP and UNICEF field offices, and the need for a blood transfusion is an additional factor to be considered whenever the question of a medical evacuation arises....

There are five Medical Directors in the "UN System" (based in Geneva, New York, Paris, Rome and Vienna). We have discussed AIDS at our annual meetings in recent years, and we maintain regular contact on what each is doing. We have a common interagency policy against routine testing for the presence of AIDS antibodies at pre-placement and periodic medical examinations. However, if we suspect someone might be serologically positive for HIV, we refer that individual to his/her personal physician for further investigations. And, if a pre-placement medical examination showed the presence of the AIDS antibodies, the Medical Services would not clear that individual for recruitment.

July 1988

... Prevention of AIDS: What I wrote last year, on this subject, is still valid. However, my medical colleagues and I now suggest, in addition, that condoms should be provided in all field offices if it is difficult to obtain them easily on the local market. I would like you to discuss this matter with your local UNFPA (UN Fund for Population Activities) and WHO colleagues. If the local supply is uncertain, condoms could possibly be obtained through a local governmental or UNFPA source (in this case, they should be free to your staff). If condoms have to be purchased from another duty station, in your region, then they should be given out at cost price. Of course, someone from the UNFPA or WHO office, the personnel in the UNDP dispensary, or one of the local UN Examining Physicians must be involved in giving advice to your staff on the proper use of condoms....

COMMENTS

Employers responsible for work populations specifically impacted by AIDS need to consider appropriate action carefully. The foregoing material is given so that those who have not done anything about AIDS in their workplace can begin before it is too late and they are in the midst of a crisis. If a health-care setting is only now employing its first AIDS educational program and setting up the necessary special precautions, pay strict attention to the CDC recommendations, and contact them or the state health department for more specific information.

NOTES

1. Mark A. Katz, *Understanding AIDS: A Personal Handbook for Employees and Managers* (Washington, DC: Employee Benefits Review, 1989), p. 28.

2. Ibid., p. 29.

3. Joint Advisory Notice, *Protection Against Occupational Exposure to Hepatitis B Virus (HBV) and Human Immunodeficiency Virus (HIV)*, Department of Labor/Department of Health and Human Services, October 19, 1987, p. 6.

4. Katz, *Understanding AIDS*, p. 27.

5. *Recommendations for Prevention of HIV Transmission in Health-Care Settings, Morbidity and Mortality Weekly Report* (U.S. Department of Health and Human Services, Public Health Service, Centers for Disease Control, August 21, 1987), p. 3S.

6. Ibid., p. 4S.

7. Service Employees International Union, AFL-CIO, CLC, *The AIDS Book*, April 1988, p. 35–5.

8. *Morbidity and Mortality Weekly Report*, p. 3S.

9. Ibid., p. 12S.

10. "Hospital Workers Need More Education and Training," AIDS Workplace Update, Vol 1, no. 9 (Greenvale NY: Panel Publishers, April 1989), p. 7.

11. Ibid., p. 4.

12. Department of Health and Human Services, Public Health Service, Centers for Disease Control, "Background Information on AIDS and HTLV-III Infection," Management of HTLV-III/LAV Infection in the Hospital, 1987, pp. 390–91.

13. Department of Health and Human Services, National Institute of Mental Health, *Coping with AIDS, Psychological and Social Considerations in Helping People with HTLV-III Infection*, 1986, pp. 15–16.

14. Laurie Goodstein, "Physician With AIDS Takes Her Case To Trial," *Washington Post*, January 7, 1990, p. A3.

15. Katz, *Understanding AIDS*, p. 27.

16. British Department of Health and Social Security and the Central Office of Information, "Government Information 1987, AIDS, Guidelines for Tattooists and Guidelines for Electrolysists" (1987).

17. Service Employees International Union, p. 38.

18. Ibid., p. 41.

19. Department of Health and Human Services, "Prevention and Beyond, A Framework for Collective Action"; A National Conference on HIV Infection and AIDS Among Racial and Ethnic Populations, Washington, DC, August 13–17, 1989, sponsored by DHHS and the Office of Minority Health, pp. 2–6.

20. Katz, *Understanding AIDS*, p. 27. ·

21. Arthur S. Leonard, "AIDS in the Workplace," in H. Dalton and S. Burris, eds., *AIDS and the Law: A Guide for the Public* (New Haven, CT: Yale University Press, 1987), p. 4.

22. The excerpts from the circulars on AIDS have been used with the kind permission of Dr. Michael Irwin.

CHAPTER 7

AIDS AND DRUGS

INTRODUCTION

This chapter on AIDS and drugs will discuss the prevalence of the HIV infection in drug users, and will consider the relationship of drugs to HIV infection and how this issue pertains to the workplace. The chapter will cover not only intravenous drug use, but also cocaine, crack, and alcohol and their connection to HIV infection. It will discuss modes of transmission of HIV infection among IV drug users and their partners, and will outline an education program designed specifically for abusers. The free needle debate will also be outlined. This will be followed by a discussion of the specific needs of the "significant others" of IV drug users. The chapter will conclude with excerpts from the 1988 Presidential Commission Report on HIV infection surrounding the issue of drug abuse and HIV infection in the United States.

Regardless of what one feels about drug use, the Rehabilitation Act of 1973, as interpreted in 1978 by the attorney general at the request of HHS Secretary Joseph Califano as well as subsequent Supreme Court decisions supporting it, have defined drug abuse clearly as a disease. It is important for CEOs, managers, and employees to understand that they must set aside their own biases toward drug abusers and must approach these individuals as people who have a disease and need to be treated accordingly. On the other hand, it is not impossible to understand the mixed feelings experienced by the employer who often has to pay the medical bills for such employees. These are excruciatingly difficult issues and must be handled from all sides with thoughtfulness and sensitivity.

PREVALENCE OF HIV INFECTION IN IV DRUG USERS

Information from the Centers for Disease Control shows that as of June 1990, 137,385 cases of adults/adolescents diagnosed with AIDS had been reported. Of these cases, 21% reported injection of an illicit substance prior to diagnosis with AIDS. Intravenous drug users are the second largest risk group for AIDS, exceeded only by homosexual and bisexual men who account for 60% of persons with AIDS. The percentage of cases involving intravenous drug abuse has increased steadily; in the spring of 1987 IV drug users accounted for 17% of the total cases of AIDS. Among new cases of AIDS reported as of January 1989, 30% have involved some form of drug abuse.

HIV INFECTION, DRUGS, AND THE WORKPLACE

Since the majority of needle-using addicts are minority members and poor, employers tend to assume that these individuals are unemployed or unemployable and therefore not in the workforce. However, this is not the case. In fact

there are many "functional" needle-using addicts who maintain jobs and, from all outward appearances, cannot be distinguished from any other working individual. ... In addition, many professionals and paraprofessionals are chemically dependent or are "recreational users" of mood-altering substances such as alcohol, sedatives, and stimulants like amphetamines. Mood-altering substances often reduce inhibitions and the likelihood of practicing safe sex is therefore decreased dramatically.[1]

THE RELATIONSHIP OF DRUGS TO HIV INFECTION

"The use of heroin, cocaine, crystal [meth] as well as alcohol and other illicit drugs has become a national epidemic. According to the National Institute of Drug Abuse (NIDA), over 1.5 million Americans are habitual users of IV drugs, and over 5 million use cocaine at least once a month."[2] Of the over 1.5 million IV drug users, 29,000 are people with AIDS. Regularly employed and valued workers who are using drugs or alcohol, whether that use is considered abusive or recreational, are at considerable risk for exposure to HIV.

"Certain drugs do direct damage to the immune system, making people more susceptible to HIV infection, and, if drug use continues after infection, speeding up the progression of illness, and eventually, death. Alcohol, cocaine, amphetamines and inhalent nitrates (often called 'poppers') are among those substances that directly injure the immune system."[3]

Observations suggest that all abused substances can be of consequence to the susceptibility of addicts to HIV and their subsequent vulnerability to development of

AIDS. The importance of this issue is emphasized by the incidence of polydrug abuse among heroin addicts (from Chicago, the rate presently is over 90%) not to mention also the pervasive problem of drug abuse in our society today, regardless of types of drugs being considered or the combinations in which they are used.[4]

IV drug users place themselves at double the risk for HIV infection. The risks are from transmission through shared needle paraphernalia, or sexual activity practiced with unsafe methods due to reduced inhibitions.

One of the most serious issues surrounding IV drug use involves the user's relationship to the "mainstream" heterosexual population.

Not only are intravenous drug abusers (IVDAs) the second most common group at risk for HIV infection after gay and bisexual males, but they represent the most likely conduit of the infection to the heterosexual community. The vast majority of female IVDAs acknowledge relying at least occasionally on prostitution to support their drug addiction. Further, IVDAs are the group most associated with the birth of HIV-infected children.[5]

OTHER DRUGS AND HIV

Alcohol and Drugs

Alcohol is considered to be a significant factor in an individual's increased risk for exposure to HIV:

(1) the cause of AIDS is a type of virus (called a retovirus) which changes the structure of the cells it attacks. It may require the presence of an already damaged immune system before it can cause disease. (2) Alcohol and drugs interfere with many types of medical and alternative therapies for AIDS. (3) Alcohol and drugs alter the judgement of the user, who may become more prone to engage in activities which put people at high risk for AIDS. (4) Alcohol and drug abuse causes stress, including sleep problems, which harms immune functioning.[6]

Marijuana

THC [tetrahydrocannabinol] may have marked suppressive effects on various components of the immune system, both cellular and humoral.... The drug also affects the ability of these cells [T and B lymphocytes and macrophage cells] to produce soluble mediators of immunity, ... which are important in various immune responses and also in resistance to viral infections, including those caused by retroviruses.... These cannabinoids, widely used by individuals who are considered at high risk for AIDS, have the ability to serve as cofactors in altering the immune status of the host and thus contributing to the increased susceptibility to retrovirus infection and eventual development of AIDS.[7]

Cocaine

Cocaine use, as reported by NIDA, is on the rise. "The dramatic rise in the use and popularity of cocaine has also caused an increased frequency in the use of needles as well as [the injection of] other illicit drugs."[8] In addition, cocaine users who inject the drug (freebasing) are at greater risk for HIV because the injection rate is more frequent than heroin users. Heroin addicts can maintain functional lives for as many as 10–20 years; cocaine addicts [lose] control of their addiction and their lives in only a few years.

Crack and AIDS

The crack epidemic has been strongly linked to the AIDS epidemic. Former Commissioner Stephen C. Joseph of the New York City Department of Health attributes the 100% rise in sexuality transmitted diseases in New York City to crack. An official from the Centers for Disease Control noted a similar correlation between HIV transmission and a rise in crack use elsewhere in the country.... Crack, a form of cocaine that is pre-based and smoked, appears to be far more addictive than regular cocaine. Uniquely marketed, crack sells for $5 or $10 a vial and is a favorite of many who can meet the price easily and, at the same time, avoid the stigma of using needles.

Crack, however, is severely destructive to the immune system as well as other parts of the human body; it produces a withdrawal that is severe and long-lasting, and current drug treatment modalities do not work with crack.

In crack houses (places where people purchase and smoke crack) youngsters, both male and female, are prostituting themselves several times each day for a pipeful of crack.[9]

Initially, crack's impact on "mainstream" society might seem remote. But consider, for example: If a heterosexual man employs the services of a prostitute who is addicted to crack and has been infected with HIV, then the virus suddenly makes its way into the "mainstream." In addition, the author in her work as an EAP evaluator has been seeing cases of crack reflected in case records in the workplace. Before 1988 this was not so. This could be an alarming reflection of the growth of the crack epidemic. It should be a major warning to employers.

TRANSMISSION

IV drug users (IVDUs) can transmit HIV in two ways: by the sharing of their drug paraphernalia with other needle users; or through sexual activity. "Small amounts of contaminated blood left in needles or syringes can carry the AIDS virus from user to user. Almost all IV drug abusers share needles at some time during their IV drug use.... Those who frequent shooting galleries (gathering places where drug users share their needles, syringes, cookers, and drugs) are particularly vulnerable."[10]

The sharing of needles is a central part of the IV drug user's culture, primarily because of economic necessity. Often, the only way for an addict to get a fix is to share someone elses' "works." Needle works can be expensive and difficult to obtain. Legally, only doctors can prescribe the equipment necessary for individuals to give themselves injections. Although the proper cleaning of one's works can prevent transmission of the AIDS virus through shared needles, cleaning is not a high priority for most addicts. Their main concern tends to involve getting as much of the drug in their system as possible. (For proper method of cleaning works, see Chapter 1.)

HIV can also be transmitted from IV drug users to their sexual partners, and from IV drug users and their sexual partners to their children prior to or during childbirth. In fact, surveillance data from the Centers for Disease Control show that most cases of heterosexually and perinatally acquired AIDS are associated with IV drug abuse. Of U.S. born AIDS cases attributed to heterosexual transmission, approximately 72% are individuals who have had sexual intercourse with IV drug users. And almost three-fourths of perinatal cases are born to IV drug users or their sexual partners.[11]

EDUCATION FOR THE IV DRUG USER

Owing to the secretive and dishonest nature of a drug addiction, the communication and educational methods used in a company AIDS program should be presented in a nonthreatening, nonjudgmental manner. This will alleviate any feelings of isolation, persecution, and paranoia—all of which are highly sensitized perceptions with a drug user. Recommendations for AIDS prevention and education activities to be incorporated into the AIDS program follow.

Widely used literature about AIDS prevention and education such as brochures and handouts are not enough. Education programs must include a comprehensive training package and should be presented on an on-going basis. The most effective change has been implemented through periodic, consistent educational approaches.

Target partners of IVDUs—These are the people most at risk for contracting the AIDS virus aside from the addicts themselves. These individuals are also more likely to be in the workforce, and therefore an employer concern. Because denial is one of the key identifying factors in drug addiction,... IV drug users are usually not willing to admit that they are or have been in the past in danger of HIV exposure. They may also deny that their sexual partner could be. It may be possible to reach the partner and effect some change in behavior in cases where the IVDU is unreachable for education. In addition, because the partner[s] of ... addict[s] are often the responsible member[s] of the households, they are in a better position to educate other members of the family, and can often be the most successful initiators for behavioral change within the family.

Personal stories are very effective—Many education programs utilize the experience of a person with AIDS who can speak to a group about his or her own personal experience. Particularly in the case of IVDUs, this may prove to be one of the most effective means for "bringing it home"

Successful recovery includes positive employment—This is one more indication of the potential impact a strong workplace education program could have. This is also important because one of the key aspects in maintaining health and a positive attitude for the person with AIDS (PWA) is their ability to continue to work.[12]

In addition, the discovery by an addict of their HIV-positive status can be a major factor in behavioral change. This is often a strong motivator for the drug-addicted employee to protect their family and loved ones through safe sex methods as well as instill an increased desire to get and stay clean to prolong their lives.

As the number of Americans who are HIV-positive rises, the risk of transmission rises exponentially. Because the use of alcohol and other drugs can impair judgment and increase impulsiveness, such use plays a pivotal role in determining an individual's likelihood to engage in risky behaviors. Thus it is recommended that specific education regarding substance abuse be incorporated into all workplace AIDS education programs.

PREVENTION OF TRANSMISSION OF HIV INFECTION FOR IV DRUG USERS

Intravenous drug use is a significant contributor to the AIDS epidemic. Therefore, IV drug users and those who are in close contact with them must be made aware of the appropriate precautions and facts pertaining to AIDS and IV drug use.

Intravenous drug users can reduce their risk of contracting AIDS by stopping the use of drugs. Those who continue to inject drugs despite the demonstrated risk to their health should refrain from sharing drugs or equipment, use only new (not re-bagged) needles, and avoid shooting galleries. Those who insist on injecting drugs may be able to reduce the risk of transmitting the AIDS virus by removing any blood or other residual material from the needle, syringe, or other "works" ... and flushing the needles and syringe at least twice with a bleach (10 parts water to 2 parts bleach). Sexual relationships with IV drug users should be avoided. At a minimum sexual partners of IV drug users should refrain from practices involving exchange of body fluids (such as blood or semen) to reduce the risk of exposure to the AIDS virus. Condoms should be used when having intimate contact with high risk individuals. It is important to know that, while condoms might make sex with an IV drug user safer, there is no such thing as "safe sex" with a person at high risk for AIDS. In addition, sexual practices that cause injury to tissue, such as anal intercourse, should be avoided.[13]

THE FREE NEEDLE DEBATE

A controversial issue in the fight to curb the spread of HIV infection among needle-using addicts involves proposals to dispense free, clean needles to addicts. The needle-dispensing concept is intended to slow the spread of the disease: "Giving addicts clean needles would, it is hoped, avoid the sharing of needles, which is a prime way the AIDS virus is transmitted. But a second and equally important element is to use the needles as a lure to force addicts to undergo counseling about how to avoid the transmission of AIDS, both during the use of drugs and during sex."[14]

Many experts in the health fields support such programs. According to Dr. Stephen C. Joseph, former commissioner of the New York City Department of Health,

the degree to which we can slow or stop the spread among intravenous drug abusers is key to the future of the AIDS epidemic.... Some data from Europe suggests that clean needles do reduce AIDS transmission. Experience in ... Scandinavia, the Netherlands, the United Kingdom, and Switzerland indicates that distribution of equipment is not followed by a rise in drug abuse. It seems prudent to undertake a medically supervised experiment on whether you can affect needle-sharing. We think there's a reasonable chance you can. Drug dealers sell pre-packaged needles as clean—in fact they're not—which command a premium price. That suggests to us that free needles will be used.[15]

This experiment has been vigorously debated and many people oppose it, including a large percentage of city and law enforcement officials. Sterling Johnson, Jr., New York City's special prosecutor for narcotics cases, states:

I think free needles just would not work. The users would get them and sell them. ... The proposal is well-meaning, but it's not the answer. First of all, addicts just will not use clean needles. Drug addicts, in the heat of the moment when they're about to insert a needle in their arms, are not about to take out a new hypo and unwrap it. They are going to take a needle and pass it around. We know this because we have raided shooting galleries with boxes of clean needles, stolen from pharmaceutical houses, all over the place, but dozens of addicts lying around with just one bloody needle among them. The needle has been and will remain a communal instrument. Slaves of addiction do not change their daily habits.[16]

The distribution of free needles is not a direct issue for the workplace. The human resources departments of companies will not be distributing free needles to addicts. However, companies must consider the free needle question when advising IV drug-using employees, or employees whose loved ones are IV drug users. The human resource and EAP departments must be knowledgeable on all current angles of the AIDS issue, and be ready to present all sides to employees seeking answers and education.

SIGNIFICANT OTHERS OF IV DRUG USERS WITH AIDS

Many IV drug users and other drug- and alcohol-addicted individuals are active and functioning in the workplace. In addition, the addicts' significant others, who are also in the workforce, are greatly affected if their loved ones are diagnosed with AIDS. The following comments are from Geoffrey Grief and Edmund Porembski.[17]

"In many cases, the significant other has become estranged from the drug abuser because of the pattern of illegal activity and irrational behavior associated with that lifestyle. Yet, when the drug abuser is diagnosed with AIDS and is in the terminal stages of the illness, the significant other may become a primary caregiver. The terminal illness of a loved one, particularly a family member, can be a powerful force in reconciling past differences. AIDS forces many family members to have to deal with the reality of drug abuse and a terminal illness for the first time. If the PWA is also homosexual, this can further complicate the dynamics of the family system.... The significant other has many feelings of his or her own that need to be considered in any treatment plan involving the PWA....

The emotional well-being of the significant other is usually linked to the health of the PWA. The repeated opportunistic infections or changing condition of the PWA can produce a roller coaster effect upon their lives. Feelings of helplessness and powerlessness are common as they watch the PWA slowly deteriorate before their eyes. This deterioration, when combined with a prolonged period of suffering prior to death, can leave an indelible and haunting scar upon the memories of the significant others....

Over time, the significant others may develop a pattern of rejecting the drug abuser. The boundaries that are drawn to exclude the abuser are challenged and partially break down when there is an AIDS diagnosis. Usually it is the parent who will cross the boundaries, but it could also be a sibling. When only one or two members of the family of origin come to the assistance of the person with AIDS, a serious rift can occur between those family members and those who continue to be rejecting. While some terminal illnesses can bring families together, the multiple problems associated with AIDS tend to make some reunions unlikely....

Drug abuse is a common though undesirable part of life in most neighborhoods. Many families have had years of exposure to the drug addict and have developed strategies for coping. When AIDS strikes, as it does increasingly, the boundaries break down. These estranged families may take on the primary responsibility of emotional and physical care because of the lack of alternative health care resources that will accept persons with AIDS."

As AIDS spreads, the workplace must plan for the needs of significant others affected by the epidemic.

THE PRESIDENTIAL COMMISSION ON THE HUMAN IMMUNODEFICIENCY VIRUS EPIDEMIC

In 1987, President Ronald Reagan formed a Presidential Commission to address the issues surrounding the AIDS epidemic. The members listened to a range of perspectives from groups, including persons with AIDS and HIV infection, federal officials, business leaders, representatives of community-based organizations, local and state government leaders, members of Congress, and experts in the field. Using this input, the Commission wrote a report outlining recommendations for the president, and delivered the report to the president in February 1988. The following are excerpts from the report regarding IV drug use:[18]

The future course of the HIV epidemic depends greatly on the effectiveness of our nation's ability to address IV drug abuse. IV drug abusers constitute [approximately] 25% of the AIDS cases in the United States. They are a major vector for the HIV infection, spreading it through needle and other drug paraphernalia sharing and sexual contacts as well as perinatally to their children. Approximately 70% of U.S. natives reporting heterosexually transmitted AIDS have had sex with an IV drug abuser, some of whom support their habits through prostitution. Seventy percent of the perinatally transmitted pediatric AIDS patients are children of IV drug abusers. The number of AIDS cases among infants and children is rapidly increasing and expected to total between 10,000 and 20,000 by 1991.

These estimates represent only the beginning of the tragedy if this nation does not act to address its drug abuse problems. The United States continues to have the highest rate of illicit drug use among young people of any country in the industrialized world. With 57% of last year's high school seniors having tried an illicit drug and over one third of all high school seniors reporting experimentation with drugs other than marijuana, drug abuse remains a significant problem that demands a dedicated and determined long-term response. Without such a response America's youth, particularly minority youth, remain vulnerable to a bleak future. . . .

In addition to the devastation that drug abuse represents for our families and communities, the cost of drug abuse is an estimated 60 billion dollars annually in health care, reduced productivity, law enforcement, theft and destruction of property. This figure does not account for the addition of the staggering costs of providing health care for drug abusers with AIDS.

Crime is also intimately related to drug abuse with studies of male arrestees in major cities finding that 66% test positive for drugs. . . .

Curbing IV drug abuse is a multifaceted challenge requiring a major commitment of the federal, state and local governments, parents, educators and community leaders working together to initiate new prevention and education programs, expanding treatment programs and building community support to eliminate drug abuse and trafficking.

In addition to focusing on the demand side of the drug abuse equation, we must not slacken in our efforts to address the supply side by including illicit domestic and international drug trafficking in our policy decisions.

COMMENTS

The HIV infection rate is rising in the drug-abusing population. Companies must recognize that many of these individuals are currently respected, valued contributors in the workforce. Companies must not ignore the issue because they stereotype drug users belonging to certain segments of society. The workplace must take the responsibility of educating all employees about AIDS and drug abuse. The workplace will then reap the benefits of helping to save the lives of their employees and of retaining the company's investment in these individuals and their families.

NOTES

1. Edith Springer, "Drug Dependency: A Conduit of AIDS," *Executive Briefing* 2, no. 6 (June 1989): 2 (A publication of the Foundation for Public Communications, DIFFA, and the National Leadership Coalition on AIDS).

2. Bryan Lawton, Thomas E. Backer, and Kirk B. O'Hara, "AIDS Handbook for EAP Professionals in the Entertainment Industry " (Los Angeles: Human Interaction Research Institute, June 1989), p. 19.

3. Springer, "Drug Dependency," p. 2.

4. T. Peter Bridge, Allan F. Mirsky, and Frederick K. Goodwin, *Psychological, Neuropsychiatric, and Substance Abuse Aspects of AIDS, Advances in Biochemical Psychopharmacology*, Vol. 44 (New York: Raven Press, 1988), p. 152.

5. Ibid., p. vii.

6. Committee on Substance Abuse and AIDS, "Alcohol Drugs and AIDS," San Francisco AIDS Foundation, October 1985, p. 1.

7. Bridge, Mirsky, and Goodwin, *Psychological, Neuropsychiatric, and Substance Abuse Aspects of AIDS*, p. 126.

8. Lawton, Backer, and O'Hara, "AIDS Handbook," p. 19.

9. Springer, "Drug Dependency," pp. 2–3.

10. "NIDA Capsules," Issued by the Press Office of the National Institute on Drug Abuse, March 1989, p. 2.

11. Ibid.

12. Lawton, Backer, and O'Hara, "AIDS Handbook," p. 21.

13. "NIDA Capsules," pp. 2–3.

14. Jeffrey Smalz, "Addicts to Get Needles in Plan to Curb AIDS," *New York Times*, January 31, 1988, p. 1.

15. "Pro & Con: Free Needles for Addicts, to Help Curb AIDS? *New York Times*, December 20, 1987, p. 2.

16. Ibid., p. 3.

17. Geoffrey L. Greif and Edmund Porembski, "Significant Others of I.V. Drug Abusers with AIDS: New Challenges for Drug Treatment Programs," *Journal of Substance Abuse Treatment* 4 (1987): 151–55.

18. Presidential Commission on the HIV Epidemic, Chairman's Recommendations, Washington, DC, February 29, 1988, pp. 4–5.

CHAPTER 8

SPECIAL POPULATIONS: WOMEN, MINORITIES, CHILDREN, AND TEENAGERS

This chapter will present special populations in our society and their relationship to HIV infection and the workplace. Relevant data for each group will be presented, and the chapter will discuss modes of transmission, education, and issues specific to each group.

WOMEN AND HIV INFECTION

Relevant Data of HIV Infection in Women

As of early November, 1986, women accounted for 6.7% of all AIDS cases. 51% of the affected women are black and 20% are Hispanic, 52% were intravenous (IV) drug users, and 21% became infected through sexual contact with infected men; 67% of these men were IV drug users. 79% of women with AIDS are 13–39 years of age and within their childbearing years.[1]

The rate of HIV infection in women has risen at a steady pace. As of June 1990, of the 137,385 cases of adult/adolescent cases of AIDS reported in the United States, 13,000 (9.5%) were women. Just over 50% were transmitted through intravenous drug use; 32% through heterosexual contact with an AIDS carrier; 10% by blood transfusions; 7% undetermined; and the remaining 1% were hemophiliacs.

Women everywhere are becoming dramatically affected by AIDS. Whether they are at direct risk for infection, or are caretaking AIDS-infected family or friends, AIDS-related issues have a profound effect on their relationships to their loved ones and their partners. In addition, as part of the parental unit, they are directly responsible for contributing to the preventive education of AIDS for their own children.

HIV Infection, Women, and the Workplace

The workplace has an obligation to educate female employees about HIV infection. Given that females comprise half the U.S. workforce, this responsibility is clear. Women are less informed about AIDS than is appropriate, and thus are more vulnerable to HIV infection. Women's ignorance about AIDS could prove to be more devastating than ignorance in any other risk group. The workplace offers an efficient and powerful setting for reaching the largest number of women possible.

Prevalence of HIV Infection in Women

More and more women are becoming infected with HIV. The stereotype of AIDS being the "gay white male disease," or "the minority male drug abuser's disease" has prevented most women from looking realistically at their own risk of infection.

The fiction that AIDS is not really a heterosexual disease has been maintained so forcefully in the United States that the Federal Centers for Disease Control (CDC) did not establish "heterosexual contact" (sex between men and women) cases as an official risk category until 1984. By late 1986, the Department of Health of New York State—the state with the greatest number of female cases—still had not added "vaginal sex" to the official list of risk behaviors.[2]

Experts suspect women are one of the fastest growing risk groups for infection. Of the 1 million individuals estimated to be carrying the HIV infection, 250,000 are estimated to be women.

Perhaps one of the reasons the CDC's low initial data relating to AIDS and women is that the AIDS virus does not affect women the exact way it affects men.

States and cities with heavy concentrations of AIDS are experiencing dramatic increases in the number of deaths of women from a variety of respiratory and infectious diseases thought to be AIDS-related, but not included in the CDC's definition of AIDS.... These increases raise major questions about the pattern of the epidemic and its true mortality rate and appropriate treatment. They indicate that in the communities hardest hit so far by AIDS, the deaths of women may be significantly undercounted because many do not survive long enough to develop or to be diagnosed as having "full-blown"AIDS used for official case counts. In addition, AIDS may manifest itself differently in women, often first appearing as a gynecological disease.

Most crucial, the CDC definition of AIDS fails to acknowledge the gynecological diseases so common among women infected with the HIV virus.... Those gynecological symptoms include chronic vaginitis, and pelvic inflammatory disease which can be so severe that it requires immediate hospitalization. Certainly in women with gynecological infections that don't respond to ordinary treatment, HIV testing should be a consideration.[3]

The demographics of female AIDS cases greatly vary according to geography. In New York City, many female AIDS cases were heterosexually transmitted with drug abusers. The women placed at the greatest risk are Hispanics and blacks. In San Francisco, on the other hand, most female AIDS cases were transmitted by heterosexual contact with bisexual men. However, for the rest of the United States,

Army studies suggest that women in other areas might be more threatened by promiscuous heterosexual men, who are usually the first to get any "new" sexual disease. Of the first ten heterosexual, non-drug-abusing male AIDS patients seen at the Walter Reed Hospital, for example, eight said they had slept with prostitutes or with fifty or more women in the previous five years.[4]

Modes of Heterosexual Transmission of HIV Infection

Another reason for the lack of knowledge about women and AIDS is the confusion about the heterosexual transmission of the virus. Misconceptions about heterosexual sexual practices from kissing and hugging to different types of intercourse have contributed to the confusion. The major route of heterosexual transmission is intercourse (penis inserted into the vagina). Other sexual practices are unlikely to transmit the virus. For example, although the virus is found in saliva, the amount is so small that kissing, including deep or "French" kissing, has been found a very unlikely means of transmission. In addition, there is now strong, direct evidence that oral sex does not transmit the virus. Several studies have shown that the homosexuals who limit their sexual activity to oral sex have not become infected. However, due to the high concentration of virus in semen, scientists still advise women not to perform oral sex on an infected man.

The major source of confusion for women in identifying the modes of heterosexual transmission have been misconceptions about anal intercourse. Because anal intercourse is the major form of transmission for homosexuals, many women have the impression that if they avoid anal intercourse they are protected from infection. AIDS education efforts directed to women must stress the differences in heterosexual and homosexual modes of transmission and consequently educate women about dangerous heterosexual behavior.

Education and Women

In the workplace and in other arenas, some educational measures must be targeted especially to women.

Educational slogans directed at women such as "don't sleep with bisexuals or drug addicts" or, more recently, "always use a condom"—are not an adequate protection policy. Women need real education programs especially for them, in settings where they feel comfortable about asking very difficult, personal questions. How, for example, do you even ask a man to put on a condom? When should you or your partner get tested? Who will help you if you insist your husband be tested and he walks out? What should you do if you're pregnant and suddenly realize that you may be at risk? How do you ask a man if he's ever had a homosexual encounter?[5]

Minority women are among the highest risk group for female AIDS cases. Many of these women are from low-income, urban areas. The workplace must take into account the various populations and demographics of these women when targeting the workplace educational programs.

Accurate information about AIDS transmission and prevention must be focused on the women at greatest risk—black and Hispanic women—and on their sex partners. Unfortunately, efforts to avoid stigmatizing these groups may have contributed to denial of their particular risk. National magazines, when dramatizing the risk of heterosexual transmission of AIDS, feature cover photographs of white teenagers, white women, and white couples support the misimpression that AIDS in heterosexuals is just a white disease, just as previous reports conveyed the false impression that AIDS is a gay disease. The evolving epidemiologic pattern of human immunodeficiency virus (HIV) infection and AIDS makes it clear that all segments of our population are at risk....

In the United States, condom advertisements and safer sex guidelines have appeared in virtually all magazines targeted at female audiences. Male-directed advertising lags far behind; none of the leading fashion or sports magazines for men has yet featured condom advertisements [as of April 1987]. A popular educational film for teenagers entitled Sex, Drugs and AIDS shows girls in a ballet class locker room discussing how they approach getting their boyfriends to wear condoms, but interestingly, the film does not depict a similar scene in the boys' locker room of boys discussing why they will wear condoms. It is no surprise that women now account for a large percentage of condom sales, and that women have sought full information about how they can best preserve their own health and the health of those with whom they have sex or to whom they give birth. But sex is a consensual act. Both sexes are responsible. Men must get the message and act on it too....

Providing appropriate education to women IV drug users poses a particularly challenging problem. Only a small percentage can be reached through treatment programs. Many are poorly educated and have little medical knowledge, and the potential future danger of AIDS is less compelling than the day-to-day problems of poverty and drug use. Therefore, to reach IV drug users, a large network must be used, including other drug users, their peers, their community, health clinics, schools, jails, music and video. The messages should be direct, preferably visual, and they should not moralize about drug use or use scare tactics. Rather, they should include constructive suggestions to maintain health, emphasizing practical considerations such as the importance of clean needles or the proper use of bleach as a disinfectant, in addition to the loftier goal of abstinence.[6]

The media, advertising, and other communities are enforcing the stereotypes about AIDs and women. At the University of Maryland, condom machines were installed in the women's bathrooms, but not the men's. Sadly, the women students did not object. If education about transmission and prevention of the AIDS virus in women is to be accurate and effective, men must also be equally informed and responsible.

A common misconception among women is that the male AIDS carrier is easily identifiable through his current behavior. This could not be further from the truth. Because HIV infection could occur from even one sexual encounter, it is imperative to know one's partners thoroughly. The chances of selecting a partner who has had one or more bisexual experiences or has experimented with IV drugs is not that remote. Just because a man is not currently an addict or engaging in homosexual practices does not mean he cannot carry AIDS. Some data suggest that individuals may be at risk for AIDS by having had sex as long ago as 10 to 15 years with partners who may have been infected with HIV. The chilling truth remains: for every person with whom one sleeps, one also has slept with all of that individual's partners.

By addressing the issues of women and AIDS, ramifications for the entire heterosexual population come into focus. These ramifications include the realization of the significant risks, and taking the proper measures to prevent and educate. These proper measures must include equal responsibility for the male heterosexual as well as the female. Sex is a mutual act. Therefore, its consequences must be treated as such.

HIV-Infected Women

The issues for the HIV-infected female differ from those of the HIV-infected male. The workplace must be aware of these issues, and education and policies should include this important, growing group.

It is important to recognize the issues that women themselves confront as infectees. ... First, is a profound sense of isolation. The infection is often kept secret, depriving women of desperately needed support from family, friends, community, and particularly from other infected women. Infected women lack the sense of community that is enjoyed by gay men, at least in certain areas. They still constitute a relatively small group and have little reason to know one another. Second, is profound grief for the loss of health, body image, sexuality, and childbearing potential. Means for sexual expression are limited, and disclosure of HIV infection to a new sexual partner can be devastating. Third, women may be too sick to fulfill their responsibilities as parents, and they may have to plan for the welfare of surviving children after their own death. Finally, in a disease that has thus far affected [predominantly] men, women may find it difficult to find primary care physicians, obstetricians, gynecologists, sex counselors, abortion counselors, and other health professionals who are educated in the issues that relate specifically to women and who are sensitive to their needs.[7]

Prostitution and HIV Infection

There has been a growing concern regarding prostitution and HIV infection. Any transmission from a prostitute has an immediate effect on three significant parties: the prostitute, her client, and her client's partner—often his wife. "In the United States, rates of infection for streetwalking prostitutes have ranged from 5% of those tested in Seattle and 6% in Los Angeles, to 19% in New York City, and 50% in Washington, D.C."[8] Prostitution has had a growing effect on the heterosexual population all over the world—especially in Africa, where use of condoms is uncommon. However, in the United States the rate of HIV infection among prostitutes is not as great as originally suspected. In Western countries, prostitutes have become increasingly aware of precautions necessary to protect themselves against HIV infection.

The primary danger involves the drug-addicted prostitute. These women are not as aware of AIDS and its lethal effects, and are less likely to follow safer sex guidelines. Prostitutes who use drugs are known to offer "condomless sex" if the client is willing to pay for it. These prostitutes are more desperate for money due to their drug habit, and much less likely to take the necessary precautions.

Minority Women and AIDS

More than 90 percent of American AIDS patients have been men, most of them white homosexuals.

Yet in black and Hispanic neighborhoods, particularly in the East Coast inner cities, the epidemic presents a very different picture. There, AIDS is a disease of both males and females; most [patients] are drug users, but many are either lovers or offspring of addicts.... Studies have found that more than 70% of AIDS cases in women occurred among blacks and Hispanics. Indeed, a woman who is black is 13 times as likely as one who is white to [become infected], and 90% of infants born with AIDS are black or Hispanic.[9]

MINORITIES AND HIV INFECTION

Relevant Data of HIV Infection in Minorities

The black population in the United States totals 11.5%. However, as of June 1990, blacks comprise a much larger proportion of persons with AIDS: 28%. This is also the case for the Hispanic population, who comprise 7% of the total population, but constitute 16% of persons with AIDS. Asian/Pacific Islanders comprise 1.6% of the population and .6% of the total

AIDS cases in the United States. American Indians constitute less than 1% of the total population, and represent .1% of total AIDS cases. However, when trying to identify the American Indian group, it must be understood that "the data for this group are underreported because of the difficulty of identifying members of this group when they live or receive medical care or counseling outside a reservation or areas where American Indians live in large groups."[10]

The statistics of the total AIDS cases and minorities is shifting dramatically. It must be understood that proportionately the highest rising population of AIDS cases is the minority population. In the first six months of 1990, the figure for the number of blacks afflicted with AIDS has increased 2%, and for Hispanics, 1%.

Minorities and the Workplace

The workplace must be aware of the issues surrounding minorities and HIV infection. The issues for minorities involve more than statistical communication and precautionary measures necessary for prevention of the spread of the virus. When educating minorities about the spread of the disease, it is necessary to be sensitive to the issue of discrimination and its repercussions. Therefore, full knowledge of all the issues surrounding minorities and AIDS is necessary for a comprehensive, effective, and accurate minority AIDS education program.

The AIDS Issue in Minority Communities

The rising rate of HIV infection in minorities disproves the initial perception of AIDS as a gay white male disease. The minority population, public health officials, and the federal government have only recently (since 1987) come to terms with the serious rate of HIV infection among minorities.

The federal response to the crisis of AIDS in minority communities has been criminally slow. The CDC held its first conference on minority AIDS in August, 1987, and established a minority section of its National AIDS Information and Education Program in December, 1987. Not until the following February did the President's AIDS Commission release a draft report acknowledging the severity of the epidemic among blacks and Hispanics. Federal money earmarked for minority AIDS is only now being released. . . .

Minority communities were left to combat AIDS on their own, without the wealthy donors and sensitivity to sexual issues that allowed the white gay community to organize in the face of prejudice and neglect. Within the last three years, dozens of minority AIDS groups have come into being, all relying overwhelmingly or exclusively on the volunteer efforts of poor and working-class people.[11]

Issues Particular to the Minority Population

Several issues come into play when discussing the reticence of minority populations to come to terms with their realistic risk of HIV infection. These issues include homophobia, genocide, and theories regarding the origin of the disease.

During the first five years of the disease, the initial data available from the CDC suggested that gay white males constituted the most "at risk" population for HIV infection. However, AIDS recognizes no color boundaries. Gay and bisexual minorities are part of this "high-risk" population. Although homophobia is an issue for all races, the black, Hispanic, and Asian/Pacific populations have had particular difficulty in accepting gay males. These populations *tend to* value a traditional "masculine" model. Therefore, to accept the growing numbers of minorities with HIV infection would threaten the perceived sexual identity. This concern has caused minority populations to distance themselves from the disease. On the other hand, minority men who are gay often hide their sexual preference. As a result many are married and often lead a double life. The threat of discovery of their sexual identity prevents them from informing their wives of their homosexuality and the possibility of their having been exposed to infection.

One of the most important issues that has surfaced in discussing AIDS has been the threat of genocide. Minorities are sensitive to this threat because of some programs aimed at reducing the AIDS risk in their populations, including distribution of free needles to addicts, abortion counseling and condom distribution, and mandatory AIDS testing. "The term [genocide] reflects the genuine suspicion of many that the AIDS virus was developed in a government laboratory for the express purpose of killing off the unwanted. This belief is helped along by HIV's curious affinity for those whom the larger society disdains."[12] This theory is further explained regarding

questions and concerns [that] persist among health officials, ethicists and members of the minority community. Of these issues, none is more explosive than the specter of population control. "Anything that touches the reproductive rights of black and Hispanic women raises issues of genocidal intent" according to Ronald Bayer, an associate for policy studies, at the Hastings Center in New York, that examines matters of medical ethics. "The not-so-distant issue of sterilization abuse has haunted this debate."[13]

Since scientists widely believed the AIDS virus originated in Africa, many whites blame the African and African-American population for the disease.

Education and Minorities

With this misdirected blame comes misplaced discrimination and anger. Minorities are aware of this and may skeptically view the usual discussion of AIDS. The task is to educate minorities to the real danger they and their children face in respect to AIDS without making it sound racist. For the workplace, persons giving educational sessions must be carefully selected and screened beforehand in how and what they present to employee groups. For further information regarding AIDS and educating minorities, contact the minority organizations listed in Appendix A at the end of this book.

CHILDREN AND AIDS

As of June 1990, the CDC had received reports of 2,380 cases of AIDS reported in children (under 13) and 541 in teens (13–19). This is an important workplace issue not only because of the emotional impact on affected employees, but also because the workplace pays the health bills for children of employees. Parents and loved ones of children with AIDS need support and information; this should be offered through the EAP and human resource departments.

Transmission

The most prevalent mode of transmission for children with AIDS is through their infected mother, either before or at birth. This transmission is passed to the child either through the mother's blood or in the birth canal. These women have been found to be intravenous drug abusers or the sexual partners of infected men. In the other cases of children with AIDS, infection has been caused by blood or blood products. However, because of the universal testing of all blood and blood products employed by hospitals in this country, transfusion and hemophilia treatment now pose a minute risk for infection. Hemophilia treatment is now safe because scientists have learned to kill the virus in the blood products needed by hemophiliacs.

Not one case of AIDS is known to have been transmitted in a school, day-care, or foster-care setting. AIDS is not spread through the kind of contact children have with each other, such as touching, hugging, or sharing meals and bathrooms. This is supported by long-term studies of family members of both adults and children with AIDS. There are no reports of household members who have become infected through routine, nonsexual contact with a family member with AIDS.[14]

TEENAGERS AND AIDS

The employees of any company will be concerned about AIDS and how it affects their lives and the lives of their families. A workplace education program should provide employees with access to information that can help them properly educate the young people in their lives about AIDS. The program should address the issue of educating oneself as well as one's children. Employers know that teenage substance abuse is costing them the largest share of their escalating mental health budget. What they have not yet perceived is that this population is also vulnerable to AIDS and may even now be carrying the virus. Employers will also be faced with the financial cost of AIDS treatment for these teens unless the behavior of the substance abusing adolescent is changed. AIDS education at the worksite must address the employees who are parents of teens.

As of June 1990, more than 28,000 people aged 20–29 have been diagnosed with AIDS. Given the fact that a person can become infected with the virus from as long as ten years before any symptoms occur, a significant portion of these young adults were infected when they were in their teen years.

The following is excerpted from the Department of Health and Human Services, Public Health Service, and the Centers for Disease Control's "AIDS Prevention Guide: For Parents and Other Adults Concerned About Youth."[15]

Many teenagers engage in behaviors that increase their risk of becoming infected.... Surveys have found that: the average age for a girl in the United States to have sexual intercourse for the first time is 16. The average age for a boy is 15.5; it is estimated that 2.5 million teens are infected with sexually transmitted diseases (venereal disease—VD) each year.... 60% of all American high school seniors have used illegal drugs. Some of these drugs are injected....

All young people need to know about AIDS and the specific actions they can take to protect themselves and their loved ones from becoming infected.

EDUCATING YOUNG PEOPLE ABOUT AIDS

Deciding What Young People Need to Know

As an adult who knows the young people you will talk with, you are in the best position to decide what they need to know about HIV infection and AIDS.

Think carefully about their knowledge and experience. How old are the children? How much do they already know about HIV infection, AIDS, and other related subjects, such as sex and drug use? Where have they gotten their information? From friends? School? Television? You? Is it likely to be accurate?

Also, ask yourself these questions: Is it possible that the young people you will be talking with are sexually active? Have they tried drugs? Do they spend time with people who do these things?

In addition, consider your family's religious and cultural values. Do you want to convey these in conversation? How will you get them across?

These are important questions. Answering them will help you stess the information that the young people in your life need to know.

COMMENTS

These special populations, especially minorities and women, are used to stereotyping and discrimination. Therefore, the presentation of generic information that does not include issues specific to their population could result in anger, skepticism, and disbelief. Consequently, the AIDS educational effort will be a failure. By addressing the special populations in the workplace and understanding their specific issues, the AIDS educational program will be comprehensive, effective, and will appeal to the workplace as a whole.

NOTES

1. Constance B. Wofsy, "Human Immunodeficiency Virus Infection in Women," *Journal of the American Medical Association* 257, no. 15 (April 17, 1987): 2074.

2. Chris Norwood, *Advice for Life: A Woman's Guide to AIDS Risks and Prevention* (New York: National Women's Health Network Guide, 1987), pp. 3–4.

3. The Ms. Reporter, *Ms Magazine*, July 1988, pp. 65, 67.

4. Norwood, *Advice for Life*, p. 90.

5. Ibid., pp. 16–17.

6. Wofsy, "Human Immunodeficiency Virus Infection in Women," p. 2075.

7. Ibid.

8. Norwood, *Advice for Life*, p. 100.

9. "AIDS and Women: Nonwhites Face the Biggest Risk," *Time*, April 27, 1988.

10. Centers for Disease Control, *HIV/AIDS Surveillance Report*, July 1989.

11. William Deresiewicz and Joe Gordon, "Against All Odds; Grassroots Minority Groups Fight AIDS," *Health/Pac Bulletin* 18 (Spring 1988): 4.

12. Harold L. Dalton, "AIDS in Blackface," *Daedulus*, Living with AIDS Part 2, Summer 1989, p. 220.

13. Jane Gross, "New York's Poorest Women Offered More AIDS Services," *New York Times*, March 5, 1988, p. 38.

14. American Red Cross, "AIDS Prevention for Youth," *America Responds to AIDS*, 1987, p. 23.

15. Department of Health and Human Services, Public Health Service, and the Centers for Disease Control, "AIDS Prevention Guide: For Parents and Other Adults Concerned About Youth," information packet, 1989.

CHAPTER 9

INTERVIEWS

Interview conducted by Dr. Dale Masi with Federal Manager of employee with AIDS

Q: Were you aware of AIDS prior to finding out that your employee had AIDS?

A: I was aware of it, yes, but not nearly to the extent that I am aware of it now.

Q: Were you prepared for supervising an employee with AIDS and handling the co-workers concerns?

A: No, not at all.

Q: How did you find out that your employee had AIDS?

A: I was told by the former supervisor of the employee that there was a life-threatening problem with the employee and he felt the employee should tell me. The employee did not tell me. After about three weeks of being his supervisor, my boss called me into his office and told me there was something I should know about the employee—that he was suffering from AIDS.

Q: How did you react to this?

A: My initial reaction was kind of shock. I was first concerned for myself—how to protect myself from catching AIDS, being contaminated. Then I got concerned for the other employees, and concerned for that employee himself, sorry for him.

Q: What did you do with this information?

A: It was late in the day when I learned about it, I went home and made the mistake of telling my wife, sharing the information with her, as she is the one that I counsel with quite frequently. She is working on her PhD in psychology and I felt she would have insight, and help walk me through this. To my surprise her reaction was shock and horror that I would be working with and potentially contaminated by this employee. After discussing it with her, I came to the conclusion that the fellow employees this AIDS victim was working with, my subordinates, had to be told. Now that I had the information I could protect myself by not using his telephone or chewing on the same pencils as the employee, washing my hands in the restroom, and so forth. However, that protection would not be afforded the other employees. Therefore, the other employees had to be told. I came back the very next morning with that conclusion.

Q: Did upper management offer you any means of support when you found out about your employee?

A: No, initially it was a matter that they felt they should just share this information with me. When I came back the next morning, I went to them and told them the other employees had to be told, that we had an obligation to those other employees. Because if somebody should come down sick, and we did not stand up and fulfill our obligation, we would potentially leave ourselves open for liability. After reeling back a few minutes, thinking about it, and realizing I was coming from a different direction than they were (they had been coming from the direction of feeling sorry for the employee, the poor thing, and we've got to do everything we can to console the employee), they admitted they had not taken into consideration the obligation to the other employees, and agreed that they must inform the other employees.

Q: Does your agency have an EAP?

A: I have since found out that now we do, but at that time when I first learned about AIDS, I was not aware that we had an EAP.

Q: So, at that point, when you were in the middle of the situation, you did not use the EAP?

A: Yes, that's correct.

Q: Did your agency have a written policy on AIDS before you found out that your employee had AIDS?

A: No, it did not, and still does not.

Q: With regard to the employee, is he or she still working?

A: Yes, the employee is still working, occasionally misses a day now and then for medical reasons, but other than that is not absent any more than a normal employee.

Q: What decisions did you as a supervisor or manager have to make?

A: The initial decision was "Do I tell the other employees?" I immediately, the day after I was told, after discussing it with my managers, confronted the employee, and verified that I had been told by the upper managers. I told him the other employees in the office had to be told. He was shocked and horrified that I had been told by the upper management, and initially resisted. He came back the next day and said he had reconsidered, and said he would tell two employees, the two that were located in the room that he is, the ones that regularly use the telephone, etc. One of the employees was pregnant, and he did tell her.

Q: What happened?

A: I called the two co-workers in, and they said they had been told, and said they had no problems continuing to work with him, including the pregnant worker, and they did not see it as a threat to themselves. They wanted to continue working and felt sorry for the employee.

Q: So they were supportive.

A: Yes.

Q: What types of situations did you face in dealing with them?

A: Nothing unusual as far as dealing with the employees themselves. I had insisted that the other nine people in our section be told, because there is very close hourly contact with these people, coming into the same room, answering the telephone, and so forth. He resisted that and threatened to sue me individually if I forced him to disclose this to the other employees. [He was] fearful that it would get all over the building and he would be earmarked as an AIDS victim and discriminated against, and people would point fingers and so forth, and he didn't want this. So at that point we then went to our legal counsel, and we got an advisory opinion from them, and I was told that we had to back off in forcing him to tell the other employees, because his right to privacy overrode the right of the other employees in the section to know.

Q: What is the impact on your life of supervising an employee with AIDS?

A: As far as the workplace is concerned, besides the initial amount of worktime that I lost which was several days—spent reading all that I could, finding out about AIDS, getting the advisory opinion, meeting with my supervisors, meeting with the employees, meeting with that employee, and the mental anguish those first few days—it has had no impact subsequently on the worksite. Everything is back to normal and continuing to function as if there is no problem. As far as me individually—having told my wife, her reaction was that she immediately moved out of the bedroom, feeling that it just was not worth the risk of my potentially being contaminated. She insisted that I get a medical examination. I was unable to find a doctor that would do this examination, being told that it would be worthless given the length of time for the test to show positive (six months), the risk that it might show positive when it is actually negative, and the fact that I might not be contaminated today, but I might potentially be contaminated tomorrow, because I am continually working with and dealing with the employee.

Q: So, it has had a tremendous impact on your personal life, even more so than at the worksite.

A: Yes, that's right.

Q: What advice would you give to a supervisor that has just found out that his or her employee has AIDS?

A: Well, he needs to educate himself about AIDS, first of all, much more in-depth than the casual information that is normally out on the street, what you might normally read and pay attention to. The second thing is concern for that individual, to try to take whatever precautions that can reasonably be taken to protect yourself and your fellow workers, recognizing the rights and privacy of the individual.

Q: What services do you wish had been available to you?

A: I wish that I'd had some counseling service. I wish there had been a policy that I could have gone to, literature that was available for me that I could rely upon.

A lot of the literature that I could find was two years old and obviously outdated because this AIDS thing is moving so rapidly, anything six months old is outdated. So, I wish that we'd had a policy, information that could have been available to me, and a written legal opinion that would be available to us.

Q: Is there anything you would like to say, besides what we have already asked you?

A: Well, nothing other than it's a real scary issue, one that I don't think there are any quick or easy answers to. It's one that society has got to start addressing, based upon what I'm reading about the estimates of the number of us that are going to have this thing, heterosexuals and so forth, over the next few years. It's the most pressing medical problem we have today, and probably the most pressing medical problem that we have worldwide.

Interview conducted by Dr. Dale Masi with Caitlin Ryan, Social Worker, Director, AIDS Policy Center, George Washington University

Q: What do you see as the main issues for the EAP professionals?

A: • The family members of the employees with AIDS or the employees who have family members at home with AIDS are under a great deal of stress; they tell no one. Frequently one will hear about "my friend, my neighbor has this problem," being afraid to say, "my husband," etc.

• EAPs must deal with the clinical issue of abused people who become infected, through rape, incest, etc.

• EAPs must be in grief, loss, or bereavement counseling, especially for the managers and co-workers coping with the loss of AIDS affected employees.

• Homophobia is an issue especially with the male EAP workers. They resist the problems of AIDS in the workplace and surrounding issues. They must confront and educate themselves to diagnose and counsel effectively those employees dealing with AIDS.

• EAPs need to learn how to take the sexual history of a client, and to analyze it in assessing risk behavior.

• EAPs must be ready to handle employees who will come forward for testing, appropriate counseling, etc. EAPs must educate themselves about alternative and anonymous testing.

• Drug treatment centers are currently AIDS unaware to EAPs need to work closely with centers when referring.

Q: What are the issues for education in the workplace?

A: • There is no on-going education for AIDS in the workplace. Those that were trained are not retrained or continually updated.

• Employees are not talking about their feelings in these education sessions.

• Fear is prevalent in the workplace, especially in the health-care settings. Support and education are needed for all workers. Training for these workers emphasizes the patient, however, not the worker. Burnout is also a prevalent issue.

Note: Caitlin Ryan has trained 45,000 employees on the subject of AIDS in the workplace. Two days after the interview, she left for a tour as a Fulbright awardee to study AIDS in Korea. When asked for the reasons behind this trip, she explained that because of the low incidence of AIDS in the Far East, it is the last part of the world where preventive education can still take place.

Excerpts from Interview conducted by Dr. Dale Masi and Robin Masi with Dr. Daniel Reardon, Dentist

Up until two years ago, there had been no incidence of a dentist being infected through the dental workplace. Currently, there is now one infected dental worker. My staff has accepted that cross-infection is minimal.

As of 1987 the CDC came out with recommended procedures for the workplace. They include wearing gloves, safety goggles, and face masks, slowing down and taking extra care in the normal hygiene procedures. After each patient, the hygienist cleans and sterilizes any areas as well as instruments where bloodspill may have occurred. In addition, one has to be slower in the actual dental procedures. There is risk of infecting oneself with sharp instruments; therefore, it is necessary to slow down during patient care.

I have been treating patients with AIDS all along. My first AIDS patient died in 1982. I continue to treat patients with AIDS, so far I've treated ten. I treat them myself, in a surgically sterile room. Due to the increase in the time necessary for the hygiene procedures, my daily patient rate decreased from 13, to 11, to its current rate of 7 patients per day. This is due to the extensive sterilization and cleaning necessary after each patient. Because of this decrease in patient load and the caring for dental patients with AIDS, I found it necessary to send out an explanatory letter to all my patients. The letter explains the CDC procedures to assuage concerned patients, as well as discusses the necessity for the increase in my fees:

Dear Patient:

Over the past eight years, the Centers for Disease Control, commonly called the CDC, has recommended specific measures to be taken to protect patients and staff from exposure and infection from the HIV virus. These measures are recommended to eliminate the risk of exposure from other bacteria and viruses as well. Since exposure to the HIV virus carries with it the possibility of a fatal consequence, the implementation of these measures has been viewed by me and my staff as absolutely mandatory.

As the CDC recommends measures, our office implements them. In order to carry out these measures, we have had to decrease our patient flow, especially in our hygiene department. It takes time to do these measures carefully. Thus, we have decreased our patient flow from 11 to 13 patients per day to 7.

Correspondingly, we are increasing the fees for this service from $47 to $60 to reflect the cost involved for careful sterilization procedures.

We know that everyone in our practice is fully aware of what is happening in our society, and we feel that our patients appreciate our concern for their safety and security, and are grateful for the measures that we have implemented.

Interview conducted by Dr. Dale Masi and Robin Masi with
B. J. Stiles, President, National Leadership Coalition on AIDS

The National Leadership Coalition on AIDS was established in May 1987 because of the growing recognition that no single segment of our society can marshal the resources required to respond to the fears and help individuals and society cope with the burdens of AIDS. The goal of the National Leadership Coalition is to bring together the collective resources of the private sector—corporate, nonprofit, and charitable—to respond to the AIDS crisis. The Coalition focuses primarily on how AIDS affects the business and labor segments of the private sector. Composed of major corporations, labor, trade and professional associations, and key civic, voluntary, religious, gay, and ethnic groups, the National Leadership Coalition reflects the diversity of american society.

Points for consideration from interview with B. J. Stiles:

- Concerning the future impact of AIDS in the workplace: There is the potential for a huge volume of employees affected by the AIDS virus. Current estimates put the HIV-positive asymptomatic estimates at 650,000. Small-and medium- sized businesses will be especially hard hit.

- Concerning the drastic implications of AIDS for the workplace: We are only *now* talking about the future of these upwardly mobile, very valuable, productive individuals, who are in their 30s and 40s who are major assets to their companies.

- Regarding new issues for case management: With the advent of AZT and the life-prolonging aspects it provides for the HIV-positive employee, what will be the case management system for the currently infected 650,000 HIV-positive, asymptomatic individuals?

- Regarding confidentiality in the workplace of the AIDS-infected employee: How will confidentiality be maintained? How well prepared are most managers to understand how to deal legally and confidentially with an infected employee?

- Concerning professions and their response to AIDS: The EAP system is not on board with the epidemic. The legal profession is also not on board. They must advise managers/supervisors, etc. what to do with the AIDS issue in the workplace. However, most are reluctant to go on the offense.

- As for the future: The decade ahead is going to be complex, costly, horrendous. We're just getting started, *Don't get tired of AIDS*. This is and will be an ongoing workplace and societal issue.

Interview conducted by Dr. Dale Masi and Robin Masi with
Dr. Michael Irwin, Director, Health Services Department, The
World Bank

Q: Regarding the material that you wrote for the United Nations on sending their employees overseas, could this apply to the private sector? (see Chapter 6 for Dr. Irwin's circulars to the UN population regarding overseas travel.)

A: If you're talking about the big groups with services overseas, yes, it will apply. IBM and Mobil will have physicians that can plug into the existing local health-care system easily. However, if smaller companies are sending employees overseas, with no service network, they are not plugged into the local medical service system. Therefore, different measures must be taken. If the company has employees who live overseas then they are using and have researched the local health facilities. However, the smaller companies must educate and prepare their employees differently than their larger counterparts.

Q: How would this education be different?

A: It would be different depending on the country one is traveling to and the length of stay.

Q: So, are you saying that different parts of the world need to be looked at differently?

A: Yes. For example, practically everywhere in Africa, medical services have gone downhill. However, in Haiti, they are going up.

Q: What about the Mideast?

A: The Mideast has adopted a medieval approach. They have a quarantine outlook with regard to AIDS. For example, the government of Saudi Arabia wants a doctor's note from every overseas traveler that they are HIV negative. In addition, the information is poor about incidence of AIDS, and vast underreporting is likely.

Q: How is the United Nations medical network set up?

A: We have 550 UN examining physicians with a contract to provide services for the UN family. There are offices in 125 countries with local and expatriate staff. The head of these offices call upon the local physicians for services provided.

Q: What kind of education does the United Nations provide to employees traveling overseas?

A: In the United Nations family, all travelers examined by our medical services are asked and screened for four–five [medical] conditions that they might fit into. They include the condition of being in a high-risk category for AIDS. If the employee answers yes to the high-risk condition, we then ask if they've checked with their own physician if it is appropriate to be traveling overseas. Just as we would ask the employee who answered yes to questions about cardiac difficulty. Then, we advise all employees to observe the following points if they are going to developing countries, such as Africa:

1. They must not use any needle unless they are going to a United Nations approved physician. We give our employees needles and syringes, and include a note for customs officials for security.

2. If there is a bad auto accident, and there must be a blood transfusion, we inform them that as of the last six months capital cities are testing for HIV. If they are in a noncapital city, we then evacuate them to a safe medical facility for treatment.

3. There is a discussion during the examination about condoms and our high recommendation of their use.

Q: How does the United Nations educate the family members of the employees traveling overseas?

A: Spouses are encouraged to be present in talks about AIDS and, hopefully, that information will be filtered to their kids. Often, we will have separate discussions for the spouses, because same-sex instructors were found to be more effective. We do not test the spouses and family members of the employees traveling overseas.

Q: What would be your advice to companies without the medical services network of the United Nations or the large U.S. corporations sending employees overseas?

A: To contact the United States or British Embassy with any questions about health care, local physicians, etc. I would *not* recommend relying on the hotel one is staying in.

Q: How does the United Nations handle the issue of testing for HIV-positive status among their employees and recruits?

A: The United Nations does not believe in outright testing of their employees. However, if through the routine examinations, and sensitive screening by the medical services staff, a recruit's HIV status is revealed as positive, we will not recruit that individual. Just as we would not recruit an individual with cardiac trouble until their condition was proved to be stabilized. The United Nations hires for life, and if we cannot guarantee that these recruits with life-threatening conditions are stabilized, they will not be recruited.

If, through the examination, an employee's HIV-positive status is revealed, we would pick and choose where we would station that employee. We would not send them to developing countries, only such places as Geneva, Tokyo, most of Europe, etc.—countries whose health facilities are able to manage and not endanger the HIV-positive employee's health.

The reason for not sending HIV-positive employees to such developing countries as Africa is that:

1. Immunizations are impossible as it introduces more elements into the system that may trigger infections which would affect the individual's health.
2. Anti-malarials increase the speed in which infection may spread.
3. HIV-positive individuals are more prone to indigenous diseases.

Q: Is there anything else you would like to add?

A: I would like to emphasize that AIDS is much more serious than we imagine. Think of how much underreporting we are discovering in this country, and then imagine how much must be occurring in developing countries. For example, last year I was involved in organizing a team of soldiers from Uganda to go to Namibia. The chief physician told me that of these soldiers, 40% were HIV positive. This is in the military, where strict testing is possible. Imagine in the civilian communities the rate of infection.... I think we must recognize how serious and underreported the disease rate is in many developing, and Western, countries.

Interview conducted by Robin Masi with Maura O'Brien, PhD in Bioethics/Philosophy; former Fulbright scholar at Monash University's Centre for Human Bioethics, Melbourne, Australia; and Medical Writer/Producer at the Network for Continuing Medical Education in Secaucus, New Jersey

Q: What were your reasons for going to Australia?

A: I wanted to focus on the issue of AIDS education, and in 1985 or 1986 there wasn't much [AIDS education] going on in the United States. For my thesis, I wanted to compare the two approaches. The interesting thing about Australia is that it's a country very much like ours—English-speaking, similar legal system and, sociopolitical issues....

Q: What were some of the issues you found in Australia?

A: What's interesting about Australia, unlike the United States, is that they recognized very early, about 1984–85, with only a few hundred national cases of AIDS, the importance of prevention through education. They realized they had no choice for public health purposes but to have really blunt, direct educational approaches. They also recognized that although the approach was tinged with moralistic concerns, from the Catholic community, right-to-lifers, and more conservative areas of the community, they really had to catagorize AIDS as a public health issue, not a moral issue.

Q: What are the demographics of the Australian AIDS cases?

A: Like the United States, the cases of AIDS early on were found in homosexual and bisexual men, even more so, 97–98%. A few were related to blood transfusions; they really did not have heterosexual or IV drug cases early on. Today, there are approximately 2,000 national AIDS cases in Australia, but 92% are still diagnosed in the gay community, and the rest are from blood transfusions. This is confusing because they developed the test that was made available to screen the virus, and it was available there in 1985 as in the United States. However, they are still seeing a lot of people who had blood transfusions before 1985.

Q: How is their blood supply?

A: There aren't any cases of anyone who has received blood recently or after the screening test was available, so it is safe and has been since 1985.

Q: What is the rate of infection through IV drug use?

A: Even though nationally they only have a small percentage, if you look at the incidence of cases from five years ago to now, the same thing is happening there that is happening in the United States: the gay cases are dropping, and the cases of heterosexuals and IV drug use are rising, even though they're rising slowly.

Q: What did you find they were doing in their workplaces?

A: They weren't doing much that was novel; if anything they looked to approaches overseas to see how they handled the issues. They had the same problems that we had of discrimination, confidentiality of test results, lack of services in the workplace, and stigmatization of AIDS, but they really only started to focus on workplace issues in 1988—they weren't really pioneers in that area.

Q: What were their approaches in AIDS education?

A: They were clearly pioneers in this area. Their whole strategy and approach are different. There are six states and two territories in Australia, and very early on they developed statewide and territory-wide councils that were independent, one for Queensland, one for Victoria, etc., to provide AIDS education and support services. Also early on they established the National AIDS Task Force, which was a big scientific, medical, research body. There is another National Advisory Committee on AIDS, called NACAIDS, and they handled more public education, counseling, support services.

So, early on they used very direct, blunt language and tried to give a somewhat graphic presentation of what the issues were in everyday language for the public. Although they did discuss monogamy, they really focused on condoms as the most realistic option for most Australians.

This is not to say that it [Australia] is this utopia, with a rational approach and no problems. It's that the people who mattered, the people who are really in charge— the government officials and the local health authorities who could really let the issue die or bring it to the forefront—did not put up with a lot of public pressure. They had to acknowledge the pressure to some extent, but they were very forceful from the beginning in saying they could respect people's personal feelings, but that they had a public health issue. They realized that people are going to continue to engage in unsafe behavior, and in order to prevent the spread of AIDS, they had no choice but to give everyone the information they need to not spread the virus.... Not only did they mention condoms as a very realistic option, but they really focused on them. They didn't just mention them in name only but really went into detail— how to use them, with pictures and print ads, where to go for more information, that you have to use water-based lubricants, use them from start to finish. It's interesting in the United States that condoms are a last resort.

Q: How was this information received?

A: Well, there was still public opposition, but it was more of a minority opposition. They just never got to the point of being powerful enough to preclude the public getting this information. The Australian Broadcasting Tribunal, which governs everything on the airwaves, said in 1987 that it would welcome commercial or public service announcements on AIDS and condoms, as long as they were "responsible." So, there were condom ads on television and in magazines. Unlike here, where we had close to 50,000 cases, and no network television stations would air condom advertisements because of moral concerns and public pressure. They [the Australian government] developed all these different methodologies. Rather than just giving information on television, they had people doing peer work on the street level, people reaching out to prostitutes, people going to the bathhouses to educate, comic books for adolescents, health authorities developed AIDS education messages on beer coasters for the general public, billboards on the highway.

Q: This was all done through the government?

A: For the most part, but there were also local councils that were not government related that also did a lot of education. But the state and territorial health authorities and the national commonwealth health departments developed a lot of it. It just seemed to be a very visible public and government commitment from the beginning.

Unlike the United States where Reagan, despite this rapidly increasing caseload, didn't utter the word "AIDS" in public until spring of 1987, and only then because the third International AIDS Conference was held in Washington, D.C. It came to the point that if he didn't acknowledge it, it could cause serious political ramifications. And when he finally did acknowledge it, he didn't focus on education and counseling or services for people with AIDS, he focused on mandatory screening for supposed high-risk groups that really weren't, such as immigrants. It's much more likely that someone coming to the United States would get infected here than somewhere else, as we have many more cases of AIDS worldwide.

Q: What is Australia's national caseload of AIDS?

A: Nationally, in terms of the numbers, it's not much, but when you consider that their total population is only 16 million people, and you look at the rate of AIDS cases proportionately, its a very high disproportionate amount.

A: Is there anything else you would like to add?

Q: The one thing that everyone thinks about when they think of AIDS education in Australia is the "Grim Reaper" commercial. The national government in 1987 aired this television ad that showed these very frightening-looking grim reapers bowling for human pins. The point of the commercial was to try to convince everyone that AIDS could affect everyone and their lives, that it's not just a gay disease. [In the commercial] they had all these upstanding members of the community literally being bowled down by these grim reapers, with very ominous music, smoke—it looked like a horror movie. It was over the top, very extreme. But it was very interesting to see that it was funded and supported by the national government and aired without any opposition at all from any of the network television stations. The strategy behind it was that people had to be literally scared into recognizing that AIDS could affect them and they had to use this apocalyptic, horror approach to do it. It was very extreme and had public opposition, but they stood behind it, followed it up, and maintained that it served its purpose.

Their whole [educational] approach was different in the sense that even though they had the same concerns and public opposition that we had here, they just never let that shape the public debate. Whereas in the United States, the surgeon general and the Department of Health and Human Services sent out the pamphlet to every home, when they listed safe behavior, they listed mutual monogamy with an un-infected partner—don't have sex, don't use needles. The approach in Australia is abstinence and monogamy are fine, but if you cannot live up to that, use condoms. It's also not "just say no," "don't use drugs," it's "don't share needles." It seemed like the American debate from the beginning, and still, is somewhat tinged with these do's and don'ts and moral concerns.

Q: What are the ethical issues for workplaces in the United States in regard to AIDS?

A: There are some people that think that living with AIDS or with HIV infection— that whole challenge—somehow tests the moral fiber of the nation. It's a matter of whether AIDS will be met with compassion or anger in the workplace, whether people who are ill or have the virus are treated with dignity or as pariahs, in terms of privacy and their right to function as employees and members of the community. It's a matter of whether reason will rule or hysteria will rule. One of the most crucial issues is the extent to which people with AIDS or HIV infection will find themselves excluded from employment, health, or life insurance. The problem is often imposed as an economic one, but it really seems to be at the base a social or moral question.

Early on, it was clear, with a lot of misinformation and hysteria, that employers would randomly and willfully fire employees who did not necessarily have HIV or AIDS, but were just perceived that way. In some workplace settings, in order for some of these people to get health insurance through their workplace, mandatory testing was required to receive it. Confidentiality safeguards, even though they existed on paper, were not the rule of the day.

The issue pertains to the health-care system, and whether or not we're going to create a class of undesirables and uninsurables who really need health care, or whether as a society, we're going to focus more on equity and try to bear the costs and the risk of higher health-care costs, proportionately among society.

There's a whole range of ethical issues pertaining to whether an individual should be tested in the workplace, whether requested by the employer, or for insurance purposes. The problems are the limitations of the test and its validity; unfortunately, it can't tell you when you will go on to develop AIDS, if tested positive; therefore, it's impossible to tell how long an employee can remain performing their work functions.

The challenge [for the employer] is to say legally and ethically that unless you're in danger of infecting someone else on the job, which you're not in the case of AIDS, unless you sleep with someone at work, or share needles with them, we have no grounds to dismiss you, and in fact, encourage you to be a part of this company for as long as your disease makes it possible for you to work here.

It just seems absurd that the last time you want to really have to take on the role of making a public statement, and citing to challenge the bureaucracy, is when you're infected with the virus, when you're even symptomatic and dying.

There are certain moral rights and responsibilities that a company has in dealing with AIDS. In terms of the rights, it is incumbent upon the company to seek a medical opinion, not to make judgments on their own based on life-style or social factors, but to have concrete medical evidence if an employee with AIDS is medically fit to work. It is the employer's right to terminate employment when [AIDS victims are] unable to perform their job function, after reasonable accommodation has been made to transfer, etc., however, with medical benefits to continue. They also have a responsibility and a right to discipline co-workers who are steadfast in their refusal to work with people with AIDS or HIV infection. Often the case is that it's not so much the employer that has the problem with it [the disease], but from the staff— people refusing to sit next to them, eat in the same cafeteria, threatening to leave their jobs.

They also have the right to make pre-employment inquiries, but only if they are related to the applicant's ability to perform the job. I think they have the right to ask for antibody testing. I don't think they have the right to require it. But they should use it only if the results are used for nondiscriminatory purposes—perhaps to project what kind of benefits this person would need, economic projections the company would make, or what kind of programs or services they might need. But they also have a responsibility to provide a safe work environment, to respond to employees with AIDS and HIV infection with compassion, sensitivity, and respect, to provide fair and equitable treatment for those employees.

They also have a responsibility to provide education for all their employees about AIDS. It's a really smart move, because that's what going to dispel misinformation and hysteria, when people really see from medical experts from the outside that you really can't catch it casually. If the government had done a better job early on, people wouldn't be as ignorant as they still are. They also have a responsibility to adopt certain policies early on, and to publicize them to the employees. They also have a responsibility to provide strict procedural safeguards about confidentiality. Employers also have the responsibility to publicize the appropriate resource department or group, to develop services for people who are infected, perhaps for family members, and so on.

Appendix A

RESOURCES

There are many resources available to provide more information about AIDS and the workplace. Resources available at the local level would be found through the local chapter of the American Red Cross, and city, state, or county health departments. Accurate information pertaining to AIDS, state and local health policies, and HIV testing sites may be obtained through the local resources and in the resources listed here. Larger cities have AIDS service agencies that can provide educational speakers and literature in addition to direct services for people with AIDS. All addresses and telephone numbers are current as of January 1990.

NATIONAL ORGANIZATIONS

Centers for Disease Control (CDC), Office of Public Inquiries, 1600 Clifton Road, N.W., Building 1, Room B63, Atlanta, GA 30333, 404–639–3534.

American Red Cross National Headquarters, AIDS Education Program, 17th and D Street, N.W., Washington, DC 20006, 202–639–3223.

National Institutes of Health (NIH), Building 1, Room 307, Bethesda, MD 20892, 301–496–5787.

U.S. Public Health Service (*Surgeon General's Report on AIDS*), Public Affairs Office, Hubert H. Humphrey Building, Room 725–H, 200 Independence Avenue, S.W., Washington, DC 20201, 202–245–6867.

Pan American Health Organization, World Health Organization (WHO), 525 23rd Street, N.W., Room A108, Washington, DC 20037, 202–861–3457.

U.S. Conference of Mayors, 1620 Eye Street, N.W., Washington, DC 20001, 202–293–7330.

Planned Parenthood Federation of America, 2010 Massachusetts Avenue, N.W.,Suite 500, Washington, DC 20036, 202–785–3351.

People with AIDS Coalition, 263A West 19th Street, New York, NY 10011, 212–532–0290.

National Lesbian & Gay Health Foundation, P.O. Box 65472, Washington, DC, 20035, 202–797–3708.

Gay Men's Health Crisis, Box 274, 132 West 24th Street, New York, NY 10011, 212–807–7517.

San Francisco AIDS Foundation, 25 Van Ness Avenue, San Francisco, CA 94102, 415–864–4376.

AIDS Project Los Angeles, 7362 Santa Monica Blvd., Los Angeles, CA 90046, 213–876–AIDS.

AIDS Action Committee, 661 Boylston Street, Boston, MA 02116, 617–437–6200.

Minnesota AIDS Project, 2025 Nicollett Avenue, South #200, Minneapolis, MN 55404, 612–870–7773.

AIDS AND THE WORKPLACE RESOURCES

OSHA Information Office, 200 Constitution Ave., S.W., Room N3647, Washington, DC 20010, 202–523–8148.

National Leadership Coalition on AIDS, Suite 202, 1150 17th Street, N.W., Washington, DC 20036, 202–429–0930.

Service Employees International Union, A.F.L.-C.I.O., 1313 L Street, N.W., Washington, DC 20005, 202–898–2300.

Workplace Health Communications Corporation/Institute for Disease Prevention in the Workplace, 4 Madison Place, Albany, NY 12202, 518–456–1854.

MINORITY AND WOMEN'S ORGANIZATIONS

National Minority AIDS Council, 714 G Street, S.E., Washington, DC 20003, 202–544–1076.

Minority Task Force on AIDS, New York City Council of Churches, 475 Riverside Drive, New York, NY 10015, 212–749–1214.

National Coalition of Hispanic Health and Human Service Organizations, 1030 15th Street, N.W., Suite 1053, Washington, DC 20005, 202–371–2100.

National Jewish AIDS Project, 1082 Columbia Road, Suite 32, Washington, DC 20009, 202–387–3097.

Hispanic AIDS Forum, c/o APRED, 853 Broadway, Suite 2007, New York, NY 10003, 212–870–1902, 212–870–1864.

Haitian Coalition, 50 Court Street, Brooklyn, NY 11201, 718–855–0972.

Mothers of AIDS Patients (MAP), c/o Barbara Peabody, 3403 E Street, San Diego, CA 92102, 619–544–0430.

AWARE (Women and AIDS), Ward 84, San Francisco General Hospital, 995 Potrero Avenue, San Francisco, CA 94110, 415–476–4091.

Stuyvesant Polyclinic, Women and AIDS Counseling Group, 137 Second Avenue, New York, NY 10003, 212–674–0267.

Women and AIDS Project, 1209 Decater Street, N.W., Washington, DC 20011, 202–387–4898.

Women's AIDS Resource Network (WARN), P.O. Box 020525, New York, NY 11202, 718–596–6007.

HEMOPHILIAC AIDS ORGANIZATIONS

World Hemophilia AIDS Center, 2400 S. Flower Street, Los Angeles, CA 90007, 213–742–1357.

National Hemophilia Foundation, Resource and Consultation Center for AIDS/HIV Infection, 110 Greene Street, New York, NY 10012, 212–219–8180.

HOTLINES

National Hotlines

National Gay and Lesbian Crisis Line	800–767–4297
National STD Hotline/American Social Health Assn.	800–227–8922
Public Health Service AIDS Hotline	800–342–AIDS
	800–342–2437

State Hotlines

Alabama	800–455–3741
Alaska	800–478–2437
Arizona	800–334–1540
Arkansas	800–445–7720
California	
Northern	800–FOR–AIDS
Southern	800–922–AIDS
Colorado	303–331–8305
Connecticut	203–566–1157
Delaware	302–995–8422
District of Columbia	202–332–AIDS
Florida	800–FLA–AIDS
Georgia	800–551–2728
Hawaii	808–922–1313
Idaho	208–334–5944
Illinois	800–AID–AIDS
Indiana	317–633–8406
Iowa	800–532–3301
Kansas	800–232–0400
Kentucky	800–654–AIDS
Louisiana	800–992–4379

Maine	800–551–AIDS
Maryland	800–638–6252
Massachusetts	800–235–2331
Minnesota	800–248–AIDS
Mississippi	800–826–2961
Montana	406–252–1212
Nebraska	800–782–2437
Nevada	
Reno	702–329–AIDS
Las Vegas	702–383–1393
New Jersey	800–624–2377
New Mexico	505–827–0006
New York	800–462–1884
North Carolina	919–733–7301
North Dakota	800–592–1861
Ohio	800–332–AIDS
Oklahoma	405–271–6434
Oregon	503–229–5792
Pennsylvania	800–692–7254
Rhode Island	402–227–6502
South Carolina	800–332–AIDS
South Dakota	800–472–2180
Tennessee	800–342–AIDS
Texas	
Dallas	214–559–AIDS
Houston	713–524–AIDS
Utah	800–843–9388
Vermont	800–882–AIDS
West Virginia	800–642–8244
Wisconsin	800–334–AIDS
Wyoming	307–777–7953

NATIONAL RESOURCE SERVICE DIRECTORIES

Educational and informational material regarding HIV and full-blown AIDS may be obtained through these services. The procedure calls for an interested party to receive a summary of their available information, and then relevant materials will be forwarded.

American Foundation for AIDS Research (AMFAR), 1515 Broadway, 36th Floor, New York, NY 10036, 212–719–0033.

National AIDS Information Clearinghouse, U.S. Dept. of Health and Human Services, P.O. Box 6003, Rockville, MD 20850, 1–800–458–5231 (multiple copies), 1–800–342–AIDS (single copies), 1–800–344–SIDA (Spanish speaking), 1–800–AIDS–TTY (TDD/TTY) (deaf and hard of hearing).

INTERNATIONAL RESOURCES

Australia/New Zealand

National AIDS Coordinating Committee, Commonwealth Department of Health, P.O. Box 100, Woden, 06, Australia.

Victorian AIDS Council, P.O. Box 174 Richmond, Melbourne 3121, Australia.

New Zealand AIDS Foundation, Auckland Hospital, Auckland, New Zealand.

Canada

AIDS Vancouver, 1033 Davie Street, Vancouver, B.C.

AIDS Committee of Toronto, 556 Church Street, Toronto, Ontario.

Centretown Community Resources, 100 Argyle Avenue, Ottawa, Ontario.

Comite SIDA du Quebec, 3757 rue Prud'homme, Montreal, Quebec.

Europe

Terrence Higgins Trust, BM AIDS, London, WCIN, England.

AIDS Policy Coordination, Burgo GVO, Prins Hendricklaan 12, 1075 BB Amsterdam, Holland.

Deutsch AIDS-Hilfe, Neibuhrstrasse 71, 1000 Berlin 12, West Germany.

SIDA STUDI, Bruc, 26, prol, 08010 Barcelona, Spain.

Mexico

CONA SIDA, Ministry of Health, Mexico, D.F.

Puerto Rico

Fundacion AIDS de Puerto Rico, Call Box AIDS, Louisa Street Station, San Juan, P.R. 00914.

VIDEOTAPED MATERIAL ON AIDS FOR THE WORKPLACE

Videotapes are available through the local AIDS agencies or the Red Cross.

"Bill: A Special Story," Council on Foundations, 1828 L Street, N.W., Washington, DC 20036, 202–466–6512.

"A Letter from Brian," American Foundation for AIDS Research, Ambrosia Home
   Video Publishing, Dept. 1087, 381 Park Ave., Suite 1601, New York, NY 10016,
   800–526–4663.
"Beyond Fear," Produced by the American Red Cross.
"Don't Forget Sherrie" (provides information for blacks and urban youth) Contact
   the American Red Cross.

GLOBAL PROGRAM ON AIDS

Statement from the Consultation on AIDS and the
Workplace, Geneva, June 27–29, 1988—World
Health Organization in Association with International
Labour Office

A Consultation on AIDS and the Workplace was convened in Geneva by the World
Health Organization's Global Programme on AIDS (GPA) in association with
WHO's Office of Occupational Health and the International Labour Office (ILO),
June 27–29, 1988. Some 36 participants from 18 countries attended, including
representatives of government, union, business, public health, medical, legal and
health education.

Three themes were addressed by the Consultation:

- Risk factors associated with HIV infection in the workplace;
- Responses by business and workers to HIV/AIDS; and
- Use of the workplace for health education activities.

The Consultation developed the following consensus statement:

I. General Statement

Infection with the human immunodeficiency virus (HIV) and the acquired immunodeficiency syndrome (AIDS) represents an urgent worldwide problem with
broad social, cultural, economic, political, ethical and legal dimensions and impact.
National and international AIDS prevention and control efforts have called upon
the entire range of health and social services. In this process, in many countries,
HIV/AIDS prevention and control problems and efforts have highlighted the weak-
nesses, inequities and imbalances in existing health and social systems. Therefore,
in combatting AIDS, an opportunity exists to re-examine and evaluate existing
systems as well as assumptions and relationships.

Today there are 2.3 billion economically active people in the world. The workplace plays a central role in the lives of people everywhere. A consideration of HIV/AIDS and the workplace will strengthen the capacity to deal effectively with the problem of HIV/AIDS at the local, national and international levels.

In addition, concern about the spread of HIV/AIDS provides an opportunity to re-examine the workplace environment. It provides workers, employers and their organizations, and where appropriate, governmental agencies and other organizations, with an opportunity to create an atmosphere conducive to caring for and promoting the health of all workers. This may involve a range of issues and concerns, not only individual behavior, but also addresses matters of collective responsibility. It provides an opportunity to re-examine working relationships in a way that promotes human rights and dignity, ensures freedom from discrimination and stigmatization, and improves working practices and procedures.

II. Introduction

Epidemiological studies from throughout the world have demonstrated that the human immunodeficiency virus (HIV) is transmitted in only 3 ways:

(a) through sexual intercourse (including semen donation);
(b) through blood (principally blood transfusions and non-sterile injection equipment; also includes organ or tissue transplant);
(c) from infected mother to infant (perinatal transmission).

There is no evidence to suggest that HIV transmission involves insects, food, water, sneezing, coughing, toilets, urine, swimming pools, sweat, tears, shared eating and drinking utensils or other items such as protective clothing or telephones. There is no evidence to suggest that HIV can be transmitted by casual, person-to-person contact in any setting.

HIV infection and AIDS (HIV/AIDS) are global problems. At any point in time, the majority of HIV-infected persons are healthy; over time, they may develop AIDS or other HIV-related conditions or they may remain healthy. It is estimated that approximately 90% of the 5–10 million HIV-infected persons worldwide are in the economically productive age-group. Therefore, it is natural that questions are asked about the implications of HIV/AIDS for the workplace.

In the vast majority of occupations and occupational settings, work does not involve a risk of acquiring or transmitting HIV between workers, from worker to client, or from client to worker. This document deals with workers who are employed in these occupations. Another consultation to be organized by the WHO Global Programme on AIDS will consider those occupations or occupational situations, such as health workers, in which a recognized risk of acquiring or transmitting HIV may occur.

The purpose of this document is to provide guidance for those considering issues raised by HIV/AIDS and the workplace. Such consideration may involve review of existing health policies or development of new ones. This document focuses upon the basic principles and core components of policies regarding HIV/AIDS and the workplace.

By addressing the issues raised by HIV/AIDS and the workplace, workers, employers and governments will be able to contribute actively to local, national and international efforts to prevent and control AIDS, in accordance with WHO's Global AIDS Strategy.

III. Policy Principles

Protection of the human rights and dignity of HIV-infected persons, including persons with AIDS, is essential to the prevention and control of HIV/AIDS. Workers with HIV infection who are healthy should be treated the same as any other worker. Workers with HIV-related illness, including AIDS, should be treated the same as any other worker with an illness.

Most people with HIV/AIDS want to continue working, which enhances their physical and mental well-being and they should be entitled to do so. They should be enabled to contribute their creativity and productivity in a supportive occupational setting.

The World Health Assembly resolution (WHA41.24) entitled "Avoidance of discrimination in relation to HIV-infected people and people with AIDS" urges Member States:

"(1) to foster a spirit of understanding and compassion for HIV-infected people and people with AIDS...;

(2) to protect the human rights and dignity of HIV-infected people and people with AIDS and to avoid discriminatory action against, and stigmatization of them in the provision, services, employment and travel;

(3) to ensure the confidentiality of HIV testing and to promote the availability of confidential counselling and other support services."

The approach taken to HIV/AIDS and the workplace must take into account the existing social and legal context, as well as national health policies and the Global AIDS Strategy.

IV. Policy Development and Implementation

Consistent policies and procedures should be developed at national and enterprise levels through consultations between workers, employers and their organizations, and where appropriate, governmental agencies and other organizations. It is recommended that such policies be developed and implemented before HIV-related questions arise in the workplace. Policy development and implementation is a dynamic process, not a static event. Therefore, HIV/AIDS workplace policies should be:

(a) communicated to all concerned;

(b) continually reviewed in the light of epidemiological and other scientific information;

(c) monitored for their successful implementation;

(d) evaluated for their effectiveness.

V. Policy components

A. Persons applying for employment: Pre-employment HIV/AIDS screening as part of the assessment of fitness to work is unnecessary and should not be required. Screening of this kind refers to direct methods (HIV testing) or indirect methods (assessment of risk behaviours) or to questions about HIV tests already taken. Pre-employment HIV/AIDS screening for insurance or other purposes raises serious concerns about discrimination and merits close and further scrutiny.

B. Persons in employment:

1. HIV/AIDS screening: HIV/AIDS screening, whether direct (HIV testing), indirect (assessment or risk behaviours) or asking questions about tests already taken, should not be required.

2. Confidentiality: Confidentiality regarding all medical information, including HIV/AIDS status, must be maintained.

3. Informing the employer: There should be no obligation of the employee to inform the employer regarding his or her HIV/AIDS status.

4. Protection of employee: Persons in the workplace affected by, or perceived to be affected by HIV/AIDS, must be protected from stigmatization and discrimination by co-workers, unions, employers or clients. Information and education are essential to maintain the climate of mutual understanding necessary to ensure this protection.

5. Access to services for employees: Employees and their families should have access to information and educational programmes on HIV/AIDS, as well as to relevant counselling and appropriate referral.

6. Benefits: HIV-infected employees should not be discriminated against, including access to and receipt of standard social security benefits and occupationally related benefits.

7. Reasonable changes in working arrangements: HIV infection by itself is not associated with any limitation in fitness to work. If fitness to work is impaired by HIV-related illness, reasonable alternative working arrangements should be made.

8. Continuation of employment relationship: HIV infection is not a cause for termination of employment. As with many other illnesses, persons with HIV-related illnesses should be able to work as long as medically fit for available, appropriate work.

9. First aid: In any situation requiring first aid in the workplace, precautions need to be taken to reduce the risk of transmitting blood-borne infections, including hepatitis B. These standard precautions will be equally effective against HIV transmission.

APPENDIX C

UPDATE: UNIVERSAL PRECAUTIONS FOR PREVENTION OF TRANSMISSION OF HUMAN IMMUNODEFICIENCY VIRUS, HEPATITIS B VIRUS, AND OTHER BLOODBORNE PATHOGENS IN HEALTH-CARE SETTINGS

INTRODUCTION

The purpose of this report is to clarify and supplement the CDC publication entitled "Recommendations for Prevention of HIV Transmission in Health-Care Settings." (The August 1987 publication should be consulted for general information and specific recommendations not addressed in this update.)[1]

In 1983, CDC published a document entitled "Guideline for Isolation Precautions in Hospitals"[2] that contained a section entitled "Blood and Body Fluid Precautions." The recommendations in this section called for blood and body fluid precautions when a patient was known or suspected to be infected with bloodborne pathogens. In August 1987, CDC published a document entitled "Recommendations for Prevention of HIV Transmission in Health-Care Settings."[1] In contrast to the 1983 document, the 1987 document recommended that blood and body fluid precautions be consistently used for all patients regardless of their bloodborne infection status. This extension of blood and body fluid precautions to *all* patients is referred to as "Universal precautions," blood and certain body fluids of all patients are considered potentially infectious for human immunodeficiency virus (HIV), hepatitis B virus (HBV), and other bloodborne pathogens.

Universal precautions are intended to prevent parenteral, mucous membrane, and nonintact skin exposures of health-care workers to bloodborne pathogens. In addition, immunization with HBV vaccine is recommended as an important adjunct to universal precautions for health-care workers who have exposures to blood.[3,4]

Since the recommendations for universal precautions were published in August 1987, CEC and the Food and Drug Administration (FDA) have received requests for clarification of the following issues: (1) body fluids to which universal precautions apply, (2) use of protective barriers, (3) use of gloves for phlebotomy, (4) selection of gloves for use while observing universal precautions, and (5) need for making changes in waste management programs as a result of adopting universal precautions.

BODY FLUIDS TO WHICH UNIVERSAL PRECAUTIONS APPLY

Universal precautions apply to blood and to other body fluids containing visible blood. Occupational transmission of HIV and HBV to health-care workers by blood is documented.[4,5] Blood is the single most important source of HIV, HBV, and other bloodborne pathogens in the occupational setting. Infection control efforts for HIV, HBV, and other bloodborne pathogens must focus on preventing exposures to blood as well as on delivery of HBV immunization.

Universal precautions also apply to semen and vaginal secretions. Although both of these fluids have been implicated in the sexual transmission of HIV and HBV, they have not been implicated in occupational transmission from patient to health-care worker. This observation is not unexpected, since exposure to semen in the usual health-care setting is limited, and the routine practice of wearing gloves for performing vaginal examinations protects health-care workers from exposure to potentially infectious vaginal secretions.

Universal precautions also apply to tissues and to the following fluids: cerebro-spinal fluid (CSF), synovial fluid, pleural fluid, peritoneal fluid, pericardial fluid, and amniotic fluid. The risk of transmission of HIV and HBV from these fluids is unknown; epidemiologic studies in the health-care and community setting are currently inadequate to assess the potential risk to health-care workers from occupational exposures to them. However, HIV has been isolated from CSF, synovial, and amniotic fluid,[6-8] and HBsAg has been detected in synovial fluid, amniotic fluid, and peritoneal fluid.[9-11] One case of HIV transmission was reported after a percutaneous exposure to bloody pleural fluid obtained by needle aspiration.[12] Whereas aseptic procedures used to obtain these fluids for diagnostic or therapeutic purposes protect health-care workers from skin exposures, they cannot prevent penetrating injuries due to contaminated needles or other sharp instruments.

BODY FLUIDS TO WHICH UNIVERSAL PRECAUTIONS DO NOT APPLY

Universal precautions do not apply to feces, nasal secretions, sputum, sweat, tears, urine, and vomitus unless they contain visible blood. The risk of transmission of HIV and HBV from these fluids and materials is extremely low or nonexistent. HIV has been isolated and HBsAg has been demonstrated in some of these fluids; however, epidemiologic studies in the health-care and community setting have not implicated these fluids or materials in the transmission of HIV and HBV infections.[13,14] Some of the above fluids and excretions represent a potential source for nosocomial and community-acquired infections with other pathogens, and recommendations for preventing the transmission of nonbloodborne pathogens have been published.[2]

PRECAUTIONS FOR OTHER BODY FLUIDS IN SPECIAL SETTINGS

Human breast milk has been implicated in perinatal transmission of HIV, and HBsAg has been found in the milk of mothers infected with HBV.[10,13] However, occupational exposure to human breast milk has not been implicated in the transmission of HIV nor HBV infection to health-care workers. Moreover, the health-care worker will not have the same type of intensive exposure to breast milk as the nursing neonate. Whereas universal precautions do not apply to human breast milk, gloves may be worn by health-care workers in situations where exposures to breast milk might be frequent, for example, in breast milk banking.

Saliva of some persons infected with HBV has been shown to contain HBV-DNA at concentrations 1/1,000 to 1/10,000 of that found in the infected person's serum.[15] HBsAg-positive saliva has been shown to be infectious when injected into experimental animals and in human bite exposures.[16–18] However, HBsAg-positive saliva has not been shown to be infectious when applied to oral mucous membranes in experimental primate studies[18] or through contamination of musical instruments or cardiopulmonary resuscitation dummies used by HBV carriers.[19,20] Epidemiologic studies of nonsexual household contacts of HIV-infected patients, including several small series in which HIV transmission failed to occur after bites or after percutaneous inoculation or contamination of cuts and open wounds with saliva from HIV-infected patients, suggest that the potential for salivary transmission of HIV is remote.[5,13,14,21,22] One case report from Germany has suggested the possibility of transmission of HIV in a household setting from an infected child to a sibling through a human bite.[23] The bite did not break the skin or result in bleeding. Since the date of seroconversion to HIV was not known for either child in this case, evidence for the role of saliva in the transmission of virus is unclear.[23] Another case report suggested the possibility of transmission of HIV from husband to wife by contact with saliva during kissing.[24] However, follow-up studies did not confirm HIV infection in the wife.[21]

Universal precautions do not apply to saliva. General infection control practices already in existence—including the use of gloves for digital examination of mucous membranes and endotracheal suctioning, and handwashing after exposure to saliva—should further minimize the minute risk, if any, for salivary transmission of HIV and HBV.[1,25] Gloves need not be worn when feeding patients and when wiping saliva from skin.

Special precautions, however, are recommended for dentistry.[1] Occupationally acquired infection with HBV in dental workers has been documented,[4] and two possible cases of occupationally acquired HIV infection involving dentists have been reported.[5,26] During dental procedures, contamination of saliva with blood is predictable, trauma to health-care workers' hands is common, and blood spattering may occur. Infection control precautions for dentistry minimize the potential for nonintact skin and mucous membrane contact of dental health-care workers to blood-contaminated saliva of patients. In addition, the use of gloves for oral examinations and treatment in the dental setting may also protect the patient's oral mucous membranes from exposures to blood, which may occur from breaks in the skin of dental workers' hands.

USE OF PROTECTIVE BARRIERS

Protective barriers reduce the risk of exposure of the health-care worker's skin or mucous membranes to potentially infective materials. For universal precautions, protective barriers reduce the risk of exposure to blood, body fluids containing visible blood, and other fluids to which universal precautions apply. Examples of protective barriers include gloves, gowns, masks, and protective eyewear. Gloves should reduce the incidence of contamination of hands, but they cannot prevent penetrating injuries due to needles or other sharp instruments. Masks and protective eyewear or face shields should reduce the incidence of contamination of mucous membranes of the mouth, nose, and eyes.

Universal precautions are intended to supplement rather than replace recommendations for routine infection control, such as handwashing and using gloves to prevent gross microbial contamination of hands.[27] Because specifying the types of barriers needed for every possible clinical situation is impractical, some judgment must be exercised.

The risk of nosocomial transmission of HIV, HBV, and other bloodborne pathogens can be minimized if health-care workers use the following general guidelines (the August 1987 publication should be consulted for general information and specific recommendations not addressed in this update):

1. Take care to prevent injuries when using needles, scalpels, and other sharp instruments or devices; when handling sharp instruments after procedures; when cleaning used instruments; and when disposing of used needles. Do not recap used needles by hand; do not remove used needles from disposable syringes by hand; and do not bend, break or otherwise manipulate used needles by hand. Place used disposable syringes and needles, scalpel blades, and other sharp items in puncture-resistant containers for disposal. Locate the puncture-resistant containers as close to the use area as is practical.

2. Use protective barriers to prevent exposure to blood, body fluids containing visible blood, and other fluids to which universal precautions apply. The type of protective barrier(s) should be appropriate for the procedure being performed and the type of exposure anticipated.

3. Immediately and thoroughly wash hands and other skin surfaces that are contaminated with blood, body fluids containing visible blood, or other body fluids to which universal precautions apply.

GLOVE USE FOR PHLEBOTOMY

Gloves should reduce the incidence of blood contamination of hands during phlebotomy (drawing blood samples), but they cannot prevent penetrating injuries caused by needles or other sharp instruments. The likelihood of hand contamination with blood containing HIV, HBV, or other bloodborne pathogens during phlebotomy depends on several factors: (1) The skill and technique of the health-care worker, (2) the frequency with which the health-care worker performs the procedure (other factors being equal, the cumulative risk of blood exposure is higher for a health-care worker who performs more procedures), (3) whether the procedure occurs in a routine or emergency situation (where blood contact may be more likely), and (4) the prevalence of infection with bloodborne pathogens in the patient population. The likelihood of infection after skin exposure to blood containing HIV or HBV will depend on the concentration of virus (viral concentration is much higher for hepatitis B than for HIV), the duration of contact, the presence of skin lesions on the hands of the health-care worker, and for HBV—the immune status of the health-care worker. Although not accurately quantified, the risk of HIV infection following intact skin contact with infective blood is certainly much less than the 0.5% risk following percutaneous needlestick exposures.[5] In universal precautions, all blood is assumed to be potentially infective for bloodborne pathogens, but in certain settings (e.g., volunteer blood-donation centers) the prevalence of infection with some bloodborne pathogens (e.g., HIV, HBV) is known to be very low. Some institutions have relaxed recommendations for using gloves for phlebotomy procedures by skilled phlebotomists in settings where the prevalence of bloodborne pathogens is known to be very low.

Institutions that judge that routine gloving for all phlebotomies is not necessary should periodically reevaluate their policy. Gloves should always be available to health-care workers who wish to use them for phlebotomy. In addition, the following general guidelines apply:

1. Use gloves for performing phlebotomy when the health-care worker has cuts, scratches, or other breaks in his/her skin.

2. Use gloves in situations where the health-care worker judges that hand contamination with blood may occur, for example, when performing phlebotomy on an uncooperative patient.

3. Use gloves for performing finger and/or heel sticks on infants and children.

4. Use gloves when persons are receiving training in phlebotomy.

SELECTION OF GLOVES

The Center for Devices and Radiological Health, FDA, has responsibility for regulating the medical glove industry. Medical gloves include those marketed as sterile surgical or nonsterile examination gloves made of vinyl or latex. General purpose utility ("rubber") gloves are also used in the health-care setting, but they are not regulated by FDA since they are not promoted for medical use. There are no reported differences in barrier effectiveness between intact latex and intact vinyl used to manufacture gloves. Thus, the type of gloves selected should be appropriate for the task being performed.

The following general guidelines are recommended:

1. Use sterile gloves for procedures involving contact with normally sterile areas of the body.

2. Use examination gloves for procedures involving contact with mucous membranes, unless otherwise indicated, and for other patient care or diagnostic procedures that do not require the use of sterile gloves.

3. Change gloves between patient contacts.

4. Do not wash or disinfect surgical or examination gloves for reuse. Washing with surfactants may cause "wicking," i.e., the enhanced penetration of liquids through undetected holes in the glove. Disinfecting agents may cause deterioration.

5. Use general-purpose utility gloves (e.g., rubber household gloves) for housekeeping chores involving potential blood contact and for instrument cleaning and decontamination procedures. Utility gloves may be decontaminated and reused but should be discarded if they are peeling, cracked, or discolored, or if they have punctures, tears, or other evidence of deterioration.

WASTE MANAGEMENT

Universal precautions are not intended to change waste management programs previously recommended by CDC for health-care settings.[1] Policies for defining, collecting, storing, decontaminating, and disposing of invective waste are generally determined by institutions in accordance with state and local regulations. Information regarding waste management regulations in health-care settings may be obtained from state or local health departments or agencies responsible for waste management.

Reported by: Center for Devices and Radiological Health, Food and Drug Administration. Hospital Infections Program, AIDS Program, and Hepatitis B, Division of Viral Diseases, Center for Infectious Diseases, National Institute for Occupational Safety and Health, CDC.

Editorial Note: Implementation of universal precautions does not eliminate the need for other category- or disease-specific isolation precautions, such as enteric precautions for infectious diarrhea or isolation for pulmonary tuberculosis.[1,2] In addition to universal precautions, detailed precautions have been developed for the following procedures and/or settings in which prolonged or intensive exposures to blood occur: invasive procedures, dentistry, autopsies or morticians' services, dialysis, and the clinical laboratory. These detailed precautions are found in the August 21, 1987, "Recommendations for Prevention of HIV Transmission in Health-Care Settings."[1] In addition, specific precautions have been developed for research laboratories.[28]

Source: Reprinted by the U.S. Department of Health and Human Services, Public Health Service, Centers for Disease Control, from *Morbidity and Mortality Weekly Report*, June 24, 1988, Vol. 37, No. 24, pp. 337–82, 387–88.

REFERENCES

1. Centers for Disease Control. Recommendations for prevention of HIV transmission in health-care settings. *MMWR* 1987;36 (suppl no. 2S).

2. Garner, J.S.; Simmons, B. P. Guideline for isolation precautions in hospitals. *Infection Control* 1983:4;245–325.

3. Immunization Practices Advisory Committee. Recommendations for protection against viral hepatitis. *MMWR* 1985;34:313–24,329–35.

4. Department of Labor, Department of Health and Human Services. Joint advisory notice: protection against occupational exposure to hepatitis B virus (HBV) and human immunodeficiency virus (HIV). Washington, DC: U.S. Department of Labor, U.S. Department of Health and Human Services, 1987.

5. Centers for Disease Control. Update: Acquired immunodeficiency syndrome and human immunodeficiency virus infection among health-care workers. *MMWR* 1988;37:229–34,239.

6. Hollander, H.; Levy, J. A. Neurologic abnormalities and recovery of human immunodeficiency virus from cerebrospinal fluid. *Annals of Internal Medicine* 1987;106:692–95.

7. Wirthrington, R. H.; Cornes, P.; Harris, J.R.W. et al. Isolation of human

immunodeficiency virus from synovial fluid of a patient with reactive arthritis. *British Medical Journal* 1987;294:484.

8. Mundy, D. D.; Schinazi, R. F.; Gerber, A. R.; Nahmias, A. J.; Randall, H. W. Human immunodeficiency virus isolated from amniotic fluid. *Lancet* 1987;2:459–60.

9. Onion, D. K.; Crumpacker, C. S.; Gilliland, B. C. Arthritis of hepatitis associated with Australia antigen. *Annals of Internal Medicine* 1971;75:29–33.

10. Lee, A.K.Y.; 1p H.M.H.; Wong V.C.W. Mechanisms of maternal-fetal transmission of hepatitis B virus. *Journal of Infectious Disease* 1978;138:668–71.

11. Bond, W. W.; Petersen, N. J.; Gravelle, C. R.; Favero, M. S. Hepatitis B virus in peritoneal dialysis fluid: A potential hazard. *Dialysis and Transplantation* 1982;11:592–600.

12. Oskenhendler, E.; Harzic, M.; Le Roux, J.-M.; Rabian, C.; Clauvel, J. P. HIV infection with seroconversion after a superficial needlestick injury to the finger (Letter). *New England Journal of Medicine* 1986;315:582.

13. Lifson, A. R. Do alternate modes for transmission of human immunodeficiency virus exist? A review. *JAMA* 1988;259:1353–56.

14. Friedland, G. H.; Saltzman, B. R.; Rogers M. F. et al. Lack of transmission of HTLV–III/LAV infection to household contacts of patients with AIDS or AIDS-related complex with oral candidiasis. *New England Journal of Medicine* 1986;314:344–49.

15. Jenison, S. A.; Lemon, S. M.; Baker, L.N.; Newbold, J. E. Quantitative analysis of hepatitis B Virus DNA in saliva and semen of chronically infected homosexual men. *Journal of Infectious Disease* 1987;156:299–306.

16. Cancio-Bello, T. P.; de Medina, M.; Shorey, J.; Valledor, M. D.; Schiff, E. R. An institutional outbreak of hepatitis B related to a human biting carrier. *Journal of Infectious Disease* 1982;146:652–56.

17. MacQuarrie, M. B.; Forghani, B.; Wolochow, D. A. Hepatitis B transmitted by a human bite. *JAMA* 1974;230:723–74.

18. Scott, R. M.; Snitbhan, R.; Bancroft, W. H.; Alter, H. J.; Tingpalapong, M. Experimental transmission of hepatitis B virus by semen and saliva. *Journal of Infectious Disease* 1980;142:67–71.

19. Glaser, J. B.; Nadler, J. P. Hepatitis B. virus in a cardiopulmonary resuscitation training course: Risk of transmission from a surface antigen-positive participant. *Archives of Internal Medicine* 1985;145:1653–55.

20. Osterholm, M. T.; Bravo, E. R., Crosson, J. T. et al. Lack of transmission of viral hepatitis type B after oral exposure to HBsAg-positive saliva. *British Medical Journal* 1979;2:1263–64.

21. Curran, J. W.; Jaffe, H. W.; Hardy, A. M. et al. Epidemiology of HIV infection and AIDS in the United States. *Science* 1988;239:610–16.

22. Jason, J. M.; McDougal, J. S.; Dixon, G. et al. HTLV–III/LAV antibody and immune status of household contacts and sexual partners of persons with hemophilia. *JAMA* 1986;255:212–15.

23. Wahn, V.; Dramer, H. H.; Voit, T.; Bruster, H. T.; Scrampical, B.; Scheid, A. Horizontal transmission of HIV infection between two siblings (letter). *Lancet* 1986;2:694.

24. Salahuddin, S. Z.; Groopman, J.E.; Markham, P. D. et al. HTLV–III in symptom-free seronegative persons. *Lancet* 1984;2:1418–20.

25. Simmons, B. P.; Wong, E. S. Guideline for prevention of nosocomial pneumonia. Atlanta: U.S. Department of Health and Human Services, Public Health Service Centers for Disease Control, 1982.

26. Klein, R. S.; Phelan, J. A.; Freeman, K. et al. Low occupational risk of human immunodeficiency virus infection among dental professionals. *New England Journal of Medicine* 1988;318:86–90.

27. Garner, J. S.; Favero, M. S. Guideline for handwashing and hospital environmental control, 1985. Atlanta: U.S. Department of Health and Human Services, Public Health Service, Centers for Disease Control, 1985 (HHS pub.no.99–1117).

28. Centers for Disease Control. 1988 Agent summary statement for human immunodeficiency virus and report on laboratory-acquired infection with human immunodeficiency virus. *MMWR* 1988;37(suppl no. S4:1S–22S).

SUMMARY OF THE AMENDMENT IN THE NATURE OF A SUBSTITUTE TO THE AMERICANS WITH DISABILITIES ACT OF 1989 (AUGUST 2, 1989)

FINDINGS, PURPOSE, AND DEFINITIONS

The purpose of the Act is to provide a clear and comprehensive national mandate to end discrimination against individuals with disabilities; provide enforceable standards addressing discrimination against individuals with disabilities; and ensure that the Federal government plays a central role in enforcing these standards on behalf of individuals with disabilities.

The term "disability" is defined to mean, with respect to an individual—a physical or mental impairment that substantially limits one or more of the major life activities of such individual, a record of such an impairment, or being regarded as having such an impairment. This is the same definition used for purposes of Section 503 and Section 504 of the Rehabilitation Act of 1973 and the recent amendments to the Fair Housing Act.

TITLE I: EMPLOYMENT

The provisions in Title I of the bill use or incorporate by reference many of the definitions in Title VII of the Civil Rights Act of 1964 (employee, employer, Commission, person, labor organization, employment agency, joint labor-management committee, commerce, industry affecting commerce). For the first two years after the effective date of the Act, only employers with 25 or more employees are covered. Thereafter, the number goes down to 15.

A "qualified individual with a disability" means an individual with a disability who, with or without reasonable accommodation, can perform the essential functions of the employment position that such individual holds or desires. This definition is comparable to the definition used for purposes of Section 504.

Using the Section 504 legal framework as the model, the bill specifies that no entity covered by the Act shall discriminate against any qualified individual with a disability because of such individual's disability in regard to application procedures, the hiring or discharge of employees and all terms, conditions, and privileges of employment.

Discrimination includes, for example: limiting, segregating, or classifying a job application or employee in a way that adversely affects his or her opportunities or status; participating in contractual or other arrangements that have the effect of subjecting individuals with disabilities to discrimination; and using criteria or methods of administration that have a discriminatory effect or perpetuate discrimination of others subject to common administrative control.

In addition, discrimination includes excluding or denying equal opportunities to a qualified nondisabled individual because of the known disability of an individual with whom the qualified individual is known to have a relationship or association.

Discrimination also includes not making *reasonable accommodations* to the known limitations of a qualified individual with a disability unless such entity can demonstrate that the accommodation would impose an *undue hardship* on the operation of the business. Discrimination also includes the denial of employment opportunities because a qualified individual with a disability needs a reasonable accommodation.

The definition of the term "reasonable accommodation" included in the bill is comparable to the definition in the Section 504 legal framework. The term includes: making existing facilities accessible, job restructuring, part-time or modified work schedules, reassignment to a vacant position, acquisition or modification of equipment or devices, appropriate adjustment or modifications of policies, examinations, and training materials, the provision of qualified readers and interpreters, and other similar accommodations.

Discrimination also includes the imposition or application of tests and other selection criteria that screen out or tend to screen out an individual with a disability or a class of individuals with disabilities unless the test or other selection criteria is shown to be job-related for the position in question and is consistent with business necessity.

The bill also includes the pre-employment inquiries provision from Section 504 which permits employers to make pre-employment inquiries into the ability of an applicant to perform job-related functions but prohibits inquiries as to whether an applicant or employee is an individual with a disability or as to the nature or severity of such disability. Employers are permitted to undertake post-offer/pre-entrance medical examinations so long as the results are kept confidential, all entering employees take the examinations, and the results are used only in accordance with the provisions of the title.

The bill also prohibits employers from conducting or requiring a medical examination and inquiries as to whether an employee has a disability or the nature or severity of the disability unless such examination or inquiry is shown to be job-related and consistent with business necessity.

The bill also specifies several defenses to charges of discrimination under the Act. First, an employer need not hire an applicant or retain an employee who it shows has a currently contagious disease or infection that poses a direct threat to the health or safety of other individuals in the workplace.

With respect to drug addicts and alcoholics, an employer may prohibit the use of alcohol or illegal drugs at the workplace by all employees; may require that employees not be under the influence of alcohol or illegal drugs at the workplace; may require that employees conform their behavior to requirements established pursuant to the Drug Free Workplace Act; and may hold a drug user or alcoholic to the same qualification standards for employment or job performance and behavior to which it holds other individuals, even if any unsatisfactory performance or behavior is related to the drug use or alcoholism of such individual. . . .

Consistent with Title VII of the Civil Rights Act of 1964, every covered entity must post notices in an accessible format describing the applicable provisions of this Act. The Commission is also directed to promulgate regulations within 1 year in an accessible format.

The bill incorporates by reference the remedies and procedures set out in Section 706, 707, 709, and Section 710 of Title VII of the Civil Rights Act of 1964.

The effective date of Title I is 24 months after the date of enactment.

TITLE II: PUBLIC SERVICES

Section 504 only applies to entities receiving Federal financial assistance. Title II of the bill makes all activities of State and local governments subject to the types of prohibitions against discrimination against a qualified individual with a disability included in Section 504 (nondiscrimination) and Section 505 (the enforcement procedures).

A "qualified individual with a disability" means an individual with a disability who, with or without reasonable modifications to rules, policies, and practices, or the removal of architectural, communication, and transportation barriers or the provision of auxiliary aids and services, meets the essential eligibility requirements for the receipt of services or the participation in programs or activities provided by a department, agency, special purpose district, or other instrumentality of a State or a local government. . . .

The bill directs the Attorney General to promulgate regulations within one year in an accessible format that implement the provisions generally applicable to state and local governments. These regulations must be consistent with the coordination of regulations issued in 1978 that governed the regulations applicable to recipients of Federal financial assistance, except with respect to "existing facilities" and "communications," in which case the Federally conducted regulations apply.

Within one year from the date of enactment, the Secretary of Transportation is directed to issue regulations in an accessible format that include standards which are consistent with minimum guidelines and requirements issued by the Architectural and Transportation Barriers Compliance Board.

This title takes effect eighteen months from the date of enactment with the exception of the provision applicable to the purchase of new buses which takes effect on the date of enactment.

TITLE III: PUBLIC ACCOMMODATIONS AND SERVICES OPERATED BY PRIVATE ENTITIES

Title III specifies that no individual shall be discriminated against on the basis of disability in the full and equal enjoyment of the goods, services, facilities, privileges, advantages, and accommodations of any place of public accommodation.

The bill lists categories of establishments that are considered public accommodations. The list includes restaurants, hotels, doctors' offices, pharmacists, grocery stores, museums, and homeless shelters. This list does not include religious institutions or entities controlled by religious institutions.

The bill includes general and specific categories of discrimination prohibited by the Act. In general, it is considered discriminatory to subject an individual or class of individuals, directly or indirectly, on the basis of disability, to any of the following:

(1) denying the opportunity to participate in or benefit from an opportunity;

(2) affording an opportunity that is not equal to that afforded others;

(3) providing an opportunity that is less effective than that provided to others;

(4) providing an opportunity that is different or separate, unless such action is necessary to provide the individuals with an opportunity that is as effective as that provided to others; however, an individual with a disability shall not be denied the opportunity to participate in such programs or activities that are not separate or different.

Further, an entity may not directly or indirectly use standards or criteria or methods of administration that have the effect of subjecting an individual to discrimination on the basis of disability or perpetuate discrimination by others who are subject to common administrative control or are agencies of the same State. Nor can an entity discriminate against an individual because of the known association of that individual with another individual with a disability.

Specific categories of discrimination include:

• The imposition or application of eligibility criteria that screen out or tend to screen out an individual with a disability unless such criteria can be shown to be necessary for the provision of the goods or services being offered.

• A failure to make reasonable modifications in rules and policies and procedures when necessary to afford meaningful opportunity unless the entity can demonstrate that the modifications would fundamentally alter the nature of the program....

Examples of discrimination include:

• the imposition or application of eligibility criteria that screen out or tend to screen out an individual with a disability;

• a failure to make reasonable modifications to criteria, provide auxiliary aids and services, and remove barriers consistent with the standards set out above;...

The bill uses the model of title II of the Civil Rights Act of 1964 (injunctive relief) and includes the pattern and practice authority (including civil penalties) from the recently enacted Fair Housing Act.

The effect date of this title is 18 months from the date of enactment....

TITLE V: MISCELLANEOUS PROVISIONS

Title V explains the relationship between Section 504 and this Act and this Act and State laws that provide greater protections. This title also explains that this bill is not to be construed as regulating the underwriting, classifying, and administering of insurance risks. Title V also includes an antiretaliation provision; a prohibition against interference, coercion, or intimidation; directs the Architectural and Transportation Barriers Compliance Board to issue minimum guidelines; and makes it clear that States are not immune under the 11th Amendment for violations of the Act.

With respect to attorney's fees, the bill specifies that in any action or administrative proceeding commenced under the Act, the court, or agency, in its discretion, may allow the prevailing party, other than the United States, a reasonable attorney's fee, including litigation expenses, and costs, and the United States shall be liable for the foregoing the same as a private individual.

*This legislation has been passed as law in 1990.

OSHA GUIDELINES: PROTECTION AGAINST OCCUPATIONAL EXPOSURE TO HEPATITIS B VIRUS AND HUMAN IMMUNODEFICIENCY VIRUS

Department of Labor
Office of the Secretary
Joint Advisory Notice; Department of Labor/Department of Health and Human Services; HBV/HIV

The Department of Labor hereby gives notice of a joint cover letter and Joint Advisory Notice, entitled "Protection Against Occupational Exposure to Hepatitis B Virus (HBV) and Human Immunodeficiency Virus (HIV)," which will be mailed on or about October 30, 1987, to health-care employers throughout the United States.

The letter and notice are attached hereto and are being mailed to approximately 500,000 employers. Signed at Washington, D.C. this 21st day of October 1987. Michael E. Baroody, Assistant Secretary for Policy, U.S. Department of Labor.

U.S. Department of Labor
Secretary of Labor
Washington, D.C.

October 30, 1987

Dear Health-Care Employer: We are writing to you about a serious health-care problem that faces all Americans but is particularly acute for health-care workers. That problem is potential exposure to hepatitis B virus (HBV), human immune deficiency virus (HIV), which causes acquired immunodeficiency syndrome (AIDS), and other blood-borne diseases.

The Centers for Disease Control (CDC), which is part of the U.S. Department of Health and Human Services (HHS), believes that as many as 18,000 health-care workers per year may be infected by the HBV. Nearly ten percent of those who become infected become long-term carriers of the virus and may have to give up their profession. Several hundred health-care workers will become acutely ill or jaundiced from hepatitis B, and as many as 300 health-care workers may die annually as a result of hepatitis B infections or complication.

Infection with the HIV in the workplace represents a small but real hazard to health-care workers. Fewer than ten cases have been reported to date, but it is not clear that these include all such infections. The CDC expects that with 1.5 million persons now believed to be infected by HIV, the number of AIDS cases in the general population may grow to as many as 270,000 by 1991 from the 40,000 which had been reported by August, 1987. The increases in AIDS cases and in the number of individuals who are infected with the virus will mean an increased potential for exposure to health-care workers.

Fortunately there are reasonable precautions which can be taken by health-care workers to prevent exposure to HBV, HIV, and other blood-borne infectious diseases. Precautions for HBV and HIV have been published by the CDC on several occasions, most recently on June 19, 1987, and on August 21, 1987. The enclosed advisory notice, entitled "Protection Against Occupational Exposure to Hepatitis B Virus (HBV) and Human Immunodeficiency Virus (HIV)," reflects many of the precautions addressed in the CDC guidelines and includes other precautions which should be considered.

It is the legal responsibility of employers to provide appropriate safeguards for health-care workers who may be exposed to these dangerous viruses. For that reason, the Occupational Safety and Health Administration (OSHA) of the U.S. Department of Labor (DOL) is beginning a program of enforcement to insure that health-care employers are meeting those needs. OSHA will respond to employee complaints and conduct other inspections to assure that appropriate measures are being followed. OSHA is currently enforcing its existing regulations and statutory provisions relating to the duty of an employer to provide "safe and healthful working conditions." OSHA is also seeking input about what additional regulatory action may be needed in Advance Notice of Proposed Rulemaking which will be published in the Federal Register.

States with approved plans to operate their own occupational safety and health program enforce standards comparable to the Federal standards and are encouraged to enforce State counterparts to the General Duty Clause. State plan standards, unlike Federal standards, apply to state, county, and municipal workers as well as to private employers.

DOL joins HHS in urging the widest possible adherence to the appropriate precautions as exemplified by the CDC guidelines and the joint advisory notice. All health-care workers who may be exposed to HBV or HIV should receive training and should utilize appropriate precautions.

If you have further questions, please contact your State public health department or OSHA office, or call the Public Health Service National AIDS Hotline, 1–800–342–AIDS. Every effort will be made to respond to your questions in a timely and informative manner. Your unions, and professional and trade associations are also available to answer your questions. We are making every effort to keep all interested parties informed.

The dangers of HBV and HIV are very real, but you can prevent or minimize those dangers for health-care workers through the utilization of the appropriate precautions recommended by the CDC.

Thank you for your time and consideration.

Very truly yours,

William E. Brock, Secretary of Labor

Otis R. Bowen, M.D., Secretary of Health and Human Services

DEPARTMENT OF LABOR/ DEPARTMENT OF HEALTH AND HUMAN SERVICES JOINT ADVISORY NOTICE: PROTECTION AGAINST OCCUPATIONAL EXPOSURE TO HEPATITIS B VIRUS (HBV) AND HUMAN IMMUNODEFICIENCY VIRUS (HIV)

I. BACKGROUND

Hepatitis B (previously called serum hepatitis) is the major infectious occupational health hazard in the health-care industry, and a model for the transmission of blood-borne pathogens. In 1985 the Centers for Disease Control (CDC) estimated that there were over 200,000 cases of hepatitis B virus (HBV) infection in the U.S. each year, leading to 10,000 hospitalizations, 250 deaths due to fulminant hepatitis, 4,000 deaths due to hepatitis-related cirrhosis, and 800 deaths due to hepatitis-related primary liver cancer (CDC, 1985c). More recently the CDC estimated the total number of HBV infections to be 300,000 per year with corresponding increases in numbers of hepatitis-related hospitalizations and deaths (CDC, 1987g). The incidence of reported clinical hepatitis B has been increasing in the United States, from 6.9/100,000 in 1978 to 9.2/100,000 in 1981 and 11.5/100,000 in 1985 (CDC, 1987g). The Hepatitis Branch, CDC, has estimated (unpublished) that 500–600 health-care workers whose job entails exposure to blood are hospitalized annually, with over 200 deaths (12–15 due to fulminant hepatitis, 170–200 from cirrhosis, and 40–50 from liver cancer). Studies indicate that 10% to 40% of health-care or dental workers may show serologic evidence of past or present HBV infection (Palmer et al., 1983). Health-care costs for hepatitis B and non-A, non-B hepatitis in health-care workers were estimated to be $10–$12 million annually (Grady & Kane, 1981). A safe, immunogenic, and effective vaccine to prevent hepatitis B has been available since 1982 and is recommended by the CDC for health-care workers exposed to blood and body fluids (CDC, 1982b, 1983b, 1984, 1985c, 1987g). According to unpublished CDC estimates, approximately 30–40% of health-care workers in high-risk settings have been vaccinated to date.

According to the most recent data available from the CDC (1987a), acquired immunodeficiency syndrom (AIDS) was the 13th leading cause of years of potential life lost (82,882 years) in 1984, increasing to 11th place in 1985 (152,595 years). As of August 10, 1987, a cumulative total of 40,051 AIDS cases (of which 558 were pediatric) had been reported to the CDC, with 23,165 (57.8%) of these known to have died (CDC, 1987f). Although occupational HIV infection has been documented, no AIDS case or AIDS-related death is believed to be occupationally related (CDC, 1987e). Spending within the Public Health Services related to AIDS has also accelerated rapidly, from $5.6 million in 1982 to $494 million in 1987, with $791 million requested for 1988. Estimates of average lifetime costs for the care of an AIDS patient have varied considerably, but recent evidence suggests the amount is probably in the range of $50,000 to $75,000.

Infection with either HBV or human immunodeficiency virus (HIV), previously called human T-lymphotropic virus type III/lymphadenopathy-associated virus (HTLVIII/LAV) or AIDS-associated retrovirus (ARV) can lead to a number of life-threatening conditions, including cancer (CDC, 1985c, 1986f, 1987g; Koop, 1986). Therefore, exposure to HBV and HIV should be reduced to the maximum extent feasible by engineering controls, work practices, and protective equipment. (Engineering controls are those methods that prevent or limit the potential for exposure at or near as possible to the point of origin, for example by eliminating a hazard by substitution or by isolating the hazard from the work environment.)

II. MODES OF TRANSMISSION

In the U.S. the major mode of HBV transmission is sexual, both homosexual and heterosexual. Also important is parenteral (entry into the body by a route other than the gastrointestinal tract): transmission by shared needles among intravenous drug abusers and to a lesser extent in needlestick injuries or other exposures of health-care workers to blood. HBV is not transmitted by casual contact, fecal-oral or airborne routes, or by contaminated food or drinking water (CDC, 1985b, 1985c, 1987g). Workers are at risk of HBV infection to the extent they are exposed to blood and other body fluids; employment without the exposure, even in a hospital, carries no greater risk than that for the general population (CDC, 1985c). Thus, the high incidence of HBV infection in some clinical settings is particularly unfortunate because the modes of transmission are well known and readily interrupted by attention to work practices and protective equipment, and because transmission can be prevented by vaccination of those without serologic evidence of previous infection.

Identified risk factors for HIV transmission are essentially identical to those for HBV. Homosexual/bisexual males and male intravenous drug abusers account for 85.4% of all AIDS cases, female intravenous drug abusers for 3.4%, and heterosexual contact for 3.8% (CDC, 1987f). Blood transfusion and treatment of hemophilia-coagulation disorders account for 3.0% of cases, and 1.4% are pediatric cases. In only 3.0% of all AIDS cases has a risk factor not been identified (CDC, 1987f). Like HBV, there is no evidence that HIV is transmitted by casual contact, fecal-oral or airborne routes, or by contaminated food or drinking water (CDC, 1985b; Koop,

1986; Vlahov & Polk, 1987), and barriers to HBV are effective against HIV. Workers are at risk of HIV infection to the extent they are directly exposed to blood and body fluids. Even in groups that presumably have high potential exposure to HIV-contaminated fluids and tissues, e.g., health-care workers specializing in treatment of AIDS patients and the parents, spouse, children, or other persons living with AIDS patients, transmission is recognized as occurring only between sexual partners or as a consequence of mucous-membrane or parenteral (including open-wound) exposure to blood or other body fluids (CDC, 1985b, 1986f, 1987e, 1987h; Gestal, 1987; Vlahov & Polk, 1987).

Despite the similarities in the modes of transmission, the risk of HBV infection in health care settings far exceeds that for HIV infection (CDC, 1985b; Vlahov & Polk, 1987). For example, it has been estimated (Grady et al., 1978; Seeff et al., 1987; Vlahov & Polk, 1987) that the risk of acquiring HBV infection following puncture with a needle contaminated by an HBV carrier ranges from 6% to 30%—far in excess of the risk of HIV infection under similar circumstances, which the CDC and others estimated to be at less than 1% (CDC, 1985b, 1987e, 1987h).

Health-care workers with documented percutaneous or mucous-membrane exposures to blood or body fluids of HIV-infected patients have been prospectively evaluated to determine the risk of infection after such exposures. As of June 30, 1987, 883 health-care workers have been tested for antibody to HIV in an ongoing surveillance project conducted by CDC (McCray, 1986). Of these, 708 (80%) had percutaneous exposures to blood, and 175 (20%) had a mucous membrane or an open wound contaminated by blood or body fluid. Of 396 health-care workers, each of whom had only a convalescent-phase serum sample obtained and tested 90 days or more post-exposure, one—for whom heterosexual transmission could not be ruled out—was seropositive for HIV antibody. For 425 additional health-care workers, both acute- and convalescent-phase serum samples were obtained and tested; none of 74 health-care workers with non-percutaneous exposures seroconverted, and three (0.9%) of 351 with percutaneous exposures seroconverted. None of these three health-care workers had other documented risk factors for infection.

Two other prospective studies to assess the risk of nosocomial acquisition of HIV infection for health-care workers are ongoing in the United States. As of April 30, 1987, 332 health-care workers with a total of 453 needlestick or mucous-membrane exposures to the blood or other body fluids of HIV-infected patients were tested for HIV antibody at the National Institutes of Health (Henderson et al., 1986). These exposed workers included 103 with needlestick injuries and 229 with mucous-membrane exposures; none had seroconverted. A similar study at the University of California of 129 health-care workers with documented needlestick injuries or mucous-membrane exposures to blood or other body fluids from patients with HIV infection has not identified any seroconversions (Gerberding et al., 1987). Results of a prospective study in the United Kingdom identified no evidence of transmission among 150 health-care workers with parenteral or mucous-membrane exposure to blood or other body fluids, secretions, or excretions from patients with HIV infection (McEvoy et al., 1987).

Following needlestick injuries, two health-care workers contracted HBV but not HIV, and in another instance a health-care worker contracted cryptococcus but not HIV from patients infected with both (Vlahov & Polk, 1987). This risk of infection by HIV and other blood-borne pathogens for which immunization is not available extends to all health-care workers exposed to blood, even those who have been immunized against HBV infection. Effective protection against blood-borne disease requires universal observance of common barrier precautions by all workers with potential exposure to blood, body fluids, and tissues (CDC, 1985b, 1987e).

HIV has been isolated from blood, semen, saliva, tears, urine, vaginal secretions, cerebrospinal fluid, breast milk, and amniotic fluid, but only blood and blood products, semen, vaginal secretions, and possibly breast milk (this needs to be confirmed) have been directly linked to transmission of HIV (CDC, 1985b, 1986a, 1987e). Contact with fluids such as saliva and tears has not been shown to result in infection (CDC, 1985b; Gestal, 1987; Vlahov & Polk, 1987). Although other fluids have not been shown to transmit infection, all body fluids and tissues should be regarded as potentially contaminated by HBV or HIV, and treated as if they were infectious. Both HBV ahd HIV appear to be incapable of penetrating intact skin, but infection may result from infectious fluids coming into contact with mucous membranes or open wounds (including inapparent lesions) on the skin (CDC, 1987h; Vlahov & Polk, 1987). If a procedure involves the potential for skin contact with blood or mucous membranes, then appropriate barriers to skin contact should be worn, e.g., gloves. Investigations of HBV risks associated with dental and other procedures that might produce particulates in air, e.g., centrifuging and dialysis, indicated that the particulates generated were relatively large droplets (spatter), and not true aerosols of suspended particulates that would represent a risk of inhalation exposure (Bond, 1986; Scarlett, 1986; Petersen, Bond, & Favero, 1979). Thus, if there is the potential for splashes or spatter of blood or fluids, face shields or protective eyewear and surgical masks should be worn. Detailed protective measures for health-care workers have been addressed by the CDC (1982a, 1983a, 1985a, 1985b, 1986a, 1986b, 1986c, 1986d, 1987e; Williams, 1983). These can serve as general guides for the specific groups covered, and for the development of comparable procedures in other working environments.

HIV infection is known to have been transmitted by organ transplants and blood transfusions received from persons who were HIV seronegative at the time of donation (CDC, 1986e, 1987c). Falsely negative serology can be due to improperly performed tests or other laboratory error, or testing in that "window" of time during which a recently infected person is infective but has not yet converted from seronegative to seropositive. Detectable levels of antibodies usually develop within 6 to 12 weeks of infection (CDC, 1987d). A recent report suggesting that this "window" may extend to 14 months is not consistent with other data, and therefore requires confirmation (Ranki et al., 1987). If all body fluids and tissues are treated as infectious, no additional level of worker protection will be gained by identifying seropositive patients or workers. Conversely, if worker protection and work practices were upgraded only following the return of positive HBV or HIV serology, then workers would be inadequately protected during the time required for testing. By producing a false sense of safety with "silent" HBV- or HIV-positive patients, a seronegative test may significantly reduce the level of routine vigilance and result in virus exposure. Furthermore, developing, implementing, and administering a program of routine testing would shift resources and energy away from efforts to assure compliance with infection control procedures. Therefore, routine screening of workers or patients for HIV antibodies will not substantially increase the level of protection for workers above that achieved by adherence to strict infection control procedures.

On the other hand, workers who have had parenteral exposure to fluids or tissues may wish to know whether their own antibody status converts from negative to positive. Such a monitoring program can lead to prophylactic interventions in the case of HBV infection, and CDC has published guidelines on pre- and post-exposure prophylaxis of viral hepatitis (CDC, 1985c, 1987g). Future developments may also allow effective intervention in the case of HIV infection. For the present, post-exposure monitoring for HIV at least can release the affected worker from unnecessary emotional stress if infection did not occur, or allow the affected worker to protect sexual partners in the event infection is detected (CDC, 1987c, 1987e).

III. SUMMARY

The cumulative epidemiologic data indicate that transmission of HBV and HIV requires direct, intimate contact with or parenteral inoculation of blood and blood products, semen, or tissues (CDC, 1985b, 1986a, 1986f, 1987e, 1987h; Vlahov & Polk, 1987). The mere presence of, or casual contact with, an infected person cannot be construed as "exposure" to HBV or HIV. Although the theoretical possibility of rate or low-risk alternative modes of transmission cannot be totally excluded, the only documented occupational risks of HBV and HIV infection are associated with parenteral (including open wound) and mucous-membrane exposure to blood and tissues (CDC, 1985b, 1987e, 1987g, 1987h; Vlahov & Polk, 1987). Workers occupationally exposed to blood, body fluids, or tissues can be protected from the recognized risks of HBV and HIV infection by imposing barriers in the form of engineering controls, work practices, and protective equipment that are readily available, commonly used, and minimally intrusive.

IV. RECOMMENDATIONS

General

"Exposure" (or "potential exposure") to HBV and HIV should be defined in terms of actual (or potential) skin, mucous-membrane, or parenteral contact with blood, body fluids, and tissues. "Tissues" and "fluids" or "body fluids" should be understood to designate not only those materials from humans, but also potentially infectious fluids and tissues associated with laboratory investigations of HBV or HIV, e.g., organs and excreta from experimental animals, embryonated eggs, tissue or cell cultures and culture media, etc.

As the first step in determining what actions are required to protect worker health, every employer should evaluate all working conditions and the specific tasks that workers are expected to encounter as a consequence of employment. That evaluation should lead to the classification of work-related tasks to one of three categories of potential exposure. These categories represent those tasks that require protective equipment to be worn during the task (Category I); tasks that do not require any protective equipment (Category III); and an intermediate grouping of tasks (Category II) that also do not require protective equipment, but that inherently include the predictable job-related requirement to perform Category I tasks unexpectedly or on short notice, so that these persons should have immediate access to some minimal set of protective devices. For example, law enforcement personnel or firefighters may be called upon to perform or assist in first aid or to be potentially exposed in some other way. This exposure classification applies to tasks rather than to individuals, who in the course of their daily activities may move from one exposure category to another as they perform various tasks.

CATEGORY I: Tasks that involve exposure to blood, body fluids, or tissues. All procedures or other job-related tasks that involve an inherent potential for mucous-membrane or skin contact with blood, body fluids, or tissues, or a potential for spills or splashes of them, are Category I tasks. Use of appropriate protective measures should be required for every employee engaged in Category I tasks.

CATEGORY II: Tasks that involve no exposure to blood, body fluids, or tissues, but employment may require performing unplanned category I tasks. The normal work routine involves no exposure to blood, body fluids, or tissues, but exposure or potential exposure may be required as a condition of employment. Appropriate protective measure should be readily available to every employee engaged in Category II tasks.

CATEGORY III: Tasks that involve no exposure to blood, body fluids or tissues, and category I tasks are not a condition of employment. The normal work routine involves no exposure to blood, body fluids, or tissues (although situations can be imagined or hypothesized under which anyone, anywhere, might encounter potential exposure to body fluids). Persons who perform these duties are not called upon as part of their employment to perform or assist in emergency medical care or first aid or to be potentially exposed in some other way. Tasks that involve handling of implements or utensils, use of public or shared bathroom facilities or telephones, and personal contacts such as handshaking are Category III tasks.

For individual Category I and II tasks, engineering controls, work practices, and protective equipment should be selected after careful consideration, for each specific situation, of the overall risk associated with the task. Some of the factors that should be included in that evaluation of risk are the following:

1. Type of body fluid with which there will or may be contact. Blood is of greater concern than urine.

2. Volume of blood or body fluid likely to be encountered. Hip-replacement surgery can be very bloody while corneal transplantation is almost bloodless.

3. Probability of an exposure taking place. Drawing blood will more likely lead to exposure to blood than will performing a physical examination.

4. Probable route of exposure. Needlestick injuries are of greater concern than contact with soiled linens.

5. Virus concentration in the fluid or tissue. The number of viruses per milliliter of fluid in research laboratory cultures may be orders of magnitude higher than in blood. Similarly, viruses have been less frequently found in such fluids as sweat, tears, urine, and saliva.

Engineering controls, work practices, and protective equipment appropriate to the task being performed are critical to minimize HBV and HIV exposure and to prevent infection. Adequate protection can be assured only if the appropriate controls and equipment are provided and all workers know the applicable work practices and how to properly use the required controls or protective equipment. Therefore, employers should establish a detailed work practices program that includes standard operating procedures (SOPs) for all tasks or work areas having the potential for exposure to fluids or tissues, and a worker education program to assure familiarity with work practices and the ability to use properly the controls and equipment provided.

It is essential for both the patient and the health-care worker to be fully aware of the reasons for the preventive measures used. The health-care worker may incorrectly interpret the work practices and protective equipment as signifying that a task is unsafe. The patient may incorrectly interpret the work practices or protective garb as evidence that the health-care provider knows or believes the patient is infected with HBV or HIV. Therefore, worker education programs should strive to allow workers (and to the extent feasible, clients or patients) to recognize the routine use of appropriate work practices and protective equipment as prudent steps that protect the health of all.

If the employer determines that Category I and II tasks do not exist in the workplace, then no specific personal hygiene or protective measures are required. However, these employers should ensure that workers are aware of the risk factors asssociated with transmission of HBV and HIV so that they can recognize situations which pose increased potential for exposure to HBV or HIV (Category I tasks) and know how to avoid or minimize personal risk. A comparable level of education is necessary for all citizens. Educational materials such as the Surgeon General's Report can provide much of the needed information (CDC, 1987b; Koop, 1986).

If the employer determines that work-related Category I or II tasks exist, then the following procedures would be implemented.

Administrative

The employer should establish formal procedures to ensure that Category I and II tasks are properly identified, SOPs are developed, and employees who must perform these tasks are adequately trained and protected. If responsibility for implementation of these procedures is delegated to a committee, it should include both management and worker representatives. Administrative activities to enhance worker protection include:

1. Evaluating the workplace to:

    a. Establish categories of risk classification for all routine and reasonably anticipatable job-related tasks.

    b. Identify all workers whose employment requires performance of Category I or II tasks.

    c. Determine for identified Category I and II tasks those body fluids to which workers most probably will be exposed and the potential extent and route of exposure.

2. Developing, or supervising the development of, Standard Operating Procedures for all Category I or II tasks. These SOPs should include mandatory work practices and protective equipment for each Category I or II task.

3. Monitoring the effectiveness of work practices and protective equipment. This includes:

    a. Surveillance of the workplace to ensure that required work practices are observed and that protective clothing and equipment are provided and properly used.

b. Investigation of known or suspected parenteral exposures to body fluids or tissues to establish the conditions surrounding the exposure and to improve training, work practices, or protective equipment to prevent a recurrence.

Training and Education

The employer should establish an initial and periodic training program for all employees who perform Category I and II tasks. No worker should engage in any Category I or II task before receiving training pertaining to the SOPs, work practices, and protective equipment required for that task. The training program should ensure that all workers:

1. Understand the modes of transmission of HBV and HIV.
2. Can recognize and differentiate Category I and II tasks.
3. Know the types of protective clothing and equipment generally appropriate for Category I and II tasks, and understand the basis for selection of clothing and equipment.
4. Are familiar with appropriate actions to take and persons to contact if unplanned-for Category I tasks are encountered.
5. Are familiar with and understand all the requirements for work practices and protective equipment specified in SOPs covering the tasks they perform.
6. Know where protective clothing and equipment is kept, how to use it properly, and how to remove, handle, decontaminate, and dispose of contaminated clothing or equipment.
7. Know and understand the limitations of protective clothing and equipment. For example, ordinary gloves offer no protection against needlestick injuries. Employers and workers should be on guard against a sense of security not warranted by the protective equipment being used.
8. Know the corrective actions to take in the event of spills or personal exposure to fluids or tissues, the appropriate reporting procedures, and the medical monitoring recommended in cases of suspected parenteral exposure.

Engineering Controls

Whenever possible, engineering controls should be used as the primary method to reduce worker exposure to harmful substances. The preferred approach in engineering controls is to use, to the fullest extent feasible, intrinsically safe substances, procedures, or devices. Replacement of a hazardous procedure or device with one that is less risky or harmful is an example of this approach. For example, a laser scalpel reduces the risk of cuts and scrapes by eliminating the necessity to handle the conventional scalpel blade.

Isolation or containment of the hazard is an alternative engineering control technique. Disposable, puncture-resistant containers for used needles, blades, etc., isolate cut and needle-stick injury hazards from the worker. Glove boxes, ventilated cabinets, or other enclosures for tissue homogenizers, sonicators, vortex mixers, etc., serve not only to isolate the hazard, but also to contain spills or splashes and prevent spatter and mist from reaching the worker.

After the potential for exposure has been minimized by engineering controls, further reductions can be achieved by work practices and, finally, personal protective equipment.

Work Practices

For all identified Category I and II tasks, the employer should have written, detailed SOPs. All employees who perform Category I or II tasks should have ready access to the SOPs pertaining to those tasks.

1. Work practices should be developed on the assumption that all body fluids and tissues are infectious. General Procedures to protect health-care workers against HBV or HIV transmission have been published elsewhere (CDC, 1982a; 1983a; 1985a, 1985c, 1986a, 1986c, 1986d, 1987g; Williams, 1983). Each employer with Category I and II tasks in the workplace should incorporate those general recommendations, as appropriate, or equivalent procedures into work practices and SOPs. The importance of handwashing should be emphasized.

2. Work practices should include provision for safe collection of fluids and tissues and for disposal in accordance with applicable local, state, and federal regulations. Provision must be made for safe removal, handling, and disposal or decontamination of protective clothing and equipment, soiled linens, etc.

3. Work practices and SOPs should provide guidance on procedures to follow in the event of spills or personal exposure to fluids or tissues. These procedures should include instructions for personal and area decontamination as well as appropriate management or supervisory personnel to whom the incident should be reported.

4. Work practices should give specific and detailed procedures to be observed with sharp objects, e.g., needles and scalpel blades. Puncture-resistant receptacles must be readily accessible for depositing these materials after use. These receptacles must be clearly marked and specific work practices provided to protect personnel responsible for disposing of them or processing their contents for reuse.

Personal Protective Equipment

Based upon the fluid or tissue to which there is potential exposure, the likelihood of exposure occurring, the potential volume of material, the probable route of exposure, and overall working conditions and job requirements, the employer should provide and maintain personal protective equipment appropriate to the specific requirements of each task.

For workers performing Category I tasks, a required minimum array of protective clothing or equipment should be specified by pertinent SOPs. Category I tasks do not all involve the same type or degree of risk, and therefore they do not all require the same kind of extent of protection. Specific combinations of clothing and equipment must be tailored to specific tasks. Minimum levels of protection for Category I tasks in most cases would include use of appropriate gloves. If there is the potential for splashes, protective eyewear or face shields should be worn. Paramedics responding to an auto accident might protect against cuts on metal and glass by wearing gloves or gauntlets that are both puncture-resistant and impervious to blood. If the conditions of exposure include the potential for clothing becoming soaked with blood, protective outer garments such as impervious coveralls should be worn.

For workers performing Category II tasks, there should be ready access to appropriate protective eyewear, or surgical masks, specified in pertinent SOPs. Workers performing Category II tasks need not be wearing protective equipment, but they should be prepared to put on appropriate protective garb on short notice.

Medical

In addition to any health care or surveillance required by other rules, regulations, or labor-management agreement, the employer should make available at no cost to the worker:

1. Voluntary HBV immunization for all workers whose employment requires them to perform Category I tasks and who test negative for HBV antibodies. Detailed recommendations for protecting health-care workers from viral hepatitis have been published by the CDC (1985c). These recommendations include procedures for both pre- and post-exposure prophylaxis, and should be the basis for the routine approach by management to the prevention of occupational hepatitis B.

2. Monitoring, at the request of the worker, for HBV and HIV antibodies following known or suspected parenteral exposure to blood, body fluids, or tissues. This monitoring program must include appropriate provisions to protect the confidentiality of test results for all workers who may elect to participate.

3. Medical counseling for all workers found, as a result of the monitoring described above, to be seropositive for HBV or HIV. Counseling guidelines have been published by the Public Health Service (CDC, 1985c, 1987d, 1987g).

Recordkeeping

If any employee is required to perform Category I or II tasks, the employer should maintain records documenting:

1. The administrative procedures used to classify job tasks. Records should describe the factors considered and outline the rationale for classification.

2. Copies of all SOPs for Category I and II tasks, and documentation of the administrative review and approval process through which each SOP passed.

3. Training records, indicating the dates of training sessions, the content of those training sessions along with the names of all persons conducting the training, and the names of all those receiving training.

4. The conditions observed in routine surveillance of the workplace for compliance with work practices and use of protective clothing or equipment. If noncompliance is noted, the conditions should be documented along with corrective actions taken.

5. The conditions associated with each incident or mucous membrane or parenteral exposure to body fluids or tissue, an evaluation of those conditions, and a description of any corrective measures taken to prevent a recurrence or other similar exposure.

REFERENCES

Bond, W. W. (1986). Modes of transmission of infectious diseases. In Proceedings of the National Conference on Infection Control in Dentistry, Chicago, pp. 29–35.

Centers for Disease Control (1982a). Acquired immune-deficiency syndrome (AIDS)—Precautions for clinical and laboratory staff. *MMWR* 31:577–80.

———. (1982b). Hepatitis B virus vaccine safety—Report of an inter-agency group. *MMWR* 31:465–67.

——. (1983a). Acquired immunodeficiency syndrome (AIDS)—Precautions for health-care workers and allied professionals. *MMWR* 32:450–52.

——. (1983b). The Safety of hepatitis B virus vaccine. *MMWR* 32:134–36.

——. (1984). Hepatitis B vaccine—Evidence confirming lack of AIDS transmission. *MMWR* 33:685–87.

——. (1985a). Recommendations for preventing possible transmission of human T-lymphotropic virus type III/lymphadenopathy-associated virus from tears. *MMWR* 34:533–34.

——. (1985b). Recommendations for preventing transmission of infection with human T-lymphotropic virus type III/lymphadenopathy-associated virus in the workplace. *MMWR* 34:681–86, 691–95.

——. (1985c). Recommendations for protection against viral hepatitis. *MMWR* 34:313–24, 329–35.

——. (1986a). Human T-lymphotropic virus, type III/lymphadenopathy-associated virus—Agent summary statement. *MMWR* 35:540–42.

——. (1986b). Recommendations for preventing transmission of infection with human T-lymphotropic virus type III/lymphadenopathy-associated virus during invasive procedures. *MMWR* 35:221–23.

——. (1986c). Recommendations for providing dialysis treatment to patients infected with human T-lymphotropic virus, type III/lymphadenopathy-associated virus. *MMWR* 35:376–83.

——. (1986d). Recommended infection-control practices for dentistry. *MMWR* 35:237–42.

——. (1986e). Transfusion-associated human T-lymphotropic virus type III/lymphadenopathy-associated virus infection from a seronegative donor—Colorado. *MMWR* 35:389–91.

——. (1986f). Update—Acquired immunodeficiency syndrome—United States. *MMWR* 35:757–66.

——. (1987a). Changes in premature mortality—United States, 1984–1985. *MMWR* 36:55–57.

——. (1987b). Facts about AIDS. U.S. Department of Health and Human Services.

——. (1987c). Human immunodeficiency virus infections transmitted from an organ donor screened for HIV antibody—North Carolina. *MMWR* 36:306–08.

——. (1987d). Public Health Service guidelines for counseling and antibody testing to prevent HIV infection and AIDS. *MMWR* 36:509–15.

——. (1987e). Recommendations for prevention of HIV transmission in health-care settings. *MMWR Supplement* 36(2S): 1S–16S.

——. (1987f). Update—Acquired immunodeficiency syndrome—United States. *MMWR Supplement* 36:522–26.

——. (1987g). Update on Hepatitis B prevention. *MMWR* 36:353–60.

——. (1987h). Update-Human immunodeficiency virus infections in health-care workers exposed to blood of infected patients. *MMWR* 36:285–89.

Gerberding, J. L., C. E. Bryant-LeBlanc, K. Nelson et al. (1987). Risk of transmitting the human immunodeficiency virus, cytomegalovirus, and hepatitis B virus to health-care workers exposed to patients with AIDS and AIDS-related conditions. *Journal of Infectious Disease* 156:1–8.

Gestal, J. J. (1987). Occupational hazards in hospitals—Risk of infection. *British Journal of Industrial Medicine* 44:435–42.

Grady, G. F. & M. A. Kane (1981). Hepatitis B infections account for multi-million dollar loss. *Hospital Infection Control* 8:60–62.

Grady, G. F., V. A. Lee, A. Prince et al. (1978). Hepatitis B immune globulin for accidental exposures among medical personnel—Final report of a multicenter controlled trial. *Journal of Infectious Disease* 138:625–38.

Henderson, D. K., A. J. Saah, B. J. Zak et al. (1986). Risk of nosocomial infection with human T-cell lymphotropic virus type III/lymphadenopathy-associated virus in a large cohort of intensively exposed health-care workers. *Annals of Internal Medicine* 104:644–47.

Koop, C. E. (1986, October). *Surgeon General's Report on Acquired Immune Deficiency Syndrome.* U.S. Department of Health and Human Services.

McCray, E. (1986). The cooperative needlestick surveillance group. Occupational risk of the acquired immunodeficiency syndrome among health-care workers. *New England Journal of Medicine* 314:1127–32.

McEvoy, M., K. Porter, P. Mortimer, N. Simmons & D. Shanson, (1987). Prospective study of clinical, laboratory, and ancillary staff with accidental exposure to blood or other body fluids from patients infected with HIV. *British Medical Journal* 294:1595–97.

Palmer, D. L., M. Barash, R. King & F. Neil (1983). Hepatitis among hospital employees. *Western Journal of Medicine* 138:519–23.

Petersen, N. J., W. W. Bond & M. S. Favero (1979). Air sampling for hepatitis B surface antigen in a dental operatory. *Journal of the American Dental Association* 99:465–467.

Ranki, S. L., M. Krohn, J. Antonen, J. P. Allain, M. Leuther, G. Franchini & K. Krohn (1987). Long latency precedes overt seroconversion in sexually transmitted human-immunodeficiency-virus infection. *Lancet* 2(8559):589–93.

Scarlett, M. (1986) Infection control practices in dentistry. In Proceedings of the National Conference on Infection Control in Dentistry, Chicago, pp. 41–51.

Seeff, L. B., E. C. Wright, H. J. Zimmerman et al. (1987). Type B hepatitis after needlestick exposure—Prevention with hepatitis B immune globulin. *Annals of Internal Medicine* 88:285–93.

Vlahov, D. & B. F. Polk (1987). Transmission of human immunodeficiency virus within the health-care setting. *Occupational Medical State of the Art Reviews* 2:429–50.

Williams, W. W. (1983). Guidelines for infection control in hospital personnel. *Infection Control* 4:326–49.

RECOMMENDATIONS FOR PREVENTION OF HIV TRANSMISSION IN HEALTH-CARE SETTINGS

INTRODUCTION

Human immunodeficiency virus (HIV), the virus that causes acquired immunodeficiency syndrome (AIDS), is transmitted through sexual contact and exposure to infected blood or blood components and perinatally from mother to neonate. HIV has been isolated from blood, semen, vaginal secretions, saliva, tears, breast milk, cerebrospinal fluid, amniotic fluid, and urine and is likely to be isolated from other body fluids, secretions, and excretions. However, epidemiologic evidence has implicated only blood, semen, vaginal secretions, and possibly breast milk in transmission.

The increasing prevalence of HIV increases the risk that health-care workers will be exposed to blood from patients infected with HIV, especially when blood and body fluid precautions are not followed for all patients. Thus, the document emphasizes the need for health-care workers to consider *all* patients as potentially infected with HIV and/or other blood-borne pathogens and to adhere rigorously to infection-control precautions for minimizing the risk of exposure to blood and body fluids of all patients.

The recommendations contained in this document consolidate and update CDC recommendations published earlier for preventing HIV transmission in health-care settings: precautions for clinical and laboratory staffs[1] and precautions for health-care workers and allied professionals;[2] recommendations for preventing HIV transmission in the workplace[3] and during invasive procedures;[4] recommendations for preventing possible transmission of HIV from tears;[5] and recommendations for providing dialysis treatment for HIV-infected patients.[6] These recommendations also update portions of the "Guideline for Isolation Precautions in Hospitals"[7] and reemphasize some of the recommendations contained in "Infection Control Practice for Dentistry."[8] The recommendations contained in this document have been developed for use in health-care settings and emphasize the need to treat blood and other body fluids from *all* patients as potentially infective. These same prudent precautions also should be taken in other settings in which persons may be exposed to blood or other body fluids.

DEFINITION OF HEALTH-CARE WORKERS

Health-care workers are defined as persons, including students and trainees, whose activities involve contact with patients or with blood or other body fluids from patients in a health-care setting.

HEALTH-CARE WORKERS WITH AIDS

As of July 10, 1987, a total of 1,875 (5.8%) of 32,395 adults with AIDS, who had been reported to the CDC national surveillance system and for whom occupational information was available, reported being employed in a health-care or clinical laboratory setting. In comparison, 6.8 million persons—representing 5.6% of the U.S. labor force—were employed in health services. Of the health-care workers with AIDS, 95% have been reported to exhibit high-risk behavior; for the remaining 5%, the means of HIV acquisition was undetermined. Health-care workers with AIDS were significantly more likely than other workers to have an undetermined risk (5% versus 3%, respectively). For both health-care workers and non-health-care workers with AIDS, the proportion with an undetermined risk has not increased since 1982.

AIDS patients initially reported as not belonging to recognized risk groups are investigated by state and local health departments to determine whether possible risk factors exist. Of all health-care workers with AIDS reported to CDC who were initially characterized as not having an identified risk and for whom follow-up information was available, 66% have been reclassified because risk factors were identified or because the patient was found not to meet the surveillance case definition for AIDS. Of the 87 health-care workers currently categorized as having no identifiable risk, information is incomplete on 16 (18%) because of death or refusal to be interviewed; 38 (44%) are still being investigated. The remaining 33 (38%) health-care workers were interviewed or had other follow-up information available. The occupations of these 33 were as follows: five physicians (15%), three of whom were surgeons; one dentist (3%); three nurses (9%); nine nursing assistants (27%); seven housekeeping or maintenance workers (21%); three clinical laboratory technicians (9%); one therapist (3%); and four others who did not have contact with patients (12%). Although 15 of these 33 health-care workers reported parenteral and/or other non-needlestick exposure to blood or body fluids from patients in the 10 years preceding their diagnosis of AIDS, none of these exposures involved a patient with AIDS or known HIV infection.

RISK TO HEALTH-CARE WORKERS OF ACQUIRING HIV IN HEALTH-CARE SETTINGS

Health-care workers with documented percutaneous or mucous-membrane exposures to blood or body fluids of HIV-infected patients have been prospectively evaluated to determine the risk of infection after such exposures. As of June 30, 1987, 883 health-care workers have been tested for antibody to HIV in an ongoing surveillance project conducted by CDC.[9] Of these, 708 (80%) had percutaneous exposures to blood, and 175 (20%) had a mucous-membrane or an open wound contaminated by blood or body fluid. Of 396 health-care workers, each of whom had only a convalescent-phase serum sample obtained and tested ≥ 90 days post-exposure, one—for whom heterosexual transmission could not be ruled out—was seropositive for HIV antibody. For 425 additional health-care workers, both acute- and convalescent-phase serum samples were obtained and tested; none of 74 health-care workers with nonpercutaneous exposures seroconverted, and three (0.9%) of 351 with precutaneous exposures seroconverted. None of these three health-care workers had other documented risk factors for infection.

Two other prospective studies to assess the risk of nosocomial acquisition of HIV infection for health-care workers are ongoing in the United States. As of April 30, 1987, 332 health-care workers with a total of 453 needlestick or mucous-membrane exposures to the blood or other body fluids of HIV-infected patients were tested for HIV antibody at the National Institutes of Health.[10] These exposed workers included 103 with needlestick injuries and 229 with mucous-membrane exposures; none had seroconverted. A similar study at the University of California of 129 health-care workers with documented needlestick injuries of mucous-membrane exposures to blood or other body fluids from patients with HIV infection has not identified any seroconversions.[11] Results of a prospective study in the United Kingdom identified no evidence of transmission among 150 health-care workers with parenteral or mucous-membrane exposures to blood or other body fluids, secretions, or excretions from patients with HIV infection.[12]

In addition to health-care workers enrolled in prospective studies, eight persons who provided care to infected patients and denied other risk factors have been reported to have acquired HIV infection. Three of these health-care workers had needlestick exposures to blood from infected patients.[13,14,15] Two were persons who provided nursing care to infected persons; although neither sustained a needlestick, both had extensive contact with blood or other body fluids, and neither observed recommended barrier precautions.[16,17] The other three were health-care workers with non-needlestick exposures to blood from infected patients.[18] Although the exact route of transmission for these last three infections is not known, all three persons had direct contact of their skin with blood from infected patients, all had skin lesions that may have been contaminated by blood, and one also had a mucous-membrane exposure.

A total of 1,231 dentists and hygienists, many of whom practiced in areas with many AIDS cases, participated in a study to determine the prevalence of antibody to HIV; one dentist (0.1%) had HIV antibody. Although no exposure to a known HIV-infected person could be documented, epidemiologic investigation did not identify any other risk factor for infection. The infected dentist, who also had a history of sustaining needlestick injuries and trauma to his hands, did not routinely wear gloves when providing dental care.[19]

PRECAUTIONS TO PREVENT TRANSMISSION OF HIV

Universal Precautions

Since medical history and examination cannot reliably identify all patients infected with HIV or other blood-borne pathogens, blood and body-fluid precautions should be consistently used for *all* patients. This approach, previously recommended by CDC, [3,4] and referred to as "universal blood and body-fluid precautions" or "universal precautions," should be used in the care of *all* patients, especially including those in emergency-care settings in which the risk of blood exposure is increased and the infection status of the patient is usually unknown.[20]

1. All health-care workers should routinely use appropriate barrier precautions to prevent skin and mucous-membrane exposure when contact with blood or other body fluids of any patient is anticipated. Gloves should be worn for touching blood and body fluids, mucous membrane, or non-intact skin of all patients, for handling items or surfaces soiled with blood or body fluids, and for performing venipuncture and other vascular access procedures. Gloves should be changed after contact with each patient. Masks and protective eyewear or face shields should be worn during procedures that are likely to generate droplets of blood or other body fluids to prevent exposure of mucous membranes of the mouth, nose, and eyes. Gowns or aprons should be worn during procedures that are likely to generate splashes of blood or other body fluids.

2. Hands and other skin surfaces should be washed immediately and thoroughly if contaminated with blood or other body fluids. Hands should be washed immediately after gloves are removed.

3. All health-care workers should take precautions to prevent injuries caused by needles, scalpels, and other sharp instruments or devices during procedures; when cleaning used instruments; during disposal of used needles; and when handling sharp instruments after procedures. To prevent needlestick injuries, needles should not be recapped, purposely bent or broken by hand, removed from disposable syringes, or otherwise manipulated by hand. After they are used, disposable syringes and needles, scalpel blades, and other sharp items should be placed in puncture-resistant containers for disposal; the puncture-resistant containers should be located as close as practical to the use area. Large-bore reusable needles should be placed in a puncture-resistant container for transport to the reprocessing area.

4. Although saliva has not been implicated in HIV transmission, to minimize the need for emergency mouth-to-mouth resuscitation, mouthpieces, resuscitation bags, or other ventilation devices should be available for use in areas in which the need for resuscitation is predictable.

5. Health-care workers who have exudative lesions or weeping dermatitis should refrain from all direct patient care and from handling patient-care equipment undil the condition resolves.

6. Pregnant health-care workers are not known to be at greater risk of contracting HIV infection than health-care workers who are not pregnant; however, if a health-care worker develops HIV infection during pregnancy, the infant is at risk of infection resulting from perinatal transmission. Because of this risk, pregnant health-care workers should be especially familiar with and strictly adhere to precautions to minimize the risk of HIV transmission.

Implementation of universal blood and body-fluid precautions for *all* patients eliminates the need for use of the isolation category of "Blood and Body Fluid Precautions" previously recommended by CDC[7] for patients known or suspected to be infected with blood-borne pathogens. Isolation precautions (e.g., enteric, "AFB"[7] should be used as necessary if associated conditions, such as infectious diarrhea or tuberculosis, are diagnosed or suspected.

Precautions for Invasive Procedures

In this document, an invasive procedure is defined as surgical entry into tissues, cavities, or organs or repair of major traumatic injuries (1) in an operating or delivery room, emergency department, or outpatient setting, including both physicians' and dentists' offices; (2) cardiac catheterization and angiographic procedures; (3) a vaginal or cesarean delivery or other invasive obstetric procedure during which bleeding may occur; or (4) the manipulation, cutting, or removal of any oral or perioral tissues, including tooth structure, during which bleeding occurs or the potential for bleeding exists. The universal blood and body-fluid precautions listed above, combined with the precautions listed below, should be the minimum precautions for *all* such invasive procedures.

1. All health-care workers who participate in invasive procedures must routinely use appropriate barrier precautions to prevent skin and mucous-membrane contact with blood and other body fluids of all patients. Gloves and surgical masks must be worn for all invasive procedures. Protective eyewear or face shields should be worn for procedures that commonly result in the generation of droplets, splashing of blood or other body fluids, or the generation of bone chips. Gowns or aprons made of materials that provide an effective barrier should be worn during invasive procedures that are likely to result in the splashing of blood or other body fluids. All health-care workers who perform or assist in vaginal or cesarean deliveries should wear gloves and gowns when handling the placenta or the infant until blood and amniotic fluid have been removed from the infant's skin and should wear gloves during post-delivery care of the umbilical cord.

2. If a glove is torn or a needlestick or other injury occurs, the glove should be removed and a new glove used as promptly as patient safety permits; the needle or instrument involved in the incident should also be removed from the sterile field.

Precautions for Dentistry

Blood, saliva, and gingival fluid from *all* dental patients should be considered infective. Special emphasis should be placed on the following precautions for preventing transmission of blood-borne pathogens in dental practice in both institutional and non-institutional settings. (General infection-control precautions are more specifically addressed in previous recommendations for infection-control practices for dentistry.[8])

1. In addition to wearing gloves for contact with oral mucous membranes of all patients, all dental workers should wear surgical masks and protective eyewear or chin-length plastic face shields during dental procedures in which splashing or spattering of blood, saliva, or gingival fluids is likely. Rubber dams, high-speed evacuation, and proper patient positioning, when appropriate, should be utilized to minimize generation of droplets and spatter.

2. Handpieces should be sterilized after use with each patient, since blood, saliva, or gingival fluid of patients may be aspirated into the handpiece or waterline. Handpieces that cannot be sterilized should at least be flushed, the outside surface cleaned and wiped with a suitable chemical germicide, and then rinsed. Handpieces should be flushed at the beginning of the day and after use with each patient. Manufacturers' recommendations should be followed for use and maintenance of waterlines and check valves and for flushing of handpieces. The same precautions should be used for ultrasonic scalers and air/water syringes.

3. Blood and saliva should be thoroughly and carefully cleaned from material that has been used in the mouth (e.g., impression materials, bite registration), especially before polishing and grinding intra-oral devices. Contaminated materials, impressions, and intra-oral devices should also be cleaned and disinfected before being handled in the dental laboratory and before they are placed in the patient's mouth. Because of the increasing variety of dental

materials used intra-orally, dental workers should consult with manufacturers as to the stability of specific materials when using disinfection procedures.

4. Dental equipment and surfaces that are difficult to disinfect (e.g., light handles or X-ray-unit heads) and that may become contaminated should be wrapped with impervious-backed paper, aluminum foil, or clear plastic wrap. The coverings should be removed and discarded, and clean coverings should be put in place after use with each patient.

Precautions for Autopsies or Morticians' Services

In addition to the universal blood and body-fluid precautions listed above, the following precautions should be used by persons performing postmortem procedures:

1. All persons performing or assisting in postmortem procedures should wear gloves, masks, protective eyewear, gowns, and waterproof aprons.

2. Instruments and surfaces contaminated during postmortem procedures should be decontaminated with an appropriate chemical germicide.

Precautions for Dialysis

Patients with end-stage renal disease who are undergoing maintenance dialysis and who have HIV infection can be dialyzed in hospital-based or free-standing dialysis units using conventional infection-control precautions.[21] Universal blood and body-fluid precautions should be used when dialyzing *all* patients.

Strategies for disinfecting the dialysis fluid pathways of the hemodialysis machine are targeted to control bacterial contamination and generally consist of using 500–750 parts per million (ppm) of sodium hypochlorite (household bleach) for 30–40 minutes of 1.5%–2.0% formaldehyde overnight. In addition, several chemical germicides formulated to disinfect dialysis machines are commercially available. None of these protocols or procedures need to be changed for dialyzing patients infected with HIV.

Patients infected with HIV can be dialyzed by either hemodialysis or peritoneal dialysis and do not need to be isolated from other patients. The type of dialysis treatment (i.e., hemodialysis or peritoneal dialysis) should be based on the needs of the patient. The dialyzer may be discarded after each use. Alternatively, centers that reuse dialyzers—i.e., a specific single-use dialyzer is issued to a specific patient, removed, cleaned, disinfected, and reused several times on the same patient only—may include HIV-infected patients in the dialyzer-reuse program. An individual dialyzer must never be used on more than one patient.

Precautions for Laboratories

Blood and other body fluids from *all* patients should be considered infective. To supplement the universal blood and body-fluid precautions listed above, the following precautions are recommended for health-care workers in clinical laboratories. (Additional precautions for research and industrial laboratories are addressed elsewhere.[22,23]

1. All specimens of blood and body fluids should be put in a well-constructed container with a secure lid to prevent leaking during transport. Care should be taken when collecting each specimen to avoid contaminating the outside of the container and of the laboratory form accompanying the specimen.

2. All persons processing blood and body-fluid specimens (e.g., removing tops from vacuum tubes) should wear gloves. Masks and protective eyewear should be work if mucous-membrane contact with blood or body fluids is anticipated. Gloves should be changed and hands washed after completion of specimen processing.

3. For routine procedures, such as histologic and pathologic studies or microbiologic culturing, a biological safety cabinet is not necessary. However, biological safety cabinets (Class I or II) should be used whenever procedures are conducted that have a high potential for generating droplets. These include activities such as blending, sonicating, and vigorous mixing.

4. Mechanical pipetting devices should be used for manipulating all liquids in the laboratory. Mouth pipetting must not be done.

5. Use of needles and syringes should be limited to situations in which there is no alternative, and the recommendations for preventing injuries with needles outlined under universal precautions should be followed.

6. Laboratory work surfaces should be decontaminated with an appropriate chemical germicide after a spill of blood or other body fluids and when work activities are completed.

7. Contaminated materials used in laboratory tests should be decontaminated before reprocessing or be placed in bags and disposed of in accordance with institutional policies for disposal of infective waste.[24]

8. Scientific equipment that has been contaminated with blood or other body fluids should be decontaminated and cleaned before being repaired in the laboratory or transported to the manufacturer.

9. All persons should wash their hands after completing laboratory activities and should remove protective clothing before leaving the laboratory.

Implementation of universal blood and body-fluid precautions for *all* patients eliminates the need for warning labels on specimens since blood and other body fluids from all patients should be considered infective.

ENVIRONMENTAL CONSIDERATIONS FOR HIV TRANSMISSION

No environmentally mediated mode of HIV transmission has been documented. Nevertheless, the precautions described below should be taken routinely in the care of *all* patients.

Sterilization and Disinfection

Standard sterilization and disinfection procedures for patient-care equipment currently recommended for use [25,26] in a variety of health-care settings—including hospitals, medical and dental clinics and offices, hemodialysis centers, emergency-care facilities, and long-term nursing-care facilities—are adequate to sterilize or disinfect instruments, devices, or other items contaminated with blood or other body fluids from persons infected with blood-borne pathogens including HIV.[21,23]

Instruments or devices that enter sterile tissue or the vascular system of any patient or through which blood flows should be sterilized before reuse. Devices or items that contact intact mucous membranes should be sterilized or receive high-level disinfection, a procedure that kills vegetative organisms and viruses but not necessarily large numbers of bacterial spores. Chemical germicides that are registered with the U.S. Environmental Protection Agency (EPA) as "sterilants" may be used either for sterilization or for high-level disinfection depending on contact time.

Contact lenses used in trial fittings should be disinfected after each fitting by using a hydrogen peroxide contact lens disinfecting system or, if compatible, with heat (78 C–80 C [172.4 F–176.0 F]) for 10 minutes.

Medical devices or instruments that require sterilization or disinfection should be thoroughly cleaned before being exposed to the germicide, and the manufacturer's instructions for the use of the germicide should be followed. Further, it is important that the manufacturer's specifications for compatibility of the medical device with chemical germicides be closely followed. Information on specific label claims of commercial germicides can be obtained by writing to the Disinfectants Branch, Office of Pesticides, Environmental Protection Agency, 401 M Street, S.W., Washington, DC 20460.

Studies have shown that HIV is inactivated rapidly after being exposed to commonly used chemical germicides at concentrations that are much lower than used in practice.[27,28,29,30] Embalming fluids are similar to the types of chemical germicides that have been tested and found to completely inactivate HIV. In addition to commercially available chemical germicides, a solution of sodium hypochlorite (household bleach) prepared daily is an inexpensive and effective germicide. Concentrations ranging from approximately 500 ppm (1:100 dilution of household bleach) sodium hypochlorite to 5,000 ppm (1:10 dilution of household bleach) are effective depending on the amount of organic material (e.g., blood, mucus) present on the surface to be cleaned and disinfected. Commercially available chemical germicides may be more compatible with certain medical devices that might be corroded by repeated exposure to sodium hypochlorite, especially to the 1:10 dilution.

Survival of HIV in the Environment

The most extensive study on the survival of HIV after drying involved greatly concentrated HIV samples, i.e., 10 million tissue-culture infectious doses per milliliter.[31] This concentration is at least 100,000 times greater than that typically found in the blood or serum of patients with HIV infection. HIV was detectable by tissue-culture techniques 1–3 days after drying, but the rate of inactivation was rapid. Studies performed at CDC have also shown that drying HIV causes a rapid (within several hours) 1–2 log (90%–99%) reduction in HIV concentration. In tissue-culture fluid, cell-free HIV could be detected up to 15 days at room temperature, up to 11 days at 37 C (98.6 F), and up to 1 day if the HIV was cell-associated.

When considered in the context of environmental conditions in health-care facilities, these results do not require any changes in currently recommended sterilization, disinfection, or housekeeping strategies. When medical devices are contaminated with blood or other body fluids, existing recommendations include the cleaning of these instruments, followed by disinfection or sterilization, depending on the type of medical device. These protocols assume "worst-case" conditions of extreme virologic and microbiologic contamination, and whether viruses have been inactivated after drying plays no role in formulating these strategies. Consequently, no changes in published procedures for cleaning, disinfecting, or sterilizing need to be made.

Housekeeping

Environmental surfaces such as walls, floors, and other surfaces are not associated with transmission of infections to patients or health-care workers. Therefore, extraordinary attempts to disinfect or sterilize these environmental surfaces are not necessary. However, cleaning and removal of soil should be done routinely.

Cleaning schedules and methods vary according to the area of the hospital or institution, type of surface to be cleaned, and the amount and type of soil present. Horizontal surfaces (e.g., bedside tables and hard-surfaced flooring) in patient-care areas are usually cleaned on a regular basis, when soiling or spills occur, and when a patient is discharged. Cleaning of walls, blinds, and curtains is recommended only if they are visibly soiled. Disinfectant fogging is an unsatisfactory method of decontaminating air and surfaces and is not recommended.

Disinfectant-detergent formulations registered by EPA can be used for cleaning environmental surfaces, but the actual physical removal of microorganisms by scrubbing is probably at least as important as an antimicrobial effect of the cleaning agent used. Therefore, cost, safety, and acceptability by housekeepers can be the main criteria for selecting any such registered agent. The manufacturers' instructions for appropriate use should be followed.

Cleaning and Decontaminating Spills of Blood or Other Body Fluids

Chemical germicides that are approved for use as "hospital disinfectants" and are tuberculocidal when used at recommended dilutions can be used to decontaminate spills of blood and other body fluids. Strategies for decontaminating spills of blood and other body fluids in a patient-care setting are different than for spills of cultures or other materials in clinical, public health, or research laboratories. In patient-care areas, visible material should first be removed and then the area should be decontaminated. With large spills of cultured or concentrated infectious agents in the laboratory, the contaminated area should be flooded with a liquid germicide before cleaning, then decontaminated with fresh germicidal chemical. In both settings, gloves should be worn during the cleaning and decontaminating procedures.

Laundry

Although soiled linen has been identified as a source of large numbers of certain pathogenic microorganisms, the risk of actual disease transmission is negligible. Rather than rigid procedures and specifications, hygienic and common-sense storage and processing of clean and soiled linen are recommended.[26] Soiled linen should be handled as little as possible and with minimum agitation to prevent gross microbial contamination of the air and of persons handling the linen. All soiled linen should be bagged at the location where it was used; it should not be sorted or rinsed in patient-care areas. Linen soiled with blood or body fluids should be placed and transported in bags that prevent leakage. If hot water is used, linen should be washed with detergent in water at least 71 C (160 F) for 25 minutes. If low-temperature (70 C [158 F]) laundry cycles are used, chemicals suitable for low-temperature washing at proper use concentration should be used.

Infective Waste

There is no epidemiologic evidence to suggest that most hospital waste is any more infective than residential waste. Moreover, there is no epidemiologic evidence that hospital waste has caused disease in the community as a result of improper disposal. Therefore, identifying wastes for which special precautions are indicated is largely a matter of judgment about the relative risk of disease transmission. The most practical approach to the management of infective waste is to identify those wastes with the potential for causing infection during handling and disposal and for which some special precautions appear prudent. Hospital wastes for which special precautions appear prudent include microbiology laboratory waste, pathology waste, and blood specimens or blood products. While any item that has had contact with blood, exudates, or secretions may be potentially infective, it is not usually considered practical or necessary to treat all such wastes as infective.[23,26] Infective waste, in general, should either be incinerated or should be autoclaved before disposal in a sanitary landfill. Bulk blood, suctioned fluids, excretions, and secretions may be carefully poured down a drain connected to a sanitary sewer. Sanitary sewers may also be used to dispose of other infectious wastes capable of being ground and flushed into the sewer.

Implementation of Recommended Precautions

Employers of health-care workers should ensure that policies exist for:

1. Initial orientation and continuing education and training of all health-care workers—including students and trainees—on the epidemiology, modes of transmission, and prevention of HIV and other blood-borne infections and the need for routine use of universal blood and body-fluid precautions for *all* patients.
2. Provision of equipment and supplies necessary to minimize the risk of infection with HIV and other blood-borne pathogens.
3. Monitoring adherence to recommended protective measures. When monitoring reveals a failure to follow recommended precautions, counseling, education, and/or re-training should be provided, and, if necessary, appropriate disciplinary action should be considered.

Professional associations and labor organizations, through continuing education efforts, should emphasize the need for health-care workers to follow recommended precautions.

SEROLOGIC TESTING FOR HIV INFECTION

Background

A person is identified as infected with HIV when a sequence of tests, starting with repeated enzyme immunoassays (EIA) and including a Western blot or similar, more specific assay, are repeatedly reactive. Persons infected with HIV usually develop antibody against the virus within 6–12 weeks after infection.

The sensitivity of the currently licensed EIA tests is at least 99% when they are performed under optimal laboratory conditions on serum specimens from persons infected for 12 weeks. Optimal laboratory conditions include the use of reliable reagents, provision of continuing education of personnel, quality control of procedures, and participation in performance/evaluation programs. Given this performance, the probability of a false-negative test is remote except during the first several weeks after infection, before detectable antibody is present. The proportion of infected persons with a false-negative test attributed to absence of antibody in the early stages of infection is dependent on both the incidence and prevalence of HIV infection in a population.

The specificity of the currently licensed EIA tests is approximately 99% when repeatedly reactive tests are considered. Repeat testing of initially reactive specimens by EIA is required to reduce the likelihood of laboratory error. To increase further the specificity of serologic tests, laboratories must use a supplemental test, most often the Western blot, to validate repeatedly reactive EIA results. Under optimal laboratory conditions, the sensitivity of the Western blot test is comparable to or greater than that of a repeatedly reactive EIA, and the Western blot is highly specific when strict criteria are used to interpret the test results. The testing sequence of a repeatedly reactive EIA and a positive Western blot test is highly predictive of HIV infection, even in a population with a low prevalence of infection. If the Western blot test result is indeterminant, the testing sequence is considered equivocal for HIV infection. When this occurs, the Western blot test should be repeated on the same serum sample, and, if still indeterminant, the testing sequence should be repeated on a sample collected 3–6 months later. Use of other supplemental tests may aid in interpreting of results on samples that are persistently indeterminant by Western blot.

Testing of Patients

Previous CDC recommendations have emphasized the value of HIV serologic testing of patients for: (1) management of parenteral or mucous-membrane exposures of health-care workers, (2) patient diagnosis and management, and (3) counseling and serologic testing to prevent and control HIV transmission in the community. In addition, more recent recommendations have stated that hospitals, in conjunction with state and local health departments, should periodically determine the prevalence of HIV infection among patients from age groups at highest risk of infection.[32]

Adherence to universal blood and body-fluid precautions recommended for the care of all patients will minimize the risk of transmission of HIV and other blood-borne pathogens from patients to health-care workers. The utility of routine HIV serologic testing of patients as an adjunct to universal precautions is unknown. Results of such testing may not be available in emergency or outpatient settings. In addition, some recently infected patients will not have detectable antibody to HIV.

Personnel in some hospitals have advocated serologic testing of patients in settings in which exposure of health-care workers to large amounts of patients' blood may be anticipated. Specific patients for whom serologic testing has been advocated include those undergoing major operative procedures and those undergoing treatment in critical-care units, especially if they have conditions involving uncontrolled bleeding. Decisions regarding the need to establish testing programs for patients should be made by physicians or individual institutions. In addition, when deemed appropriate, testing of individual patients may be performed on agreement between the patient and the physician providing care.

In addition to the universal precautions recommended for all patients, certain additional precautions for the care of HIV-infected patients undergoing major surgical operations have been proposed by personnel in some hospitals. For example, surgical procedures on an HIV-infected patient might be altered so that hand-to-hand passing of sharp instruments would be eliminated; stapling instruments rather than hand-suturing equipment might be used to perform tissue approximation; electrocautery devices rather than scalpels might be used as cutting instruments; and, even though uncomfortable, gowns that totally prevent seepage of blood onto the skin of members of the operative team might be worn. While such modifications might further minimize the risk of HIV infection for members of the operative team, some of these techniques could result in prolongation of operative time and could potentially have an adverse effect on the patient.

Testing programs, if developed, should include the following principles:

- Obtaining consent for testing.
- Informing patients of test results, and providing counseling for seropositive patients by properly trained persons.
- Assuring that confidentiality safeguards are in place to limit knowledge of test results to those directly involved in the care of infected patients or as required by law.
- Assuring that identification of infected patients will not result in denial of needed care or provision of suboptimal care.
- Evaluating prospectively (1) the efficacy of the program in reducing the incidence of parenteral, mucous-membrane, or significant cutaneous exposures of health-care workers to the blood or other body fluids of HIV-infected patients and (2) the effect of modified procedures on patients.

Testing of Health-Care Workers

Although transmission of HIV from infected health-care workers to patients has not been reported, transmission during invasive procedures remains a possibility. Transmission of hepatitis B virus (HBV)—a blood-borne agent with a considerably greater potential for nosocomial spread—from health-care workers to patients has been documented. Such transmission has occurred in situations (e.g., oral and gynecologic surgery) in which health-care workers, when tested, had very high concentrations of HBV in their blood (at least 100 million infectious virus particles per milliliter, a concentration much higher than occurs with HIV infection), and the health-care workers sustained a puncture wound while performing invasive procedures or had exudative or weeping lesions or microlacerations that allowed virus to contaminate instruments or open wounds of patients.[33,34]

The hepatitis B experience indicates that only those health-care workers who perform certain types of invasive procedures have transmitted HBV to patients. Adherence to recommendations in this document will minimize the risk of transmission of HIV and other blood-borne pathogens from health-care workers to patients during invasive procedures. Since transmission of HIV from infected health-care workers performing invasive procedures to their patients has not been reported and would be expected to occur only very rarely, if at all, the utility of routine testing of such health-care workers to prevent transmission of HIV cannot be assessed. If consideration is given to developing a serologic testing program for health-care workers who perform invasive procedures, the frequency of testing, as well as the issues of consent, confidentiality, and consequences of test results—as previously outlined for testing programs for patients—must be addressed.

Management of Infected Health-Care Workers

Health-care workers with impaired immune systems resulting from HIV infection or other causes are at increased risk of acquiring or experiencing serious complications of infectious disease. Of particular concern is the risk of severe infection following exposure to patients with infectious diseases that are easily transmitted if appropriate precautions are not taken (e.g., measles, varicella). Any health-care worker with an impaired immune system should be counseled about the potential risk associated with taking care of patients with any transmissible infection and should continue to follow existing recommendations for infection control to minimize risk of exposure to other infectious agents.[7,35] Recommendations of the Immunization Practices Advisory Committee (ACIP) and institutional policies concerning requirements for vaccinating health-care workers with live-virus vaccines (e.g., measles, rubella) should also be considered.

The question of whether workers infected with HIV—especially those who perform invasive procedures—can adequately and safely be allowed to perform patient-care duties or whether their work assignments should be changed must be determined on an individual basis. These decisions should be made by the health-care worker's personal physician(s) in conjunction with the medical directors and personnel health service staff of the employing institution or hospital.

Management of Exposures

If a health-care worker has a parenteral (e.g., needlestick or cut) or mucous-membrane (e.g., splash to the eye or mouth) exposure to blood or other body fluids or has a cutaneous exposure involving large amounts of blood or prolonged contact with blood—especially when the exposed skin is chapped, abraded, or afflicted with dermatitis—the source patient should be informed of the incident and tested for serologic evidence of HIV infection after consent is obtained. Policies should be developed for testing source patients in situations in which consent cannot be obtained (e.g., an unconscious patient).

If the source patient has AIDS, is positive for HIV antibody, or refuses the test, the health-care worker should be counseled regarding the risk of infection and evaluated clinically and serologically for evidence of HIV infection as soon as possible after the exposure. The health-care worker should be advised to report and seek medical evaluation for any acute febrile illness that occurs within 12 weeks after the exposure. Such an illness—particularly one characterized by fever, rash, or lymphadenopathy—may be indicative of recent HIV infection. Seronegative health-care workers should be retested 6 weeks post-exposure and on a periodic basis thereafter (e.g., 12 weeks and 6 months after exposure) to determine whether transmission has occurred. During this follow-up period—especially the first 6–12 weeks after exposure, when most infected persons are expected to seroconvert—exposed health-care workers should follow U.S. Public Health Service (PHS) recommendations for preventing transmission of HIV.[36,37]

No further follow-up of a health-care worker exposed to infection as described above is necessary if the source patient is seronegative unless the source patient is at high risk of HIV infection. In the latter case, a subsequent specimen (e.g., 12 weeks following exposure) may be obtained from the health-care worker for antibody testing. If the source patient cannot be identified, decisions regarding appropriate follow-up should be individualized. Serologic testing should be available to all health-care workers who are concerned that they may have been infected with HIV.

If a patient has a parenteral or mucous-membrane exposure to blood or other body fluid of a health-care worker, the patient should be informed of the incident, and the same procedure outlined above for management of exposures should be followed for both the source health-care worker and the exposed patient.

REFERENCES

Reprinted by the U.S. Department of Health and Human Services, Public Health Service, Centers for Disease Control, from *Morbidity and Mortality Weekly Report* (Supplement) 36, no. 2S (August 21, 1987).

1. CDC, Acquired immunodeficiency syndrome (AIDS): Precautions for clinical and laboratory staffs, *MMWR* 1982;31:577–80.

2. CDC, Acquired immunodeficiency syndrome (AIDS): Precautions for health-care workers and allied professionals, *MMWR* 1983; 32:450–51.

3. CDC, Recommendations for preventing transmission of infection with human T-lymphotropic virus type III/lymphadenopathy-associated virus in the workplace, *MMWR* 1985;34:681–86, 691–95.

4. CDC, Recommendations for preventing transmission of infection with human T-lymphotropic virus type III/lymphadenopathy-associated virus during invasive procedures, *MMWR* 1986;35:221–23.

5. CDC, Recommendations for preventing possible transmission of human T-lymphotropic virus type III/lymphadenopathy-associated virus from tears, *MMWR* 1985;34:533–54.

6. CDC, Recommendations for providing dialysis treatment to patients infected with human T-lymphotropic virus type III/lymphadenopathy-associated virus infection, *MMWR* 1986;35:376–78, 383.

7. J. S. Garner and B. P. Simmons, Guideline for isolation precautions in hospitals, *Infection Control* 1983;4 (suppl):245–325.

8. CDC, Recommended infection control practices for dentistry, *MMWR* 1986;35:237–42.

9. E. McCray, The Cooperative Needlestick Surveillance Group. Occupational risk of the acquired immunodeficiency syndrome among health-care workers, *New England Journal of Medicine* 1986;314:1127–32.

10. D. K. Henderson, A. J. Saah, B. J. Zak et al., Risk of nosocomial infection with human T-cell lymphotropic virus type III/lymphadenopathy-associated virus in a large cohort of intensively exposed health care workers, *Annals of Internal Medicine* 1986;104:644–47.

11. J. L. Gerberding, C. E. Bryant-LeBlanc, K. Nelson et al., Risk of transmitting the human immunodeficiency virus, cytomegalovirus, and hepatitis B virus to health care workers exposed to patients with AIDS and AIDS-related conditions, *Journal of Infectious Disease* 1987;156:1–8.

12. M. McEvoy, K. Porter, P. Mortimer, N. Simmons, and D. Shanson, Prospective study of clinical, laboratory, and ancillary staff with accidental exposure to blood or other body fluids from patients infected with HIV, *British Medical Journal* 1987;294:1595–97.

13. Anonymous, Needlestick transmission of HTLV-III from a patient infected in Africa, *Lancet* 1984;2:1376–77.

14. E. Oksenhendler, M. Harzic, J. M. Le Rous, C. Rabian, and J. P. Clauvel, HIV infection with seroconversion after a superficial needlestick injury to the finger, *New England Journal of Medicine* 1986;315:582.

15. C. Neisson-Vernant, S. Arfi, D. Mathez, J. Leibowitch, and N. Monplaisir, Needlestick HIV seroconversion in a nurse, *Lancet* 1986;2:814.

16. P. Grint and M. McEvoy, Two associated cases of the acquired immune deficiency syndrome (AIDS), PHLS *Communicable Disease Report* 1985;42:4.

17. CDC, Apparent transmission of human T-lymphotropic virus type III/lymphadenopathy-associated virus from a child to a mother providing health care, *MMWR* 1986;35:76–79.

18. CDC, Update: Human immunodeficiency virus infections in health-care workers exposed to blood of infected patients, *MMWR* 1987; 36:285–89.

19. R. S. Kline, J. Phelan, G. H. Friedland et al., Low occupational risk for HIV infection for dental professionals (Abstract), in: Abstracts from the III International Conference on AIDS (Washington, DC: June 1–5, 1985): 155.

20. J. L. Baker, G. D. Kelen, K. T. Sivertson and T. C. Quinn, Unsuspected human immunodeficiency virus in critically ill emergency patients, *JAMA* 1987;257:2609–11.

21. M. S. Favero, Dialysis-associated diseases and their control, in: J. V. Bennett, and P. S. Brachman, eds. *Hospital Infections* (Boston: Little, Brown, 1985); 267–84.

22. J. H. Richardson, and W. E. Barkley, eds., *Biosafety in Microbiological and Biomedical Laboratories* 1984 (Washington, DC: US Department of Health and Human Services, Public Health Service, HHS publication no. (CDC) 84–8395.

23. CDC, Human T-lymphotropic virus type III/lymphadenopathy-associated virus: Agent summary statement, *MMWR* 1986;35:540–42, 547–49.

24. Environmental Protection Agency, *EPA Guide for Infectious Waste Management* (Washington, DC: U.S. Environmental Protection Agency, May 1986). Publication no. EPA/530–SW–86–014.

25. M. S. Favero, Sterilization, disinfection and antisepsis in the hospital, in: *Manual of clinical microbiology*, 4th ed (Washington, DC: American Society for Microbiology, 1985): 129–37.

26. J. S. Garner, and M. S. Favero, *Guideline for Handwashing and Hospital*

Environmental Control (Atlanta: Public Health Service, Centers for Disease Control, 1985). HHS publication no. 99–1117.

27. B. Spire, L. Montagnier, F. Barre-Sinoussi, and J. C. Chermann, Inactivation of lymphadenopathy associated virus by chemical disinfectants, *Lancet* 1984;2:899–901.

28. L. S. Martin, J. S. McDougal, and S. L. Loskoski, Disinfection and inactivation of the human T lymphotropic virus type III/lymphadenopathy-associated virus, *Journal of Infectious Disease* 1985; 152:400–3.

29. J. S. McDougal, L. S. Martin, S. P. Cort et al., Thermal inactivation of the acquired immunodeficiency syndrome virus-III/lymphadenopathy-associated virus, with special references to antihemophilic factor, *Journal of Clinical Investigation* 1985;76:875–77.

30. B. Spire, F. Barre-Sinoussi, D. Dormont, L. Montagnier, and J. C. Chermann, Inactivation of lymphadenopathy-associated virus by heat, gamma rays, and ultraviolet light, *Lancet* 1985;1:188–89.

31. L. Resnik, K. Veren, S. Z. Salahuddin, S. Tondreau, and P. D. Markham, Stability and inactivation of HTLV-III/LAV under clinical and laboratory environments, *JAMA* 1986;255:1887–91.

32. CDC, Public Health Service (PHS) guidelines for counseling and antibody testing to prevent HIV infection and AIDS, *MMWR* 1987;3:509–15.

33. M. A. Kane, and L. A. Lettau, Transmission of HBV from dental personnel to patients, *Journal of the American Dental Association* 1985; 110:634–36.

34. L. A. Lettau, J. D. Smith, D. Williams et al., Transmission of hepatitis B with resultant restriction of surgical practice, *JAMA* 1986; 255:934–37.

35. W. W. Williams, Guideline for infection control in hospital personnel, *Infection Control* 1983;4 (suppl):326–49.

36. CDC, Prevention of acquired immune deficiency syndrome (AIDS): Report of inter-agency recommendations, *MMWR* 1983;32:101–3.

37. CDC, Provisional Public Health Service inter-agency recommendations for screening donated blood and plasma for antibody to the virus causing acquired immunodeficiency syndrome, *MMWR* 1985;34:1–5.

BIBLIOGRAPHY

Abramowitz, Michael. "Justice Limits Job Protection for AIDS Victims." *Washington Post*, June 24, 1986.

"AIDS and Women: Nonwhites Face the Biggest Risk." *Time*, April 27, 1988.

Allstate Forum on Public Issues. *Corporate America Responds*, October 1987.

American Foundation for AIDS Research. *AIDS Education: A Business Guide*, 1988.

American Red Cross. "AIDS Prevention for Youth," *America Responds to AIDS*, 1987.

Anderson, Beverly J. and Edward A. Lemerise. "The Role of the EAP Practitioner in Managing AIDS." Aids Workplace Update. Greenvale, NY: Panel Publishers, October 1988.

Backer, Thomas E. "AIDS/HIV Infection and the Workplace: Emerging Issues," Unpublished notes from NIDA-sponsored conference on AIDS/HIV Infection, November 17, 1989.

Balkam, Cliff. "New HR Policies." Aids Workplace Update. Greenvale, NY: Panel Publishers, February 1989.

Banta, William F. *AIDS in the Workplace: Legal Questions and Practical Answers.* Lexington, MA: D. C. Heath, 1988.

Bass, Thomas. "Interview, Luc Montagnier." *Omni.* December 1988.

Bohl, Don L., Eric Rolfe Greenberg, Anne Skagen, and Yvette DeBow. "AIDS: The New Workplace Issues," American Management Briefing. New York: American Management Association, 1988.

Bridge, T. Peter, Allan F. Mirsky, and Frederick K. Goodwin. *Psychological, Neuropsychiatric, and Substance Abuse Aspects of AIDS.* Advances in Biochemical Psychopharmacology, Vol. 44. New York: Raven Press, 1988.

British Department of Health and Social Security and the Central Office of Information. "Government Information 1987, AIDS, Guidelines for Tattooists and Guidelines for Electrolysists," 1987.

Brown, Kathleen C. and Joan G. Turner. *AIDS, Policies and Programs for the Workplace.* New York: Van Nostrand Reinhold, 1989.

Bunker, John F., Michael P. Eriksen, and Jennifer Kinsey. "AIDS in the Workplace: The Role of EAPs." *The Almacan*, September 1987.

Buraff Publications. *AIDS Policy and Law*. Various issues March–May 1989. Washington, DC.

Centers for Disease Control. *HIV/AIDS Surveillance Report*. July 1989.

Committee on Substance Abuse and AIDS. "Alcohol, Drugs and AIDS." San Francisco AIDS Foundation, October 1985.

Dalton, Harold L. "AIDS in Blackface," *Daedulus*, Living with AIDS Part 2, Summer 1989.

Dartnell Corporation. *AIDS in the Workplace: A Guide for Management*. Chicago, 1987.

Department of Health and Human Services. "Acquired Immunodeficiency Syndrome (AIDS) among Blacks and Hispanics—United States." *Morbidity and Mortality Weekly Report*, 35, no. 42 (October 24, 1986).

———. *Facts About AIDS*. Public Health Control, Spring 1987.

———. "Prevention and Beyond, A Framework for Collective Action"; A National Conference on HIV Infection and AIDS Among Racial and Ethnic Populations. Washington, DC, August 13–17, 1989. Sponsored by DHHS and the Office of Minority Health.

———"Human Immunodeficiency Virus in the United States: A Review of Current Knowledge" *Morbidity and Mortality Weekly Report* 36, No. S–6 (December 18, 1987).

Department of Health and Human Services, Public Health Service, "Update: Universal Precautions for Prevention of Transmission of Human Immunodeficiency Virus, Hepatitis B Virus, and Other Bloodborne Pathogens in Health-Care Settings." *MMWR*, June 24, 1988.

Department of Health and Human Services, Public Health Service, Centers for Disease Control. "Background Information on AIDS and HTLV-III Infection." Management of HTLV-III/LAV Infection in the Hospital, 1987.

———. "AIDS Prevention Guide: For Parents and Other Adults Concerned About Youth." Information Packet, 1989.

Department of Health and Human Services, National Institute of Mental Health. *Coping with AIDS, Psychological and Social Considerations in Helping People with HTLV-III Infection*, 1986.

Deresiewicz, William and Joe Gordon. "Against All Odds; Grassroots Minority Groups Fight AIDS." *Health/Pac Bulletin* 18 (Spring 1988).

EAP Digest. May/June 1988. With permission of Performance Resource Press, Inc., 2145 Crooks Road, Suite 103, Troy, Michigan 48084. Paraphrased by Bryan Lawton, Thomas E. Backer, and Kirk B. O'Hara, in "Aids Handbook for EAP Professionals in the Entertainment Industry." Los Angeles: Human Interaction Research Institute, June 1989.

Ellison-Sandler, Yvonne. "AIDS/HIV Infection and the Workplace Workgroup." Unpublished notes from NIDA-sponsored conference on AIDS/HIV Infection, November 17, 1989.

Essex, Max and Phyllis J. Kanki. "The Origins of the AIDS Virus." *Scientific American*, October 1988.

Fineberg, Harvey V. "Education to Prevent AIDS: Prospects and Obstacles." *Science* 239 (February 5, 1988).

Fortune Magazine and Allstate Insurance (1988). "Business Response to AIDS: A National Survey of U.S. Companies." In Kathleen C. Brown and Joan G. Turner, *AIDS, Policies and Programs for the Workplace.* Van Nostrand Reinhold, 1989.

Fromer, Margot J. "Counseling Employees About Experimental Drugs." Aids Workplace Update. Greenvale, NY: Panel Publishers, March 1989.

Gadsby, Patricia. "AIDS Watch," *Discover,* April 1988.

Gallo, Robert C. and Luc Montagnier. "AIDS in 1988." *Scientific American,* October 1988.

Garry, Robert F., Maryls H. Witte, A. Arthur Gottlieb, Memory Elvin-Lewis, Charles L. Witte, Steve S. Alexander, William R. Cole, and William L. Drake, Jr. "Documentation of an AIDS Virus Infection in the United States in 1968." *Journal of the American Medical Association* 260, no. 14 (October 14, 1988).

Goldberg, A. "Acquired Immune Deficiency Syndrome: Workplace Issues." Speech given at the American Management Association Executive Briefing of "AIDS on the Workplace" in New York, April 12, 1989.

Goodstein, Laurie. "Physician With AIDS Takes Her Case To Trial." *Washington Post,* January 7, 1990.

Grief, Geoffrey L. and Edmund Porembski. "Significant Others of I.V. Drug Abusers with AIDS: New Challenges for Drug Treatment Programs." *Journal of Substance Abuse Treatment* 4 (1987).

Gross, Jane. "New York's Poorest Women Offered More AIDS Services." *New York Times,* March 5, 1988.

Guinan, Mary E. and Ann Hardy. "Epidemiology of AIDS in Women in the United States." *Journal of the American Medical Association* 257, no. 15 (April 17, 1987).

Hamburg, Margaret A., and Anthony S. Fauci. "AIDS: The Challenge to Biomedical Research." *Daedulus,* Winter 1989.

Herold, David. "Employees' Reactions to AIDS in the Workplace." Center for Work Performance Problems, College of Management, Georgia Institute of Technology, February 1988.

Hiratsuka, Jon. "AIDS Being Treated as a Chronic Disease." *NASW News,* October 1989.

"Hospital Workers Need More Education and Training." AIDS Workplace Update, Vol 1, no. 9. New York: Panel Publishers, April 1989.

Joint Advisory Notice. *Protection Against Occupational Exposure to Hepatitis B Virus (HBV) and Human Immunodeficiency Virus (HIV).* Department of Labor/Department of Health and Human Services, October 19, 1987.

Katz, Mark A. *Understanding AIDS, A Personal Handbook for Employees and Managers.* Washington, DC: Employee Benefits Review, 1989.

Kelly, James and Pamelia Sykes. "Helping the Helpers: A Support Group for Family Members of Persons with AIDS." *Social Work,* May 1989.

Krueger, Guenther. "Helping the Employee with ARC or AIDS," *The Almacan,* September 1987.

Lawton, Bryan. "How to Develop a Successful AIDS Policy That Can Help Both the Company and Its Employees." Personnel Manager's Letter, February 1, 1988.

———. "Personnel Directive on AIDS." AIDS, The Crisis for American Business Conference, November 2–3, 1987.

Lawton, Bryan, Thomas E. Backer, and Kirk B. O'Hara. "Aids Handbook for EAP Professionals in the Entertainment Industry." Los Angeles: Human Interaction Research Institute, June 1989.

Leonard, Arthur, "AIDS in the Workplace." In H. Dalton and S. Burris, eds., *AIDS and the Law: A Guide for the Public.* New Haven, CT: Yale University Press, 1987.

Levi Strauss and Co. "Talk about AIDS." Videotape distributed by the San Francisco AIDS Foundation, 1987.

Mann, Jonathan M., James Chin, Peter Piot, and Thomas Quinn. "The International Epidemiology of AIDS." *Scientific American,* October 1988.

Maryland Center for Business Management, Inc. "AIDS in the Workplace and Other Catastrophic Diseases." Joint presentation by the Maryland Center for Business Management, Inc., and M. Rosenberg and Co., The Johns Hopkins University School of Hygiene and Public Health, and The Educational Center of Sheppard Pratt, Division of Employee Assistance Programs, October 22, 1987.

Maryland Department of Health and Hygiene. "AIDS, Teaching/Learning Module." 1987.

———. "Report on Acquired Immune Deficiency Syndrome," 1987.

Masi, Dale A. "AIDS in the Workplace, What Can Be Done?" American Management Association, Periodicals Division, 1987.

———. "AIDS: What Can Be Done ... What Should Be Done ... What Is Being Done Now." Personnel Manager's Letter, February 1, 1988.

———. *Designing Employee Assistance Programs.* New York: AMACOM, 1984.

———. *Drug Free Workplace: A Guide for Supervisors.* Washington, DC: Buraff Publications, 1987.

———. "EAP Actions and Options." *Personnel Journal.* June 1988.

Mayer, Stephen S. "Legal Aspects of AIDS in the Workplace." In Richard Waldstein and Jo-Ann Heyer, eds., *AIDS in the Workplace: Here are the Answers You Must Have.* Englewood Cliffs, NJ: Prentice Hall, 1988.

Measham, Anthony R. "Subject: World Health Organization/Global Programme on AIDS (WHO/GPA) Management Committee Meeting, Geneva, December 6–8, 1989." The World Bank/IFC/MIGA Office Memorandum.

Merrigan, Daniel M. "NIDA Meeting: HIV/AIDS in the Workplace." Unpublished presentation at NIDA-sponsored conference on AIDS/HIV Infection, November 17, 1989.

———. *"Recommendations for Prevention of HIV Transmission in Health-Care Settings.* U.S. Department of Health and Human Services, Public Health Service, Centers for Disease Control, August 21, 1987.

Ms. Reporter, *Ms. Magazine,* July 1988.

National Coalition Leadership on AIDS: "Private Sector Leadership Conference on AIDS." September 16, 1988.

National Institute on Alcohol Abuse and Alcoholism. "Acquired Immune Deficiency Syndrome and Chemical Dependency." U.S. Department of Health and Human Services, Report of Symposium, Joint AMSAODD/NCA National Meeting, San Francisco, April 1986.

"NIDA Capsules." Issued by the Press Office of the National Institute on Drug Abuse, March 1989.

Norwood, Chris. *Advice for Life: A Woman's Guide to Aids Risks and Prevention.* New York: National Women's Health Network Guide, 1987.

Office of Personnel Management. "AIDS in the Workplace, Guidelines for AIDS Information and Education and for Personnel Management Issues," March 1988.

Presidential Commission on the Human Immunodeficiency Virus Epidemic, Chairman's Recommendations. Washington, DC, February 29, 1988.

"Pro & Con: Free Needles for Addicts, to Help Curb AIDS?" *New York Times,* December 20, 1987.

Puckett, Sam B. and Alan R. Emery. *Managing AIDS in the Workplace.* Reading, MA: Addison-Wesley, 1988.

Quinn, Thomas C., Fernando R. K. Zacarias, and Ronald K. St. John. "AIDS in the Americas: An Emerging Public Health Crisis." *New England Journal of Medicine* 320, no. 15, (April 13, 1989).

Report of the Surgeon General's Workshop with Children with HIV Infection and Their Families. U.S. Department of Health and Human Services, April 1987.

Ritter, David B. and Ronald Turner. "AIDS: Employer Concerns and Employer Options." In Richard Waldstein and Jo-Ann Heyer, eds., *AIDS in the Workplace: Here Are the Answers You Must Have.* Englewood Cliffs, NJ: Prentice Hall, 1988.

Rougan, Jan and Paul Haussler. "The Case Management Approach to Catastrophic Care," *Corporate Commentary* 2, no. 3 (Fall 1986) (Washington, DC).

Rowe, Mona. "Workers' Rights to Know: Managing the Issues." *AIDS Workplace Update* 1, no. 6. Greenvale, NY: Panel Publishers, January 1989.

Ryan, Caitlin. "Helping Co-Workers Deal with an Employee with AIDS." AIDS Workplace Update. Greenvale, NY: Panel Publishers, October 1988.

———. "The Social and Clinical Challenges of AIDS." *Smith College Studies in Social Work* 59, no. 1 (November 1988).

Ryan, Caitlin and Ellen Ratner. "EAPs and AIDS: Meeting the Challenge." Elizabeth Danto and Robert McConaghy, eds., *New Concepts in Employee Assistance Programs; Designing Today's EAP.* Englewood Cliffs, NJ: Prentice Hall, 1989.

San Francisco Chamber of Commerce. "AIDS in the Workplace: Suggested Guidelines for the Business Community," June 1987.

Schatz, Benjamin. "Employee Discrimination." In P. Alpert, L. Graff, and B. Schatz, eds., *AIDS Practice Manual: A Legal and Educational Guide,* 2nd ed. San Francisco: National Gay Rights Advocates and National Lawyer Guild AIDS Network, 1988.

Service Employees International Union, AFL-CIO, CLC. *The AIDS Book.* April 1988.

Sloan, Irving J. *AIDS Law: Implications for the Individual and Society.* New York: Oceana, 1988.

Smalz, Jeffrey. "Addicts to Get Needles in Plan to Curb AIDS." *New York Times,* January 31, 1988.

Springer, Edith. "Drug Dependency: A Conduit for AIDS." *Executive Briefing* 2, no. 6 (June 1989). A publication of the Foundation for Public Communications, DIFFA, and the National Leadership Coalition on AIDS.

Sullivan, Barry et al. *AIDS: The Legal Issues Discussion Draft of the American Bar Association AIDS Coordinating Committee.* Washington, DC: American Bar Association, August 1988.

Surgeon General's Report on Acquired Immune Deficiency Syndrome. U.S. Department of Health and Human Services and the American Red Cross, 1987.

"Transmission of the AIDS Virus." *Science* 239, no. 4840 (February 5, 1988).

Turk, Harry N. "AIDS in the Workplace." In J. Parry and D. Rapoport, eds., *Legal, Medical and Governmental Perspectives on AIDS as a Disability.* Washington DC: American Bar Association Commission on the Mentally Disabled, 1987.

UAW-FM Human Resource Center, AIDS Information Network. "Dealing with AIDS," 1988.

Weddington, William, "Summary." Unpublished notes from NIDA-sponsored conference on AIDS/HIV Infection, November 17, 1989.

Wofsy, Constance B. "Human Immunodeficiency Virus Infection in Women." *Journal of the American Medical Association* 257, no. 15 (April 17, 1987).

INDEX

About the Author

DALE A. MASI is Professor of Social Work at the University of Maryland and President of Masi Research Consultants, Inc., a firm which specializes in the design and evaluation of Employee Assistance Programs and corporate training. Dr. Masi is the author of four other books and over forty scholarly articles.